WOMEN'S ETHNICITIES

WOMEN'S ETHNICITIES

Journeys Through Psychology

edited by

Karen Fraser Wyche

<small>BROWN UNIVERSITY</small>

Faye J. Crosby

<small>SMITH COLLEGE</small>

**with a Foreword by Elizabeth R. Cole
and Abigail J. Stewart**

WestviewPress
A Division of HarperCollins*Publishers*

Copyright © 1996 by Westview Press, Inc., A Division of HarperCollins Publishers, Inc.

Published in 1996 in the United States of America by Westview Press, Inc., 5500 Central Avenue, Boulder, Colorado, 80301-2877, and in the United Kingdom by Westview Press, 12 Hid's Copse Road, Cumnor Hill, Oxford OX2 9JJ

A CIP catalog record for this book is available from the Library of Congress.
ISBN 0-8133-2372-X; ISBN 0-8133-2373-8 (pbk.)

The paper used in this publication meets the requirements of the American National Standard for Permanence of Paper for Printed Library Materials Z39–1984.

10   9   8   7   6   5   4   3   2   1

To Floretta, Lorraine, and the sister fellows and staff of
The Mary Ingraham Bunting Institute of Radcliffe College
—Karen Fraser Wyche

To Sara, Edie, and Sally
—Faye J. Crosby

Contents

PART 3
GENDER, CULTURE, AND VALUES   125

Foreword: Transgressions in Psychology—Daring to Look at Ethnicity and Gender

Mythology tells us that for women, looking is a transgression. Pandora, the first woman, was unable or unwilling to contain her curiosity. She looked into the forbidden box, unleashing all evil upon the world. Lot's wife (we know her only by her husband's name) looked back at the city as she fled and was turned into a pillar of salt. Even the Gorgon Medusa, whose frightful demeanor turned all who looked upon her into stone, was undone by gazing at her own reflection in a mirror. In these stories, the protagonist who defies the order to look away is invariably punished, often in such a way that she is literally paralyzed. These myths, then, communicate the message that boxes of unknown contents are better off sealed, that history and self ought to remain unexamined, and that those who choose instead to look will be condemned.

As a discipline, much of psychology implicitly shares these prohibitions, particularly concerning the subject of race and ethnicity. Even today, when university politics often focuses on whether and how to achieve "diversity," many scholars consider the race and ethnicity of the people they study to have little or no relationship to the interpretation of their findings. For these psychologists, race and ethnicity remain unopened boxes. Indeed, the prospect of revealing their contents may be worrisome. Similarly, relatively few psychologists attend to the historical contexts of their work and of the people they study. Their unwillingness to "look back" means that their scholarship floats in a kind of historical vacuum, abstracted from the larger contexts that may give meaning both to the research and to the lives of the people studied. Finally, the ideal of scholarly "objectivity" dictates that researchers strive to divorce themselves from their own backgrounds of race, ethnicity, and gender. This principle suggests that the scholar who looks reflexively upon the self will, like the Gorgon, be frozen in the attempt to generate knowledge. However, without such insight into the self, we may, like Medusa, remain unaware of the nature of our impact on the people upon whom we direct our stare!

In this volume, women scholars dare to break these commandments, audaciously turning their gaze on the previously forbidden topic of women's ethnicity. Like Pandora, they have opened the box, in this case marked "race and ethnicity," potentially unleashing the complexity of the subject upon the discipline, forever changing it. They confirm that it matters, in simple and complex ways. For example, Guadalupe Gutierrez found that the Mexican American men and women in her sample were, as a group, conscious of power differences in the world around them—"they felt that there were clear lines drawn between themselves and persons in power." At the same time, there were differences in their reactions to those power structures: Women, more than men, sought nontraditional relations between traditional dominants and subordinates. One thing we learn from the authors who opened this box, then, is that the contents cannot be described in simple terms. Among people with the "same" racial-ethnic background, there are many differences in just how that background matters to them.

Like Lot's wife, the scholars in this volume look behind them, to understand the ways in which the discipline of psychology has been partial and incomplete because of its blindness to history, race, and ethnicity. For example, Mary Brabeck "looks back" to discover a U.S. history shaping psychologists' individualistic assumptions of individualism and looks back on a violent Guatemalan history shaping ordinary adolescents' experience of everyday danger as well as their communal orientations. Like others in this book, she dares to think through the ways in which the past is present in her own worldview as well as in the worldviews of those she studies.

Finally, like Medusa, the authors of these chapters turn their critical glance upon themselves, scrutinizing their own reflections in an effort to understand how they have been "blind" to certain ways of seeing, and reveal the "in-sight" they have gained through opening the boxes of their constructs and turning the lenses of history and self-reflection on their research. For example, Sandra Tangri describes how in her multiethnic, cross-cultural study of women's lives, ethnicity complicates both collaboration and assessment and interpretation. She outlines difficulties that face those who try to hold on to their own positive ethnic identities while appreciating others' differences, and she reminds us that achieving mutual understanding is hard and often painful work. We learn from her, and the other authors here, not only that we study women's ethnicity from particular standpoints but also that we must be willing to try to understand our own inevitably obstructed views.

What is the fate of these intrepid scholars who refuse to look away? In her chapter, Brenda Allen suggests that there may indeed be professional costs to those who not only look but also speak about what they see. There will also be gains—for ourselves, for psychology, even for these authors—if we dare to listen to what they have to say.

Elizabeth R. Cole
Northeastern University

Abigail J. Stewart
University of Michigan

About the Editors and Contributors

Brenda A. Allen received her M.A. in 1981 and her Ph.D. in Developmental Psychology from Howard University in 1988. She completed a three-year postdoctoral fellowship at Yale University, where she also held a lecturer appointment for two years in the Departments of Psychology and African American Studies. Currently she is an Assistant Professor in the Department of Psychology at Smith College in Northampton, Massachusetts. She will be reviewed for tenure and promotion in fall 1995. She self-identifies as an African American woman.

Mary M. Brabeck is Professor of Counseling and Developmental Psychology and Associate Dean of the School of Education at Boston College. She earned her Ph.D. in Educational Psychology from the University of Minnesota in 1980. Her research is on ethical sensitivity and the moral self, professional ethics, and interprofessional collaborations. She self-identifies as a White, middle-class woman.

Rosario E. Ceballo earned her Ph.D. in Developmental and Clinical Psychology at the University of Michigan. She is currently Assistant Professor of Women's Studies and Psychology at the University of Michigan. Her research focuses on the effects of poverty and community violence on children's development. She self-identifies as a Hispanic woman.

Faye J. Crosby is Professor of Psychology at Smith College. She earned her Ph.D. in Social Psychology in 1976. Her research focuses on the relationships between objective and subjective reality and especially on perceptions of fairness. She self-identifies as a White woman.

Amy J. Dabul earned her Ph.D. in Social Psychology from Arizona State University in 1995. She is a faculty member in the Department of Psychology at Phoenix College. She currently conducts research examining the influence of gender, culture, and social context on achievement behavior in educational and occupational settings. She self-identifies as a biracial (half Hispanic, half Anglo) woman.

Guadalupe Gutierrez is a doctoral candidate in Clinical Psychology at the University of Michigan. Her research interests are in the development of an ethnopsychology for Mexican Americans focusing on value orientations and in the area of appropriate diagnosis of psychological disorders for the Latino populations in the United States. She self-identifies as a California Chicana.

Kimberly Kinsler is Associate Professor with the Department of Educational Foundations at Hunter College. She obtained her Ph.D. in Educational Psychology from the Graduate Center of the City University of New York. Her research focuses on studying the effects of culture and ethnicity on learning and cognitive development. She self-identifies as an African American woman.

Julie Kmiec received her B.A. from Smith College in 1995. She intends to pursue a career in psychology. Her research interests include feminism and also depression. She self-identifies as a White woman.

Debra Lobato is Clinical Psychologist and Clinical Associate Professor in the Department of Psychiatry at Rhode Island Hospital and the Brown University Program in Medicine. She obtained her Ph.D. in psychology from the University of Massachusetts, Amherst, in 1981. Her research focuses on family adaptation in chronic illness and disability. She self-identifies as a Spanish American woman.

Donna K. Nagata is Associate Professor of Psychology at the University of Michigan, Ann Arbor. She earned her Ph.D. in Clinical Psychology at the University of Illinois, Urbana-Champaign. Her research interests include Asian American mental health, the psychosocial consequences of the World War II Japanese American internment, and family processes. She self-identifies as a Japanese American woman.

Sheryl L. Olson is Associate Professor of Psychology at the University of Michigan. She obtained her Ph.D. in Clinical Psychology from Indiana University. Her research focuses on cultural, familial, and peer-group contexts of social-emotional maladjustment in young children. She self-identifies as a second-generation Swedish American woman.

Nancy Felipe Russo is Professor of Psychology and Women's Studies at Arizona State University. She obtained her Ph.D. in Social and Developmental Psychology from Cornell University in 1970. Her research focuses on relationships between women's roles and status and their performance and well-being. She is present editor of *Psychology of Women Quarterly*. She self-identifies as a Hispanic woman of Basque heritage.

Elizabeth E. Sparks is Assistant Professor in the Counseling, Developmental Psychology, and Research Methods Department at Boston College. She earned her Ph.D. in Counseling Psychology at Boston College in 1988. Her research interests stem from her clinical career in community mental health and focus on interpersonal, assaultive violence in African American youth and issues in multicultural counseling and training. She self-identifies as an African American woman.

Sandra Schwartz Tangri is Professor of Psychology at Howard University. She earned her Ph.D. in Social Psychology in 1969. Her research interests are women's career development and integration of multiple roles, discrimination, sexual harassment, and affirmative action. She self-identifies as a progressive Jewish feminist.

Judith Worell is Professor and Chair in the Department of Educational and Counseling Psychology at the University of Kentucky. She received her M.A. and Ph.D. in Clinical Psychology from Ohio State University. Her research interests center on the construction of gender in close relationships, including friendships, long-term committed relationships, and client-therapist interactions. She self-identifies as ethnic Jewish.

Karen Fraser Wyche is Assistant Professor of Education and Afro-American Studies at Brown University. She obtained her M.S.W. at the University of Maryland and her Ph.D. in Clinical Psychology from the University of Missouri–Columbia. Her research interests include social supports in minority women and gender and ethnic understanding in children. She self-identifies as an African American woman.

Sue Rosenberg Zalk is Professor in the Department of Educational Foundations and Counseling Programs at Hunter College. She is on the faculty of the Ph.D. Programs in Social/Personality Psychology and Educational Psychology at the Graduate School and University Center of City University of New York, where she also serves as Ombuds Officer. She is present editor of *Sex Roles: A Journal of Research,* and her research interests include gender role attitudes and behaviors and the development of racial prejudice in children. She self-identifies as a Jewish American woman.

1

Introduction: Coming Together

Faye J. Crosby and Karen Fraser Wyche

Periodically, social scientists notice that the life circumstances, experiences, or behaviors of women and men are not always identical. Somewhat less frequently, social scientists look for differences without thinking of deficiencies (Travis, 1992). When social scientists exhibit both of these behaviors, the research is feminist (Unger and Crawford, 1992).

Since the 1970s, academics have debated various tenets of feminism. Indeed, the very term seems to hold numerous, sometimes contradictory meanings among those of different scholarly traditions. Sometimes the debates reach a level of intensity unknown to most ivory-tower disagreements. Despite the squabbles, every academic researcher appears to accept one central tenet of feminism: Gender constitutes a fundamental category of analysis. To understand a person's life, you need to know whether the person is a man or a woman.

The feminist focus on gender has its own problems. The most serious is essentialism, or the tendency to think that all women are essentially the same as each other. In looking at the differences between the genders, psychologists, sociologists, political scientists, and others can lose sight of the variations among women. The very category "woman" means that different women's experiences—and their conditions of living—are essentialized, at least to some degree.

The problem has not escaped notice. Questions have arisen. We have begun to consider the extent to which the experiences of all women have been squeezed into a mold that fits only the most privileged. We have even begun to wonder if there are any ways in which knowledge of White, highly educated, middle-class, heterosexual women can not only leave us uninformed about other women but can also actually blind us to the circumstances and the phenomenologies of women who enjoy little access to power and to the chroniclers of power, including ourselves.

Such concerns lead to others. How is it possible, we must now ask, to avoid essentialism when we use categories of analysis such as gender and ethnicity? Can we speak of women? Or only of White women and women of color? If we speak of White women, do we assume that all White women have the same experiences as each other, regardless of age, social class, education, sexual orientation, and disability status? If we speak of Asian American, African American, Native American, and Latina women, do we assume homogeneity? If not, where do we make distinctions and how do we avoid making so many distinctions that we are left without categories? The dilemma is not easy to resolve.

Our volume, *Women's Ethnicities: Journeys Through Psychology,* aims to contribute to the colloquy. All of us in the book are psychologists, we are all women, and we are all American. All of us have agreed to confront, each in her own way, issues of epistemology and of ethics. We all, furthermore, openly acknowledge that every woman's own experiences as a human being shape the questions she asks about human behavior and the methods she employs for finding answers.

For us, community, identity, and professional work are all inextricably intertwined. We are all committed to the common effort to engage in research that is simultaneously feminist and nonessentialist. And we all struggle in the effort.

Looking over the chapters in the volume, one can detect four means by which this collection of authors are able to focus on gender without engaging in essentialism. First, a researcher can use categories that are smaller than the simple categories of gender and ethnicity. The research can explicitly consider whether poor White women, for example, live in circumstances that make them behave in ways that differ from more affluent White women. Second, the researcher can treat various dimensions—such as skin pigmentation or age or education—as characteristics rather than categories. Aside from gender, there are virtually no truly dichotomous variables among the living. Some people even challenge whether gender is dichotomous. For scholars like us who have been trained to place people in discrete conceptual boxes, seeing the world as strings of continua is not always easy. But it is possible, and it is fruitful. Third, the researcher can strive for awareness of her initial assumptions or axioms. No research is value free, and every project starts with some self-evident truth. Being conscious of the starting assumptions is a useful exercise because discussion of the assumptions often leads to the discovery that any given "truth" is not, after all, self-evident to everyone. Finally, researchers can collaborate with others who differ from the self in meaningful ways. Sometimes the collaboration involves working together closely, and sometimes it entails simply attentive reading of each other. Whatever the form, collaboration is essential if diversity is to be embraced and solipsism is to be avoided.

You do not need to be a rocket scientist to see that this book is ripe with collaboration. Seven of the eleven chapters are coauthored, and the book has two coeditors. Authors allude to each other's work. Not readily apparent from the printed text, however, is a deeper collaboration among all the authors. This book grew out of a special conference that took place in summer 1994 on Martha's Vineyard, for which Karen Wyche and Faye Crosby served as co-leaders. The process was communal.

Because of its impact on the book that you are now holding, the meeting deserves at least a brief description here. In spring 1994, four White women and four women of color, all of whom were psychologists, were asked to come to Martha's Vineyard to spend several days talking, eating, and living together. The invitation came with strings attached. First, each recruited guest had to bring with her a female friend of the other designation: Each woman of color came with a white "buddy," and each White woman came with a buddy who was a woman of color. All the guests—recruits and buddies both—were asked to bring an open heart and mind and also a specific dilemma or problem relevant to issues of gender and ethnicity that bothered her as a feminist. More than one participant, for instance, brought problems of miscommunication and spoke of how they had inadvertently offended someone or been offended by someone. In the calm and magic air of the Vineyard, the group confronted, without pretense or protection, some of the problems we have faced in our journeys through psychology.

At the end of the meeting, we invited each participant to contribute a chapter to this volume. Each potential author was given permission to obtain coauthors. At least one author from each of the present chapters attended the 1994 meeting. We asked those writing chapters to present their own research in the chapter and, in addition, to address two questions in any fashion that seemed appropriate. The questions were

- How do gender and ethnicity, conceptualized as categories of analysis, figure in the work reported in the chapter?
- How does one's own gender and ethnicity influence one's conceptualizations of gender and ethnicity?

Chapter drafts arrived in winter 1994, and we worked side by side to provide feedback to the authors. By May 1995, all authors had turned in completed manuscripts. Between the two of us, one had decades of publishing experience and the other less experience. But never has the process of confronting thorny issues been so easy and enjoyable.

While working on the final draft of the book, we came across a chapter by bell hooks on feminism. In it, hooks says:

Small groups of people coming together to engage in feminist discussion, in dialectical struggle make a space where the "personal is political" as a starting point for education.... All efforts at self-transformation challenge us to engage in ongoing critical self-examination and reflection about feminist practice, about how we live in the world. This individual commitment, when coupled with engagement in collective discussion, provides a space for critical feedback which strengthens our efforts to change and make ourselves new.

hooks goes on to say: "It is in this commitment to feminist principles in our word and deeds that the hope of feminist revolution lies" (hooks, 1992, p. 190).

We hope that the sense of dialogue that undergirds this book can continue. Of course, our hopes and desires are only part of the story. We've said our piece. It's your turn now.

References

hooks, b. (1992). Feminism: A transformational politic. In D. Rhode (Ed.), *Theoretical Perspectives on Sexual Differences* (pp. 185–193). New Haven, CT: Yale University Press.

Travis, C. (1992). *The mismeasure of woman.* New York, NY: Simon and Schuster.

Unger, R., and Crawford, M. (1992). *Women and gender: A feminist psychology.* New York, NY: McGraw-Hill.

PART ONE

Education Is Political

Education is a process in which the end result is learning. There are several ways this can happen. Learning can take place when teachers choose to impart certain types of knowledge to those without that knowledge. This is the traditional way we think of teaching. Education can occur when knowledge is gained for a particular purpose by self-learning. Also, learning can be unplanned and unexpected. Here something becomes learned, although the expected outcome was quite different. The last way, often painful, leaves a lasting impression.

Although education can happen in all these ways, the authors of Part 1 remind us that the process of education is political. This means that what is taught, how it is taught, how studies are designed, and what scholarship is used in teaching are influenced by the ideology of the teacher, researcher, and larger academic community.

How do the politics of the academy influence the professional life of an academic? How acceptable are research findings that support minority children having improved academic performance over White children? These are some of the questions that Brenda Allen discusses in Chapter 2. The ways in which academics play a gatekeeping function in perpetuating the status quo is seen clearly in the personal account of her experiences. Allen chronicles the barriers she faced as a graduate student and faculty member in gaining acceptance of her work for publication and funding. Several of her studies examining children's learning in a "movement-expressive" context find consistently that African American children outperform White children under these conditions. We learn that these findings become problematic for those who question the results. Brenda Allen's chapter challenges us to examine biases regarding research with same-race participants, the standards by which psychology accepts difference, and the political power used within the profession to shape the scholarship that becomes disseminated.

Is teaching a political act? To answer this question, Kimberly Kinsler and Sue Rosenberg Zalk discuss the inherently political nature of teaching. In Chapter 3 they argue that instructors make political choices in what theories and research to include in their courses. The politics of this decision-making is often hidden, as teachers present facts or theories as neutral to unsuspecting students. These daily curricula decisions limit the range of interactive discourse and thus may change the content of such courses.

Kinsler and Zalk wish to make their teaching both multicultural and feminist. Using themselves as examples, they explain how, as faculty members of the same department, they teach major theories of learning and development with a focus on cultural content. However, they vary in the emphasis placed on feminist and ethnic perspectives, although both are covered: Kinsler emphasizes ethnic aspects and Zalk focuses on issues of gender. They both recognize their own political agenda in their teaching and wish to challenge their students to become critical thinkers. For them professional integrity comes from acknowledging to students that what and how they teach is not neutral and in evaluating with them the biases and contrary evidence to dominant group theories and research.

Do feminist professors put into practice their ideological commitments, especially when claiming a strong adherence to feminist pedagogy? Do they "walk the talk" or just "talk the talk?" In Chapter 4, Julie Kmiec, who is a student, and her professor, Faye Crosby, present a collaborative study with Judith Worell (a professor at another institution) to test that question. Through both interviews and questionnaires, seventy-seven women professors of psychology who are members of Division 35 (The Psychology of Women) of the American Psychological Association responded to an invitation to be in the study. It was interesting to find that there was little association between attitudes and behaviors among the sample. Those professors of psychology who said they were highly committed to feminist pedagogy did not behave differently from others in the sample. All engaged in behaviors that were promotive of learning.

These authors wonder if their findings are influenced by who they are as researchers—their homogeneity as White women. Does the lens through which they experience and understand feminism focus in a particular way? Kmiec, Crosby, and Worell lead the reader on a journey of self-reflection. They wonder if the study would have been developed differently if they were not all White and female. That is, would different samples have been chosen? Would the questions asked and the conceptions of feminism have been different?

What themes run through these chapters? We see several:

- All the authors acknowledge that what they do, teaching or research, is political. These behaviors frame the way in which they ask research questions, have their findings accepted, or impart knowledge to students.
- Research and teaching are self-reflective processes. Feminist psychologists critically evaluate their work and are not afraid to show their vulnerabilities.
- The product of these authors' work is always in the context of a larger social network. This network takes several forms: collaborative research, mentoring, and peer consultation. The result is a constant exchange of ideas to help improve their research or teaching.

These themes in Part 1 reflect that the writings, teaching, and research of psychologists are never neutral. The process is political. The chapters of these six women help us to understand that the questions they ask in their studies, the evaluation of their results, and the types of knowledge they choose to emphasize are all included in this political process. They have much to tell us about how they think about this process, the risks they take, and the problems they encounter along the way.

2

Staying Within the Academy

Brenda A. Allen

In the landmark case of *Brown v. the Board of Education of Topeka, Kansas,* Thurgood Marshall convinced the Supreme Court that Black Americans would continue to be located at the lower end of the economic ladder if something was not done to improve access to educational resources. Marshall argued that school segregation violated the Constitution. He won his case. Since 1954 segregated educational facilities have been illegal. The civil rights movement of the 1950s and 1960s brought continued changes. Formal barriers that had previously blocked the access of large numbers of African Americans to certain educational opportunities were now dismantled. But some informal barriers remained. Blacks have continued to be less successful in and more alienated from the educational enterprise than Whites. The question is, why?

The present chapter presents one African American woman's view of why the apparent change in racial climate has not been fully successful at balancing the scales of equity in the academic arena. Using my research on African American schoolchildren as a vehicle for discussion, I attempt to show that although American society is more tolerant than it used to be, it is a long way from being cured of racism. I speak of my own career not because I imagine I am unique. On the contrary, I go into some detail because I think that what has happened to me happens to many Black scholars and researchers throughout academia. There are systematic forces at work. In looking at my own career, I am simply giving some concrete detail to these abstract forces.

I believe that the nature of racism in America has generally changed from overt acts of race superiority to subtle acts that perpetuate the status quo, and I will use my own experiences to illustrate the latter. I argue that this new form of racism can be as—if not more—damaging to the success of

African American people as the earlier overt forms of racism, especially when people of color and White people remain separated from each other outside of formal occupational settings.

One peculiarity of my narrative should not escape notice. It is the connection between my own situation and the situation of those whom I study. Looking at how African American youngsters become alienated from the American school system, I must reflect on how I, as a highly educated adult with "good" credentials, often feel unwelcome in the White academy and often distrust the rhetoric of racial equality that seems so pervasive among White liberals today. Given the parallels between my subject matter and my life, this chapter sprinkles reflections about myself and my career through descriptions of my work. Throughout the chapter, I examine the lessons to be learned from the struggle.

When Often Is Heard a Discouraging Word

My major research interest pertains to the influence of culture on learning. I am interested in this phenomenon as it relates to educationally disadvantaged children generally and more particularly to those African Americans who are at risk for especially poor academic performance. Indeed, it has been my commitment to the understanding of African American children's educational plight that has led me to the study of culture and cognition.

Upon entering graduate school, I was plagued by the question, Why do African American children fare so poorly in academic situations? In an attempt to answer this question, I began to study what seemed to me to be a vast array of information offered within the field of psychology. Even though various explanations were offered in a variety of subject areas such as motivation, learning, and personality, a common theme emerged, and I became increasingly aware of a major trend present in the study of Black children and their school performance. Although the literature was clearly divided between genetic and environmental explanations, regardless of the psychological process implicated, both views began with the general assumption of Black inferiority. On the one hand, the genetic explanation, which is best characterized by the work of Arthur Jensen (1969, 1973, 1980), assumes that an inferior genetic code accounts for African American children's academic ills. On the other hand, the environmental view (Deutsch, 1967; Hunt, 1975; Katz, 1973) assumes an inferior home environment as the major culprit in Black children's academic plight.

The educational implications of each of these views left much to be desired. Neither camp seemed to offer an alternative that preserved the viability and integrity of African American people or the viability and integrity of the African American experience. Jensen (1969, 1973, 1980) argued, quite passionately, that Black people should not be expected to learn information that they simply do not have the mental capacity to understand. Instead, he asserted, the educational system should work to improve Black people's use of lower-level processing and to prepare them for their place in the natural order of things. Now what was I supposed to do with that line of reasoning?

The environmental approach offered an alternative that was just as unsettling for me. Specifically, advocates of the environmental view propose that the intellectual functioning of Black people can be enhanced if steps are taken to expose children to the types of experiences characteristic of the life-styles possessed by those who perform well in schools, in this case white middle-class children. As a solution, the compensatory educational programs developed during the Johnson administration's War on Poverty were generated. These programs, known as Head Start, Title One, and more recently Chapter One, are designed to counter the assumed disadvantaged home experiences of low-performing children with enriching experience derived from the cultural ethos of the White middle class. In more extreme cases, projects such as Home Start (Miller, 1983) were developed, where the environmental intervention commences at birth instead of in the fourth and fifth year of life. That is, an attempt is made to intercept the assumed debilitating effects of the home environment before they affect children's intellectual growth. Although this line of thinking was more palatable to the liberal conscious, was the implication that the Black cultural experience offered *nothing* in the way of intellectual stimulation?

As I plunged on through the literature, I noticed an ever growing body of work dedicated to presenting persuasive criticisms of both of these lines of thinking (see Allen, 1978; Bradley and Bradley, 1977; Caplan and Nelson, 1973; Howard and Scott, 1981; Gould, 1981, 1994; Kamin, 1974, 1995; Persell, 1977; Ryan, 1971). The genetic stance has been criticized for many things, especially for making illogical leaps from differences within groups to differences between groups (Gould, 1994) and for using correlational data to infer cause-and-effect outcomes (Kamin, 1995). The environmental view has been criticized for being limited and myopic in scope by focusing upon individual rather than universal change (Persell, 1977; Ryan, 1971). Environmental explanations have offered empirically weak constructs that have not held up under close scrutiny (Bradley and Bradley, 1977; Howard and Scott, 1981). The most far-reaching criticism of both views is that neither has been successful at generating programs that suffice in improving the academic performance of African American children (Barclay and Allen, 1982; Boykin, 1986; Gould, 1994; Ogbu, 1978; Springle and Schaefer, 1985). It appeared that explanations for Black children's academic ills would lie elsewhere than in the traditional psychological literature.

Fortunately, I soon began training under my mentor, A. Wade Boykin. Boykin presented me and the other graduate students at Howard University with an integrative conceptual framework that uses cultural context as an overarching explanatory system. Boykin proposed that the poor academic behavior of African American children is a result more of motivation than of cognitive ability per se (see Allen and Boykin, 1991, 1992; Boykin, 1983, 1986, 1994a, 1994b).

Boykin's analysis starts with a depiction of the African American's cultural reality that acknowledges the complexity and diversity inherent in a group of people who possess differing degrees of contact with and participation in mainstream U.S. culture. Gutierrez and Nagata (this volume) point out that a direct focus on minority groups reveals intragroup variations that are obscured when the minority group is seen only as a foil to the majority. Boykin's work is no exception.

More specifically, Boykin portrays African American culture as encompassing three realms of experiences: the mainstream, the minority, and the Afro-cultural. Briefly, the mainstream experience entails beliefs, values, and behavioral styles common to most members of the United States whereas the minority experience refers to certain coping strategies and defense mechanisms developed by most minority groups in order to face life in an oppressive environment. The Afro-cultural experience, which is essentially the link between contemporary African Americans and the traditional West African worldview, includes certain beliefs, values, and behaviors common to most Black people throughout the diaspora. It is maintained that not all Black families participate in each of the three realms to the same degree. Thus we witness a great deal of heterogeneity within the African American population (Allen and Boykin, 1992; Boykin, 1983, 1986). Yet those African American children who are most at risk academically tend to come disproportionately from the low-income stratum of the African American population. The life experiences of low-income African Americans are heavily characterized by the Afro-cultural realm of the African American cultural experience. Such appears to be the case primarily because the economic circumstances of this particular group of people essentially serve to isolate them from the everyday practices of mainstream society. Boykin (1983, 1986, 1994a, 1994b) argues that it is this cultural reality that may best account for the academic problems faced by these Black children.

There exists a general disparity between the Afro-cultural experience and the mainstream White experience. In the former, a premium is placed on audio stimulation and movement (Young, 1970, 1974). In the latter, quiet is revered (Wachs, Uzgiris, and Hunt, 1971). Whereas rhythms are essential to Afro-cultural life, White America stresses that which is linear and unidirectional (with the direction being from the top down) (Shade, 1991). Within the Afro-cultural mores, group interconnectedness is prized, whereas the mainstream places a premium on the individual (Sampson, 1979). Verbal interactions in the Afro-cultural context are characterized by more of a give and take than is true of those in the Euro-cultural context

(Brice-Heath, 1990; Gay, 1987; Botan and Smitherman, 1991). Afro-cultural music employs syncopation more than Euro-cultural music does (Thompson, 1984). (Refer to Boykin, 1983, for a more systematic contrast between the mainstream and Afro-cultural experiences.) It should be noted that no one cultural experience is completely devoid of particular beliefs, values, and styles. Indeed, most if not all cultural systems value, for example, movement expression along with movement compression. What is important, however, is the patterning of these cultural motifs. Greater emphasis is given to certain aspects over others, depending upon the cultural system of the group. In plain words, the Afro-cultural experience is not the only context in which music and movement, for instance, are venerated. Yet, this cultural system incorporates these aspects of experience much more interactively and frequently in its daily routines than does the culture of the mainstream in American society.

Such cultural incongruence has direct implications for schooling. The U.S. educational system is based upon the cultural ideas of the mainstream. If the Afro-cultural experience is the most salient in the everyday lives of low-income Black children, then the cultural context of the school will be relatively unfamiliar. Unfamiliarity can undermine motivation (Banks, McQuater, and Hubbard, 1979; Tharp, 1989). Everyone benefits by learning in a manner that is familiar, and everyone learns less well in "foreign" situations than in "homey" ones (Cole, 1988; Vygotsky, 1962). Thus Boykin (1983, 1986) reasoned that these Black children may be performing less well in the school context not because they lacked the ability but because they lacked the will.

I knew that if Boykin's ideas were correct, low-income Black children could perform better than they currently do. I reasoned that if task contexts were designed to reflect more closely the Afro-cultural experience than is usually the case, then low-income Black children may be more motivated to engage in the task at hand and consequently would learn more (Allen and Boykin, 1992). It was at this point that I began to study the possible motivational effects of rhythmic movement, music, and percussion on low-income Black children's learning.

I chose these particular variables for several reasons. Although the positive effects of general movement on learning had already been established in the literature (G. Humphrey, 1952; J. Humphrey, 1962, 1969), the special importance of rhythmic movement, music, and percussion to the Afrocultural experience had been clearly delineated (Abrahams and Swed, 1983; Hale, 1982; Gordon, 1982; Morgan, 1980; Thompson, 1984; Young, 1974). Also, the use of music as a source of background stimulation could help to expand earlier work on the facilitative effects of high sensate stimulation on low-income Black children's learning primarily because much of the stimulation present in the African American home environment extends from the presence of music and movement (Boykin, 1979, 1982). Finally, and perhaps most important, a focus on movement as a cultural dimension might help explain why a disproportionate number of African American children are clinically diagnosed as hyperactive (Lansdorf, 1979; Spring, Blunder, Lawrence, and Yellin, 1977). This focus might eventually have very positive effects in helping clinicians understand how movement is a part of some children's natural behaviors and should not be interpreted as dysfunctional. I reasoned that if a context of learning aided by rhythmic movement, music, and percussion could be used to facilitate Black children's learning, then such a context could someday serve as a viable alternative to drug-induced movement control.

With the help of my mentor, I devised an experiment to see if we could increase the performance of low-income Black children, aged six and nine, on an academic task. The children engaged in a paired associate learning task. In any session, an adult taught two or three children twelve sets of animal-food pairs (e.g., bear-cake) and then used a matching pictures task to test the children's retention. After an interval of five minutes, the children were tested again. The adult who was present for testing was blind to the experimental condition of the children.

Of critical importance was one variable: the learning context. One-half of the children were taught the picture pairs in a learning context that was designed to be familiar to someone from an Afro-cultural home. The other half were taught in the more standard Euro-cultural fashion. Because the research entered virgin territory, I decided to make the two learning contexts as different from each other as I could. This meant that several different aspects of the situations were varied. More specifically, in the Afro-cultural learning context

> the children were told to stand around the experimenter while they listened to a rhythmic percussive tune. Then they were told the experimenter would call out either a pair of words or only one word, while displaying the corresponding poster. If the experimenter called out a pair of words, the children were to respond by calling back the pair; if the experimenter called out only one word in the pair, they were to respond by calling back the appropriate word to complete the pair. (Boykin and Allen, 1988, p. 339)

In the Euro-cultural learning context, music was not present and the children, sitting in chairs, were instructed to repeat each pair after it was orally presented by the experimenter. For example, the experimenter would say "bear-cake," and the children would repeat "bear-cake."

At the close of the experimental session, which consisted of two learning trials, the children were interviewed and given two questionnaires to take home. From the answers, we were able to code the degree to which the home environment matched the prototypical Afro-cultural environment and the extent to which the child engaged in motorically active behaviors.

This project served as my master's thesis, and to conduct the study required four months. The analyses revealed that, as predicted, African American children in the Afro-cultural learning condition retained significantly more information than did their peers in the Euro-cultural learning condition. The difference was most marked among the older children (nine-year-olds) and after the second trial. We also found that enhancement of learning occurred most for children whose home environment was especially like the Afro-cultural prototype and who were, themselves, motorically active. We also found evidence of a link between the amount of sensate stimulation afforded in one's home environment, as well as the amount of motorically active behavior displayed by the child, and enhanced performance under the "movement-expressive" learning context.

The results of the study were rewarding in that our initial expectations obtained some validation. We believed that the study merited publication because it was grounded in a theoretical base, the design was experimentally sound, and the analyses were appropriate to the questions posed. So the thesis was revised to conform to the traditional journal publication style and submitted to a prominent American Psychological Association (APA) journal in fall 1984. Four years and four journal submissions later, the paper was finally published (see Boykin and Allen, 1988).

I wished to convince myself that all publications take time, but four years seemed a bit much. The publication process was one that definitely left me with feelings of suspicion. My alienation seems especially strong when I recall the rejection letters for my article submissions to APA journals. The paper was never criticized for lacking experimental integrity. On the contrary, the paper was consistently praised for its experimental sophistication. But I was also consistently told that the homogeneous nature of my subject population, that is, eighty low-income Black children, did not warrant my conclusions about the cultural nature of my findings. Basically, I was told that I could not make conclusions about culture without a White control group.

How valid was the criticism? In my discussion section, I cautioned readers about concluding that the results proved that all children learn best in an environment that mimics their home environment. So surely there was some validity to the criticism. Yet I thought that my findings should have provoked interest. The Black children performed better in the movement and music condition than in the condition without these factors. The prediction was made, and the results were consistent with the prediction. They corroborated a theory. So the lack of a control group as the major basis for rejecting the article for publication struck me as strange. This was especially so because I had kept abreast of psychological journals and could see that

99 percent of the articles presented samples of White middle-class populations only but made generalizations to all people. Where were the Black
control groups?

I asked myself: Why is it that Black people must always check their psychological reality against that of White people but the psychological reality
of White people automatically stands for the psychological reality of all
people? It became clear to me that the assumption of universality based
upon the performance of White subjects was a major racist supposition that
did not go away with greater racial tolerance and that such an assumption
has had a direct effect on my progress. That is, I did not receive my first
publication until the year that I left graduate school because I was spending
time between my studies revising and resubmitting the paper from my master's thesis. Upon entering the job market, this process put me at a disadvantage compared to my contemporaries who were able to move more eas-
ily their work from the laboratory to the journal publications.

And the Skies Are Quite Cloudy All Day

The episode of my master's thesis convinced me that my findings may have
been more of a threat to "the way things are" than I had initially perceived,
but it did not make me abandon my work. On the contrary, the findings of
the inaugural study—and the resistance to those findings among journal editors—helped me to realize that Boykin and I may possibly have identified
something that could be very useful to education in general and to the education of African American children in particular. So I charged onward.

The first study left many questions unanswered. For example, like my
critics, I questioned whether the context of rhythmic movement, music, and
percussion would elicit similar cognitive facilitation in all children, regardless of cultural orientation. Further, I questioned the actual psychological
underpinnings for improved performance under such a movement-expressive context. I wanted to know whether the enhanced motivation that presumably underlay enhanced performance could be measured directly. I also
questioned whether an Afro-cultural testing context would enhance performance as much as the Afro-cultural learning context had.

I sought the answers to some of these questions in my doctoral dissertation. More specifically, I expanded my previous work by examining the effects of Afro-cultural setting (which afforded rhythmic movement, music,
and percussion) on both learning and recall. In addition, I added a comparative group of low-income White children. In my dissertation, 32 White
and 40 Black low-income first and second graders from a large northeastern school district learned picture pairs, as the children had in my master's
thesis. Both sexes were well represented in the sample.

First, half of the children learned one set of materials in the Afro-cultural context, with rhythm, movement, and interaction. Then, a week later, children learned another set of materials in the Euro-cultural context, with no music and movement opportunity. For the other half of the children, the order was reversed. Testing immediately followed learning, and there were two testing trials within each learning context. For half of the children, a rhythmic tune was played during testing; for the other half, no music was played during testing. Thus, my dissertation experiment employed a 2 × 2 × 2 × 2 fully crossed design in which the independent variables were ethnicity (Black or White), testing context (music or no music), learning context (Afro-cultural or Euro-cultural), and trial (1, 2).

My results showed that Black and White children from similar socioeconomic backgrounds do respond differently within Afro-cultural and Euro-cultural contexts. Music and movement during learning helped the Black children but hindered the White children. The interaction can be seen in Table 2.1, which displays the mean number of correct matches made by the White and Black children in the Euro-cultural and Afro-cultural learning contexts. Analyses also showed that the White children performed less well than the Black children in an Afro-cultural learning situation, regardless of recall context factors. As for the Black children, stimulation at either the moment of learning or the moment of testing proved helpful. My dissertation seemed to have corrected for the major criticism given by reviewers of the first paper. I included a White control group, and the obtained results lent credence to my cultural interpretation. I did not suggest that the cultural argument was proven, only that it was supported by the data.

The work of the dissertation also expanded the work of the master's thesis by looking at the testing context and not just the learning context. We found that music played during testing helped the Black children to recover from a "no music and movement" learning environment. For the White children, factors at testing seemed not to be as powerful as factors present during learning. The Black children performed about the same on the task

TABLE 2.1   Mean Number of Correct Matches in Learning Context

	Learning Context	
Child's Ethnicity	*Afro-Cultural*	*Euro-Cultural*
African American	5.71	5.07
Euro American	4.56	6.33

NOTE: Possible range is 0–12 for number of correct matches. Post hoc tests revealed that within ethnic group, the only means that differed significantly were White children's Euro-cultural versus Afro-cultural performance. Black children did not show a difference in performance by learning context until the trials factor entered the equation. Across ethnic groups, post hoc tests revealed that White children outperformed Black children in the Euro-cultural context, and Black children outperformed White children in the Afro-cultural context.

whenever music was present, be it at learning only, at testing only, or at learning and testing. The Black children's worst performance was in the "no music and movement" learning context coupled with the "no music" testing environment. The White children did better when no music and movement were present at learning than when these factors were present at learning, irrespective of music or no music at testing.

So why then did it take another four years for this paper to appear in print? Several factors may have been important. One problem is that the results were complex and were thus less clear cut than is sometimes the case in published work. I obtained a statistically significant four-way interaction, for example, and reviewers hate four-way interactions because they mean that the central results—in my case the two-way interaction between cultural orientation and learning context—can be said to be true under some conditions and not under others. But the interpretation of the mean difference implied by the four-way data fits well with the theory guiding the inquiry. The complex nature of my findings could not, therefore, have provided the full explanation for the rejection because many articles published in mainstream journals are complex and do lack clear-cut findings.

What else could have been happening? One factor might have been that, like all authors, I sometimes expressed my ideas in a somewhat impenetrable fashion. Again, possible verbal infelicity could not have been the only force at play because, I am told, many manuscripts that are accepted by APA journals need stylistic improvement and clarification before going to press. One of my current colleagues reviews manuscripts for a number of APA journals, consulting on a total of fifty to seventy-five manuscripts a year. She tells me that even the six or so articles she recommends for publication each year often need major rewriting. Judging from the range of reviews received for this study, I wondered if I might have been held to a higher or a different standard than I would have been if the findings did not contain some threatening material. The paper was submitted to three journals, one of which was a special edition devoted to work on minority populations. The reasons for rejection ranged from the simple—the results are too complicated—to questions about whether I had done enough previous work to warrant publication of this one investigation. That is, execute your entire empirical program and then we will publish your work (if the manuscript is not too long).

The most telling comment came in a rejection letter from one editor. He wrote something to the effect that he must agree with one of the reviewers, that it was not clear whether the experimenter (me) had somehow done something in the two learning contexts to bias the outcome. He wondered, that is, if I had somehow made one or the other context more pleasant for one or the other group of children. I realized that there might be many ways to interpret the editor's comment, but one of them was extremely hurtful. His comment questioned my integrity as a person and my integrity as a researcher. Here I was presenting to a journal a well-conceived, well-executed study that was successful at yielding an interaction so complex that some journals refused to publish it, yet it was assumed that I did not understand the very basic lesson of research methods 101, controlling for confounds across my experimental conditions.

Would all work have received such criticism? Is this harsh way of speaking simply typical of the review process? I did not know, but I strongly suspected that the objection lay with what I had found and not how I had found it. Not only did my results show that Black and White children can have comparable performance if certain cultural factors are taken into consideration in task context, but they also showed that in certain conditions— namely, the Afro-cultural learning context—Black children can outperform White children on an academic task. A literature search revealed that such a finding had never been published. I began to think that maybe my research findings went against some deeply held racial stereotype about why Black and White people perform differently in school. If reviewers and editors could not fathom the notion of superior performance by Black children, then they would have been even harsher on the first draft of my paper than they would have been on some other, equally imperfect but less upsetting submission.

I abandoned the major APA journals and submitted the paper to an international journal at the suggestion of a new female mentor, Carol Camp Yeakey, who had become very instrumental in my professional development. In our discussions, she made me realize that issues of racial and cultural difference in the international arena were seen as less of a personal threat to scholars than seems to be the case in our society. The review process for the international journal took only six weeks (as compared to four to six months with U.S. journals), and to my surprise, the only revisions requested by the international reviewers were to change the words Black and White to Afro American and Euro American. Remember that this was the same, exact paper that received the criticisms mentioned above: None of the previous reviews were helpful in improving upon the text of the paper, so it had remained unaltered. The paper was published in less than six months (see Allen and Boykin, 1991).

The treatment I received from the European journal did not make me rethink my questions about the assumptions of U.S. gatekeepers. It certainly did seem that people assumed that Black children can never do anything academic better than White children. All of this could have been conceived of as a figment of my imagination if I had not run more fully into this assumption several years later, when I applied for grant money.

Out, Out of the Range

In 1989 at a national meeting, a representative of Smith College invited me to apply there for a job. One year later I began life as an assistant professor at the liberal arts women's college. I was one of two people of color in a department with twelve full-time faculty members and several adjuncts and associates.

With the encouragement of my senior colleagues in the Psychology Department, I submitted a grant proposal to an agency that provides research support for developing scholars. The grant could have greatly affected my career in that it would have provided five years of reduced teaching as well as summer research support. Receiving such a grant would have made a major difference in the rate at which my research career could have developed.

My grant proposal made it through the first round of cuts. Only eleven finalists out of hundreds of applicants were chosen. Being a finalist meant that I would be given a thirty-minute interview with the selection committee, after which the final decisions would be made. Only five of the eleven finalists were actually to receive awards.

I traveled three hours by train to reach my interview. I had planned to arrive early, and as it turned out, I arrived an hour and a half before my appointment. While waiting I was able to observe three of the other finalists being escorted to and from the interviewing room. Each finalist was promptly ushered in on the half hour and promptly ushered out thirty minutes later. When my time rolled around I was ushered in, but I did not emerge from the room until close to an hour later and that was only because the chairperson of the selection committee insisted that I be excused.

What did they have to talk to me about for so long? Primarily the interview focused on the findings I had obtained for my control group. I was extensively questioned about my thoughts on why the White children in the study had not performed well under my movement-expressive context. We discussed how my choice of music for the movement-expressive context created ethnic boundaries that the White children may not have been able to cross. I said that the type of music was part of the experimental question; they said that it created a situation that was unduly biased toward the Black children. Silently, I was thinking "given that same logic, the context devoid of movement and music then is unduly biased against the Black children, and as such supports my point." But very few of the reviewers wanted to discuss the performance of the Black children. Most wanted to explore why the White children had not performed well. I had never stated anywhere in my proposal that the goals of my research was to understand the control group. The White children, which all the reviewers of my first paper said I needed, were just that, a control group. My research questions have and continue to be focused on alleviating the educational difficulties of African American children through the use of *their* proactive life experiences. I sought to discern whether the cultivation of music and movement orientations within the African American community had any pedagogical significance. Implicit in this question is an orientation derived from a specific cultural experience where the music implied also has a cultural link. If the music was not linked culturally to the context, the nature of my question would have been dramatically different. Nonetheless, in my interview I was forced to discuss my control group at the expense of discussing the heuristic value of my research for African American children.

I did not feel that the selection committee and I communicated very effectively with one another. Would the communication have been more complete had the selection committee included someone who is deeply familiar with the Afro-centered culture of the diaspora? I cannot be sure, but I think so.

Not surprisingly, I was not awarded one of the five grants. I was, however, awarded a small grant to test issues relevant to the committee's concerns. To receive the money, I had to restate my research question so that it would be in line with the concerns of the selection committee. They were mainly interested in whether the effects yielded for the White populations were more particular to the type of music employed than to the music and movement context per se. They wondered: Would the White children's performance be just as good as the Black children's performance if the music was less "Black"?

I explored their agenda in an experiment with three types of learning conditions. The first afforded the opportunity for movement along with a musical tune characterized by highly syncopated (i.e., Black) rhythmic patterns (Thompson, 1984). The second condition afforded movement opportunity along with a musical tune characterized by nonsyncopated (i.e., White) rhythmic patterns (Tharp, 1989). Finally, there was a context devoid of music and movement opportunity. The study utilized the same paired-associate learning task used in the previous studies where performance was measured by the number of pairs correctly recalled. The subjects were twenty White children. The results showed that the best performance of these children was again in the no-music condition. Both music latent contexts seemed to adversely affect performance (Allen, in preparation). So the effects seem to be much deeper then simply the type of music (as I had suggested in my original proposal).

In my opinion, my experience with the granting agency was mixed. The work that I was "funded into doing" provided more evidence for my line of reasoning and as such can be looked upon as a positive outcome. That I was denied the larger opportunity was discouraging. I also felt discouraged because the selection committee's actions essentially said that their questions were the right questions and if I wanted to get anywhere in this academic world I must acquiesce to the status quo. This seemed to me to bring politics into science in a way that feels ethically uncomfortable.

Where the Deer and the Antelope Play

There are days when I think that dropping out of the academy, or at least decreasing my efforts to be highly productive, would feel like a blessed relief. Communicating across the racial barriers is often difficult. This is because the academy as an institution and I as an individual do not seem to share many of the same basic assumptions about how the world operates. This difference in worldview often makes doing my job feel like an unrewarded chore.

If I did drop out, I would be a statistic in American higher education. At all moments beyond high school, like the moments of high school and the moments prior to high school, the prospects for Blacks are dim.

The retention rates of African Americans in predominantly White educational institutions are dismal. In 1985, Black students represented 7 percent of all incoming first-year students; in 1989, however, they represented only 3 percent of all graduates. Allen (1978, 1988) has shown that Black students leave predominantly White colleges after their first two years at a rate of three to one when compared to their White counterparts. Black students more than white students report frustration and lack of social and academic support as their major reasons for leaving school.

The picture becomes even more bleak when we look at graduate training. The statistics are the most disheartening in my own area, the sciences. Blacks earn fewer Ph.D.s now than they did twenty years ago, and only 1 percent of all science doctorates are awarded to African Americans (Pool, 1990). As Pool (1990) noted, it is nearly impossible in certain fields to find a Black candidate for a job opening. In 1988, the number of African Americans to receive doctorates in mathematics and computer science was one each. Needless to say, these statistics mean that the presence of African Americans in the academy is slight.

Once in the academy, African Americans are still located disproportionately at the lower levels. Consider that although African Americans make up only 4.7 percent of all full-time faculty, over 60 percent of these African Americans are located at the level of assistant professor or below (National Center for Educational Statistics, 1993). Moreover, those in associate and full professor positions represent only 3.2 percent of this population as compared to the 90.4 percent representation by their White counterparts (National Center for Educational Statistics, 1993). Thus, lack of success in the academic arena does not stop at the differential rate of earning degrees.

Despite feelings of discouragement, I—unlike the low-income Black youth whom I want to help—do not allow my feelings of alienation to immobilize me. In looking at the factors that keep me going, one may discover some clues to the puzzle of Black underachievement. Primarily, that I work in a supportive proximal environment aids my ability to keep the larger issues in perspective. I do not feel the racial pressures or racial insensitivities from the outside on a daily basis. The collegial support extended to me within my department allows me to receive objective feedback about my work, and I do not have to question the intent of the criticism. Moreover, I am able to share critiques from the outside world, which provides me with other interpretations of those criticisms. So I am able to assess whether I am reading too much into what the reviewers are saying or whether my perceptions are pretty much on target or at least shared by my co-workers. In addition, my colleagues provide for me the type of critical scrutiny that my work is likely to receive from review committees, and when necessary they help me to reframe the issues so that the phrasing of my work does not put off reviewers before they consider its scientific integrity. Such a supportive and mentoring environment helps me stick with climbing the tenure ladder at my institution.

Equally important has been my continued relationship with my original mentor and other Black scholars around the country. I have been adopted into the mentoring families of many African American researchers and I try to pay my debt by extending my academic and professional knowledge to those less informed than I am. Being cultivated into a scholar and helping to cultivate a community of African American scholars allow me to see that as long as we continue to train the soldiers and remain an integral part of the struggle for intellectual freedom, then the fight for equity becomes less burdensome for any given individual.

Finally, the successes in my life help me to continue the pursuit. Every time a paper is published, a presentation provokes lively discussion, a grant receives critical scrutiny of the methods and not the philosophy, or a student says "I never thought about it quite like that," I feel that I am winning some of the battles and that the fight is worth fighting.

References

Abrahams, R. D., and Swed, J. F. (Eds.) (1983). *After Africa*. New Haven, CT: Yale University Press.

Allen, B. A., and Boykin, A. W. (1991). The influence of contextual factors on Black and White children's performance: Effects of movement opportunity and music. *International Journal of Psychology, 26*, 373–387.

Allen, B. A., and Boykin, A. W. (1992). African American children and the educational process: Alleviating cultural discontinuity through prescriptive pedagogy. *School Psychology Review, 21*(4), 586–596.

Allen, W. R. (1978). The search for applicable theories of Black family life. *Journal of Marriage and Family, 40*, 117–129.

Allen, W. R. (1988). Black students in US higher education: Toward improved access adjustment and achievement. *Urban Review, 20*(3), 165–188.

Banks, W. C., McQuater, G. V., and Hubbard, J. L. (1979). Toward a reconceptualization of social-cognitive bases of achievement orientations in Blacks. In A. W. Boykin, A. J. Franklin, and J. F. Yates (Eds.), *Research directions of Black psychologists* (pp. 294–311). New York, NY: Russell Sage Press.

Barclay, A., and Allen, J. (1982). Effects of Head Start Programs on factor structure of mental ability. *Psychological Reports, 51,* 512–514.

Botan, C., and Smitherman, G. (1991). Black English in the integrated workplace. *Journal of Black Studies, 22,* 168–185.

Boykin, A. W. (1979). Psychological/behavioral verve: Some theoretical explorations and empirical manifestations. In A. W. Boykin, A. J. Franklin, and J. F. Yates (Eds.), *Research directions of Black psychologists* (pp. 351–367). New York, NY: Russell Sage Press.

Boykin, A. W. (1982). Task variability and the performance of Black and White schoolchildren. *Journal of Black Studies, 12,* 469–485.

Boykin, A. W. (1983). The academic performance of Afro-American children. In J. Spence (Ed.), *Achievement and achievement motives* (pp. 321–371). San Francisco, CA: W. Freeman.

Boykin, A. W. (1986). The triple quandary and the schooling of Afro-American children. In U. Neisser (Ed.), *The school achievement of minority children* (pp. 57–92). Hillsdale, NJ: Erlbaum.

Boykin, A. W. (1994a). Afro-cultural expression and its implications for schooling. In E. Hollins (Ed.), *Teaching diverse populations*. Albany, NY: State University of New York Press.

Boykin, A. W. (1994b). Harvesting talent and culture. In R. Rossi (Ed.), *Schools and students at risk: Context and frameworks for positive change* (pp. 116–139). New York, NY: Teacher's College Press.

Boykin, A. W., and Allen, B. A. (1988). Rhythmic movement facilitation of learning in working class Afro-American children. *Journal of Genetic Psychology, 149,* 335–348.

Bradley, L., and Bradley, G. (1977). The academic achievement of Black students in desegregated schools: A critical review. *Review of Educational Research, 47,* 399–449.

Brice-Heath, S. (1990). The children of Trackton's children: Spoken and written language in social change. In J. W. Stigler, R. A. Shweder, and G. Herdth (Eds.), *Cultural psychology: Essays on comparative human development* (pp. 496–519). New York, NY: Cambridge University Press.

Caplan, N., and Nelson, S. (1973). On being useful: The nature and consequences of psychological research on social problems. *American Psychologist, 28,* 199–211.

Cole, M. (1988). Cross-cultural research in the sociohistorical tradition. *Human Development, 31,* 137–157.

Deutsch, M. (1967). The disadvantaged child and the learning process. In M. Deutsch (Ed.), *The disadvantaged child* (pp. 39–58). New York, NY: Basic Books.

Gay, G. (1987). Ethnic identity development and black expressiveness. In G. Gay and W. L. Baber (Eds.), *Expressively Black: The cultural basis of ethnic identity* (pp. 35–74). New York, NY: Praeger.

Gordon, B. (1982). Towards a theory of knowledge acquisition for Black children. *Journal of Education, 74,* 90–108.

Gould, S. J. (1981). *The mismeasure of man.* New York, NY: Norton.

Gould, S. J. (1994, November 14). Curveball. *New Yorker,* 139–149.

Hale, J. (1982). *Black children: Their roots, culture and learning styles.* Provo, UT: Brigham Young Press.

Howard, A., and Scott, R. (1981). The study of minority groups in complex societies. In R. H. Munroe, R. L. Munroe, and B. B. Whitings (Eds.), *The handbook of cross-cultural human development* (pp. 113–152). New York, NY: Garland.

Humphrey, G. (1952). *Thinking: An introduction to experimental.* New York, NY: Wiley.

Humphrey, J. (1962). A pilot study of the use of physical education as a learning medium in the development of language concepts in third grade children. *Research Quarterly, 33,* 136–138.

Humphrey, J. (1969). Active games as a learning medium. *Academic Therapy, 5,* 345–348.

Hunt, M. J. (1975). Social class and preschool language skills. *Genetic Psychology Monographs, 91,* 281–298.

Jensen, A. R. (1969). How much can we boost IQ and scholastic achievement? *Harvard Educational Review, 39*(10), 1–127.

Jensen, A. R. (1973). *Educability and group differences.* New York, NY: Harper and Row.

Jensen, A. R. (1980). *Bias in mental testing.* New York, NY: Basic Books.

Kamin, L. J. (1974). *The science and politics of IQ.* Baltimore, MD: Erlbaum.

Kamin, L. J. (1995). Behind the curve. *Scientific American, 272,* 99–103.

Katz, I. (1973). Alternative to personality deficit interpretation of Negro underachievers. In P. Watson (Ed.), *Psychology and race.* Chicago, IL: Aldine.

Landsdorf, R. (1979). Ethnicity, social class and perception of hyperactivity. *Psychology in the Schools, 16*(2), 293–298.

Miller, P. (1983). *Theories of developmental psychology.* San Francisco, CA: W. H. Freeman.

Morgan, H. (1980). How schools fail Black children. *Social Policy, 11,* 49–54.

National Center for Educational Statistics (1993). *Digest of Educational Statistics, 1993.* Washington, DC: U.S. Department of Education, Office of Educational Research and Improvement.

Ogbu, J. (1978). *Minority education and caste: The American system in cross-cultural perspective.* New York, NY: Academic Press.

Persell, C. (1977). *Education and inequality: A theoretical and empirical synthesis.* New York, NY: Free Press.

Pool, R. (1990). A lost generation. *Science, 248,* 434–435.

Ryan, W. (1971). *Blaming the victim.* New York, NY: Vintage Books.

Sampson, J. (1979). The American ideal. *Journal of Personality and Social Psychology, 36,* 37–52.

Shade, B. (1991). African American patterns of cognition. In R. Jones (Ed.), *Black Psychology,* 3d ed. (pp. 231–247). Berkeley, CA: Cobb-Henry.

Spring, C., Blunder, S., Lawrence, M., and Yellin, A. (1977). Validity and norms of a hyperactivity rating scale. *Journal of Special Education, 11,* 313–321.

Springle, J. E., and Schaefer, L. (1985). Longitudinal evaluation of effects of two compensatory preschool programs on fourth through sixth grade students. *Developmental Psychology, 21,* 702–708.

Tharp, R. (1989). Psychocultural variables and constants: Effects on teaching and learning in school. *American Psychologist, 44,* 349–359.

Thompson, R. F. (1984). *Flash of the spirit: African and Afro-American art and philosophy.* New York, NY: Vintage Books.

Vygotsky, L. S. (1962). *Thought and language.* Cambridge, MA: MIT Press.

Wachs, T. D., Uzgiris, I. C., and Hunt, J. M. (1971). Cognitive development in infants of different age levels and from different environmental backgrounds: An exploratory investigation. *Merrill Palmer Quarterly, 17,* 283–316.

Young, V. (1970). Family and childhood in a southern Negro community. *American Anthropologist, 72,* 269–288.

Young, V. (1974). A Black American socialization pattern. *American Ethnologist, 1,* 405–413.

3

Teaching Is a Political Act: Contextualizing Gender and Ethnic Voices

Kimberly Kinsler and Sue Rosenberg Zalk

It is the first meeting of an educational psychology class in a teacher preparation program for elementary school teachers in an inner city. In response to the professor's question, "Why do you want to become teachers?" a young male Puerto Rican student states: "I want to teach Latinos. I understand them, particularly Latino males. I think I could make a difference."

In this instance, the instructor may follow up on the student's remarks in a range of ways, from the seemingly benign to the most overtly opinionated and political. At the seemingly neutral end are statements indicating simple acknowledgment, acceptance, and encouragement, expressed, perhaps, with words such as "good," "that's admirable," or a supportive "I'm sure you will."

Alternatively, the instructor may choose to use this interaction to talk about the influence of culturally based factors on learning and instruction. The student's remarks may be placed in the context of the literature of the various subdisciplines composing culture studies. Thus, on the one hand, the instructor might elect to pursue an analysis based on ethnicity. This discourse might, for example, begin by the teacher tracing a brief history of the struggles of ethnic minorities to obtain an equal and equitable education. The discussion might then proceed to a presentation of the literature on the cultural biases inherent in the system's curriculum and assessment procedures, research on the often negative attitudes toward the educational system held by many inner-city Latino youths and their subsequent high dropout rates, and the facilitative effects on learning when instructors use students' culturally based learning styles and interaction patterns (Ogbu, 1991; Apple, 1990; Oakes, 1985; Hale-Bensen, 1982). Playing devil's advocate, the teacher might also discuss how both these data and the student's own admirable goals can be taken to their logical extreme and be used to support a separatist system of education, that is, "people should teach their own." Indeed, recent examples of the creation of a school exclusively for Native American children in Colorado and the proposal to create schools for African American boys might be given. This discourse might conclude on a conciliatory note by the teacher proposing a social reconstructionist position similar to that advocated by Sleeter and Grant (1988).

On the other hand, the teacher's response may be framed from the perspective of gender studies. Accordingly, the instructor could comment on the underrepresentation of Puerto Rican male teachers in the public school system. Providing a historical dimension, the instructor could point out that in the 1960s and 1970s there was a concerted effort to encourage more males to enter the teaching profession, consistent with the belief that boys require male role models in the schools. To support this argument, the teacher might note the literature that suggests that males might be at a disadvantage in the elementary and secondary school system. Both systems are female dominated, and, as some have asserted, the schools encourage "feminine" behavior (e.g., physical passivity, conformity, and obedience) that stereotypically conflicts with boys' temperaments (Sexton, 1969). Following this reasoning, the instructor might continue the discussion by presenting the literature on same-gender role models and suggest that if the student became a teacher, his presence could serve to counter some of the negative effects of gender-based conflicts. Conversely, and once more playing devil's advocate, the instructor could focus on the student's preference for teaching male students and challenge the reasoning cited above. The instructor could conclude by noting the research that suggests that female and male elementary school teachers are similar in their behavior toward children in the classroom, although both respond differently to girl and boy students (see, for example, Wilkinson and Marrett, 1985).

We started this chapter with an incident that took place in a class of chapter author Kimberly Kinsler. She, too, chose among the many possible responses she could give to the student. Selectively drawing upon many of the issues raised in ethnic studies, she demonstrated how the logical outcome of following the student's line of reasoning was school segregation and discussed the possible implications this could have for students of color. However, had the situation posed itself to chapter author Sue Rosenberg Zalk, she may very well have chosen to discuss gender implications and question the student about how he thinks his experiences as a Latino male would influence his teaching of Latino girls. She may also have discussed literature on ethnic gender role expectations and the possible influence of these expectations on classroom interactions and outcomes.

This incident was chosen to illustrate how each day instructors, whether or not they regard themselves or their teaching as political in nature, constantly reproduce in their classrooms the very political struggles that avowed combatants wage in public. One such struggle is whether multicultural perspectives should be introduced into traditional curriculum courses and, if so, what their place should be in that curriculum and which of the various subdivisions, or "voices," should be privileged. Each of the responses cited above represents a position in the current "culture wars" over the school curriculum. Early curricular battles, which could be likened to world wars, were between those who advocated the existence of autonomous culture studies programs and the infusion of these literatures throughout the traditional curriculum and traditionalists who challenged this position (e.g., D'souza, 1991; Schlesinger, 1992). This latter group argued for the superiority, timelessness, and universality of the existing canon. These struggles are currently being won, as colleges and universities nationwide are adopting diversity or culture studies requirements as part of their instructional core. Civil wars now have emerged among former allies over the organization of culture studies programs, the relative privileging of various voices, and debates over who can ventriloquize for whom in teaching the curriculum (Roman, 1993). At present, feminist and ethnic studies vie for prominence.

The first response in the example above, that of acknowledgment and simple support, implies a belief on the part of the teacher that cultural issues have no place in this dialogue. There was no direct attention given to the implication of the student's remarks for the field, regardless of whether the instructor appreciates the student's desire to use both his formal education and personal cultural knowledge to effect positive change in his community. The teacher's response denies the student's culturally based motivation in this academic setting. Although endorsing the student's agenda, the instructor ignores the political motivation. Would the instructor be more reticent in accepting a white middle-class student's assertion that he wants to teach white males like himself?

Responses based on ethnic and gender studies validate the presence and support the significance of culture and culture studies in the college curriculum. The student's remarks become contextualized in the literature of the various subdisciplines this field comprises. Intentionally or unintentionally choosing to pursue a particular voice within culture studies to the exclusion of another equally valid subfield ranks and privileges a field. Even if the educator were to contextualize the student's remarks in more than one explanatory literature, the relative weight given to each area would still imply a hierarchical ordering of these areas. Moreover, if instructors are not members, either by birth or advocacy, of one or more of the groups making up culture studies, their ability and legitimacy to speak in the name of a field is questioned.

The point here is that in daily curricular decisions involving choices about what to include and exclude (and thereby what to make legitimate or illegitimate) and how to variously privilege available discourses, instructors are making political decisions. They make many of the same decisions every day in their classes regardless of whether they are asked to declare their politics, for example, by voting for or against the inclusion of culture studies in the school's curriculum. These daily decisions are the ones that may have the deepest and most lasting effect on students. For unlike public votes and political demonstrations, which are overt in their political nature and for which students engage the content as such, teachers' politics in the classroom are hidden, characteristically presented as neutral fact and/or theory, and as such may be regarded by students as gospel.

It is the purpose of this chapter to raise the awareness of both instructors and students to the inherently political nature of teaching and schools. We intend to demonstrate this, to argue that it cannot be otherwise, and to encourage teachers to own their politics in the practice of teaching (see, for example, Gordon, Miller, and Rollock, 1990). Toward this end, the next section briefly reviews the three major sociological views on the purposes or functions of school and schooling. We then broach the issue of advocacy, qua "preaching," in the classroom and the need to achieve balance. In the following section, we discuss our own evolution as teachers and our current teaching practices. And in the final section, we explore some of the tensions between feminist and ethnic perspectives within culture studies.

The Politics of Schooling

In modern society, the educational system, or the institution of schooling, is a complex enterprise with several significant functions. Theorists disagree, however, on the exact nature of these functions and on whether the system is intended to serve the interests of the entire society or dominant groups within it. Three major views have emerged to explain and to describe the social role of education: Parsonianism, various forms of Marxism, and Weberianism. Although these views are sociological, they clearly reveal the political nature of teaching and so provide a useful context within which to frame our own views and work in the teaching of psychology. These theories are, therefore, briefly described below.

Parsonian/Functionalist Theory

Parsonians, or functionalists, regard society as an interrelated set of institutions, each with specialized functions that facilitate the survival of the society and maximize benefits to its members. Accordingly, the primary functions of school are said to be the transmission of culturally based knowledge and the allocation and integration of individuals to their adult roles in society. Parsonians would assert that the school's function is neutral and egalitarian in nature. However, when these goals are examined in terms of their reality for historically disenfranchised groups, a different, more political agenda emerges relative to the role of the school.

The Transmission of Knowledge. To perpetuate any society, the knowledge held by its adults must be passed to the next generation. Moreover, the transmission of knowledge that is deemed critical to a society's survival, advancement, and status becomes a societal responsibility and therefore the task of one of its key institutions—the school. The major questions in this regard are what knowledge, within the realm of possible content, is necessary and worthy of intergenerational transfer in the school and who should determine what this knowledge should be.

Parsonians would assert that these determinations are objective, and guided solely by consideration for the advancement of society, but outcome data would suggest more political motives. Much has been said about the canon. On the one hand, it has been argued that it constitutes a neutral foundational knowledge, essential for more advanced learning in all of the liberal arts disciplines. For example, the classics and philosophy are claimed to promote critical thinking, cognitive rigor, logical thought, and "a disciplined mind." Conversely, it has been claimed that this knowledge is not neutral but based on the latent assumption that Western European-American culture and its works provide the best foundations for and examples of intellectual rigor that have been provided thus far. Why is this political? Teaching based on the belief that one culture (i.e., Western) can and should set the standard against which all other cultures and knowledge are to be judged is not politically neutral. It not only disregards the very class, gender, and racial biases upon which much of the canon is based (e.g., the ancient Greek concept of "citizen"), but it also advocates and perpetuates the ideological dominance of these assumptions (see, for example, Zalk and Kelter-Gordon, 1992).

The Preparation of Youth for Adult Roles. Few would argue against every society preparing its youth to occupy the various positions in the society and to perform the tasks necessary for its continuation and development. Historically, a variety of ascribed or inherited characteristics, including family background, race, religion, and gender, have been used by many societies to allocate individuals to the various positions or to decide which groups of individuals will have an opportunity to compete for certain privileged positions. As the school has increasingly taken from the family the responsibility of socializing the young, Parsonians assert that through the school, it has become possible for any child to acquire the skills necessary to fulfill virtually any position in society within the limitations of individual ability. Thus, more and more, the school becomes society's great equalizer in blindly recognizing and nurturing talent and ability and, in a more balanced fashion, determining which individuals are given advanced forms of knowledge and thereby access to life's various paths and professions (Goslin, 1965/1990).

However, the image of the school as society's great equalizer has not been borne out in fact. Bowles and Gintis (1976) wrote that if all schools rewarded and advanced students solely based on ability and not ascribed traits, that class, race, and gender differences would soon be eradicated. Although there has been some narrowing of the educational and professional disparities existing between groups, large differences remain. Many assert that the seeming intractability of these disparities results, in no small part, from the continued use by schools and teachers of ascribed traits as the primary criteria for sorting students (e.g., Apple, 1990). Thus teachers are said to differentially nurture and discourage particular traits in students. They select specific qualities to cultivate and to instill and, conversely, to ignore and to eliminate. Characteristically, these judgments are usually based on often classist, racist, and sexist assumptions about which traits and behaviors are appropriate and necessary for individuals or groups to assume productive adult roles. These are not neutral acts but rather are political in nature. The continued use of these assumptions and criteria to track and sort individuals for the various career paths has perpetuated extant disparities between members of society's interest groups in their academic and vocational preparation. For example, students who are speakers and writers of nonstandard English continue to be regarded by teachers as less intelligent and less capable of critical and abstract thought than speakers of standard English. Therefore, they are tracked disproportionately at the primary and secondary school levels into special education classes. At the college level, they are regarded with disdain and given little encouragement or hope of succeeding (Oakes, 1985). Similarly, teachers have historically placed less importance on the professional achievement and ambitions of female students than on male students and are more likely to discourage their pursuit of excellence in areas requiring analytical or mathematical thinking (Ehrhart and Sandler, 1987; Sadker and Sadker, 1986). These practices continue to relegate historically disenfranchised populations to lesser job paths and careers.

Whereas a traditional Parsonian perspective would deny the interest group bias inherent in the very nature of the school, other theories directly assert the political nature of educational content and practices.

Marxist and Weberian Theory

Unlike Parsonians, Marxists and Weberians posit far less democratically motivated objectives for the school. Marxists contend that the primary objective of the school is the production and reproduction of existing class stratifications through the transmission of capitalist ideology or needed economy-based skills and attitudes. However, Marxists differ among themselves on the means by which these ends are attained. Weberians extend Marxist views to assert that not only dominant socioeconomic status (SES) groups but also other dominant interest groups (e.g., religious, political, and cultural) seek to maintain their wealth, power, and prestige by variously restricting subordinate groups' access to needed jobs, credentials, and cultural capital and by schooling subordinate groups in the society's dominant cultures (Collins, 1971, 1977; Dougherty and Hammack, 1990). Both these views of schooling assert the inherently political nature of teaching and would contend that educators who teach the traditional canon, making no effort to "politicize" the curriculum, nonetheless are engaged in the political activity of perpetuating, if not actively supporting, existing class, race, and ethnic privileges.

If teaching the canon is, by its very nature, advocacy of dominant ways of thinking, acting, and knowing, then what do we as teachers do? If we, like the vast majority of teachers, view the profession in neutral Parsonian terms, we would continue to teach the canon, blind to or in agreement with the system's underlying assumptions and privileging criteria. However, if we are radicalized educators, for example, feminists and those who focus on race and class politics, or have merely alternative theoretical interpretations and belief systems, how do we give voice to our views and beliefs? How do we arouse and inform society of the possibility of these credos? Are we obligated to do the bidding of the dominant culture and to teach traditional theories and beliefs, to reward and to privilege dominant attitudes and behaviors, and to muzzle our minds and mute our voices when addressing content that we believe is sexist, racist, and classist? Or, to borrow from the title of another chapter in this volume (see the chapter by Kmiec, Crosby, and Worell), do we in our teaching and valuative actions "walk the walk and talk the talk" of our own political agenda, consciously attempting to counter and/or balance not only society's but our own stereotypes of appropriateness and legitimacy?

Teaching as Preaching

One of the greatest compliments a teacher can receive is to be told by a student that the teacher was tremendously influential in the student's life—assuming, of course, that the student was influenced in ways consistent with the teacher's ideals, values, and beliefs. For example, if a student informs us (the authors) that as a result of one of our classes, she or he has decided to go on to law school and perhaps specialize in civil rights law, we would feel truly gratified. If, however, the student was to declare that our course had been decisive in making the decision to go to Hollywood to write and produce Black sexploitation films, we would undoubtedly feel a sense of abject failure. Picking ourselves up off the floor, we would puzzle: How could my class have influenced in such a way?

Obviously, we do not want to have an influence, qua influence, on our students' lives, but to be able to influence them in particular ways; that is, to help them develop specific categories of knowledge, critical belief systems, and ways of thinking and viewing the world that, though not necessarily identical to our own, are consistent with these views. In this sense, we hope, consistent with Meyer (1977), that the school and we as teachers can influence significantly people's lives and help to shape society. To the extent that we serve some social or instructive purpose, it is not essentially by providing job-relevant skills but by providing students with a means to organize and to interpret societal events and information. We seek to create categories of knowledge and ways of knowing that people defer to. In so doing, we as educators seek to socialize not only our students but also society, not through direct inculcation but rather through acceptance of our categories of knowledge and ways of viewing the world and by generating behaviors consistent with these values. Meyer described this view of instruction as "religion" or "myth," for, like religion, it seeks to provide legitimating accounts of a perspective's competency, the authority of its elites, and the adequacy or necessity of the social system to achieve it (Meyer, 1977; Dougherty and Hammack, 1990). Teachers have the task of "conversion," for want of a better term. Although many educators do not readily nor openly admit to such a position, is this not the essence of successfully "influencing" students and, in fact, the larger society?

Does Balance Exist?

Probably, our reluctance to adopt this view is because it runs counter to our training as "scientists," "objectively" researching variables and reporting findings toward a greater approximation and understanding of the "truth." This is despite our knowledge that every theory and research question is embedded in theorists' belief systems, sociopolitics, and cultural and research history of their time (Gordon, Miller, and Rollock, 1990). Yet the concept of "preaching" feels somehow morally wrong. Many would rather assert that the educator's role is to present the facts and theories as "objectively" and "neutrally" as possible and to allow the student and society to be independent and critical consumers of this knowledge.

But can this be done? We as educators are obligated to present the dominant traditional theories in our respective areas. But as this knowledge base is not neutral, without a contrary position, by default students will be led to adopt or strongly favor its underlying assumptions. The question is: Do we share with students our belief systems, our research questions, and the paths of our own political and intellectual development, particularly if we know that the dominant position presents a one-sided picture or omits significant bodies of information? Moreover, do we attempt merely to balance the equation and to fill in the gaps or to proselytize? We know that our own beliefs are political and oriented in a particular direction (we certainly believe they are more closely approximating the truth) and that the dominant traditional views are, similarly, political and oriented toward a certain perspective. Additionally, knowing that dominant views constantly bombard the public, do we simply offer our own opposing positions or seek to "make a case"? For example, the public is constantly exposed to a cultural-deficit view of underachievement for racial minorities (e.g., in the media and in texts), and recently genetic-deficit views received profuse nationwide attention (i.e., Hernstein and Murray, 1994). These theories are not neutral and have serious implications for social change, public policy, and human behavior. Is a mere statement of a cultural-difference view adequate to balance this equation?

This is not to imply that educators should teach only their own positions and perspectives but rather that they should teach with political awareness and with knowledge. Despite that no position seems to have grasped truth or universality, students nonetheless seek absolutes. As neither traditionally dominant views nor our own theories and beliefs are unbiased, and as there are few clear and unqualified answers to any question, particularly in the field of psychology, fair-minded teachers search for compasses to guide their teaching and pedagogic interactions. And on the basis of good faith they set out in a direction that they hope will achieve a balance not only in their instructional content but also in their lives. Within this context, we make decisions about what facts and theories to present and what to omit; how to order this material; what points to emphasize, support, and challenge; and how to respond to students' queries. In a land where there is no absolute balance, we seek our own.

Our Journey Through the Teaching of Psychology: Our Personal Growth

In arriving at this position, we have evolved in our own personal beliefs about psychology and the ways the field addresses both of our respective areas of interest and teaching. As individuals, we are committed to using or developing a psychology for social reconstruction. It is our position that the greatest value of psychology lies in the field's ability to reveal the psychological processes perpetuating social injustices and to correct the social systems that have an unjust impact on the quality of people's lives. Of paramount concern are explorations into the beliefs, behaviors, and institutions that oppress people. Consequently, we are strong advocates of civil rights. In our teaching, we seek to reveal the psychosocial mechanisms of racism, sexism, and classism. Our aim is to help students identify their role in these processes so as to resist tacit participation and to become agents for change. Admittedly political, we believe that we can and do consciously work toward these ends without compromising our integrity as psychologists and as scholars.

We came to these positions from two totally different routes. The author Kimberly Kinsler, being a woman of color, went into the field to answer personal questions of individual and group differences in school success and achievement. Having witnessed, with increasing helplessness, the growing mental anguish, societal alienation, and personal demise of siblings she felt to be brighter and bolder than herself, she searched for answers in the realm of the human mind. The explanations that were so authoritatively offered did not, however, seem consistent with her experiences and interpretations of familial events. At the time she was pursuing doctoral studies in educational psychology. Cultural-deficit explanations of group and individual differences in academic achievement were in favor. The culture of her siblings was no more deficit than her own. Although decidedly working class, it certainly was not deprived; it was not devoid of values, caring, and a concern and hope for the academic and professional success of all the children and for African Americans in general. Yet, knowing that one or even a few personal exceptions do not constitute a valid theoretical challenge, and aggressive protest not then being her nature, she continued to absorb this knowledge without denial or refutation. In her own mind she became, in the words of Greenlee (1969), like "the spook that sat by the door," that is, someone almost without race, absorbing the knowledge of the oppressor in hopes that at some later time she could use this information as tools, if not weapons, to discredit these theories and to provide more insightful and "truthful" explanations of the oppression of her people.

The author Sue Rosenberg Zalk got into the field in the early 1970s and initially started doing research on racial attitudes in children. By the mid 1970s, she was exploring children's development of gender attitudes. During this period, she believed that psychology was a neutral and unbiased science. Its methodological rigor eschewed subjectivity so as to permit the acquisition of objective knowledge. There was also a strong belief that through such rigorous science, knowledge could be generated that was indeed apolitical, and with it social scientists would, in fact, increasingly approximate the "truth." Later and through the writings of feminists, she came to recognize how society defined her, personally, as a woman, and the ways in which the social sciences contributed to these definitions and their ongoing and potential influence on them. She recognized that the content and direction of their influence was not fixed, but a function of the politics of the times and the field. As a result, she came to recognize that there are no innocent questions when it comes to the study of human behavior and that all social science knowledge is political. She finally acknowledged that she could not claim, as others have done, that the study of gender, or race or any other socially created category, is neutral and apolitical or that she could pursue research designed to advance equality detached from a political agenda. Nor could she claim, or want to claim, that all of this did not influence her in the classroom. People who made this claim were suspect.

Quite independently, we both came to the understanding that nearly all theories and research have political implications. In the questions that are (and are not) asked, in the configurations of the subject populations, and in the interpretation of data, almost invariably, disenfranchised populations are "scientifically" found responsible for their circumstances. Eventually we began to see that much psychological information is built upon often unstated assumptions about the basic superiority of male, middle-class, European-American values, behaviors, and ways of thinking. And although many sociologists readily acknowledge these biases—indeed, major schools of thought (e.g., Marxism and Weberianism) are based upon and actively study the implications—psychologists seem reluctant to acknowledge the privileged status given to these groups in their theories, research, and institutional practices (see, for example, Parlee, 1992a). As a result, we found ourselves increasingly pondering the fact that psychological theory had been and continues to be used as a primary means to justify and support racist, classist, and sexist ideology.

What to do with this understanding became burdensome and presented us with a dilemma. Silently, we each pondered whether to betray our training and openly challenge the field's assertion of objectivity or to betray what we knew to be "truth" about our interest groups. It was like a catch-22: We felt that we were "damned if we did and damned if we didn't." Each perceived the need to give critical voice to our political realizations, but with each level of advancement within the system, we felt that we were being asked to pay with our silence if not our commitment to its belief system. Consistent with the work of Bourdieu and Passeron (1977), we felt that as new college professors, albeit with academic freedom, that

> the freedom the educational system allows the teacher is the best guarantee that he will serve the system, the freedom allowed to the educational system is the best guarantee that it will serve the perpetuation of the relations prevailing between the classes, because the possibility of the redirection of ends is inscribed in the very logic of a system which never better fulfills its social function than when it seems to be exclusively pursuing its own ends. (p. 126)

The solution to this dilemma is not limited freedom but rather that this freedom be used to defend and support multiple voices.

How Politics Informs Our Teaching

As a result of these personal growth processes, our own teaching has gone through an evolution.[1] When we began college-level teaching, we both believed that we could disseminate psychological content from a neutral perspective. As the educational curriculum that we teach mandates that the major theories of learning and development be covered, as well as their applications to the school setting, we believed that this had to be done objectively and that valid alternative interpretations, qualifications, and challenges to these views could be provided with disassociation—lest students regard the major theories as sacrosanct and truly universal. Consequently, biological, cognitive, and socialization theories competed with equal time. All were dispassionately laid out before our students and they were advised that in their personal adoption of theories and applications, they should understand the strengths and weaknesses of each and accordingly choose among them.

Yet, as our own political awareness and our knowledge of the hidden assumptions of much of psychological theory increased, several things became clear: Despite our efforts to balance information, the politics of these theories remained masked, we were not neutral about their social implications, and many of our students did not yet have sufficient theoretical backgrounds to evaluate the mass of material. As a result, we felt a need to guide them through this morass of information. To do this, decisions had to be made about what to include and exclude, how to order and sequence this knowledge, and what points to stress and which to de-emphasize. Again, independently of each other, we set as our goals for classroom instruction to help students develop a critical knowledge of psychology that could further, in action as well as thought, the equitable treatment of all individuals and to facilitate their understanding of both the psychological, sociopolitical, and institutional mechanisms that perpetuate existing inequalities. Once these were openly acknowledged, we were forced to admit to ourselves that our aim is to "convert" students.

We are now much more overtly political, and our politics may be seen in our specific classroom practices. Their manifestations may be found in our selection of content and its organization, its presentation, and in our interpretations of content.

Content Selection and Organization

As previously stated, content selection and organization are very political and ideologically based acts. In setting up our courses and in our daily responses to student's questions, we make decisions concerning the inclusion and the exclusion of material, not unlike those debated publicly in the current "culture wars" over the curriculum. For both of us, the issue is not whether to interject culturally based content—we in our minds have already resolved this conflict—but rather the relative privilege or ranking to give to each of the various subdisciplines. It is here that we disagree most, each believing in the superior explanatory ability of our own subdiscipline.

Thus the first author, Kimberly Kinsler, in selecting course content begins the class with a discussion on how theories are products of theorists' sociopolitical contexts, for example, their historical era and their personal and political beliefs. In presenting any theory of development, explanations are organized as follows: The major theory is first presented, followed by a discussion of general challenges to that theory with an emphasis on their cultural biases, and then information is provided on the theory's sociopolitical implications for nontraditional populations. Students are then asked to brainstorm strengths and weaknesses of the theory as well as the applicability of the theory to urban schools. A unit on Culture and Cognition is always included as one selected topic. In this lesson the first author discusses intelligence tests: their origins, biases, and implications for nontraditional students. As explanatory theories, genetic-deficit, cultural-deficit, and cultural-difference models are introduced. In the context of genetic-deficit theory, the racist and classist writings of Cyril Burt are discussed along with his knighthood by the British government and the subsequent finding that his data were fraudulent. The cultural-deficit model is similarly treated, as are many current-day psychologists' (e.g., Arthur Jensen and now Hernstein and Murray) rigid adherence to deficit hypotheses. When considering cultural-difference theories of academic performance, the literature on learning styles and the work of Hale-Bensen (1982) are presented, as well as the research by Ogbu (1991), as a means to explain the underachievement of nontraditional populations. The ways in which school practices have historically followed upon these views (e.g., segregation and tracking, compensation, and "multicultural education") are included. The session ends with strong caveats about stereotypes of any kind, and students are asked in parting to think about how they would address the issue of cultural differences in their classrooms.

In contrast, the second author, Sue Rosenberg Zalk, in an overview of theories, uses Kohlberg's (1964, 1969) and Gilligan's (1982) work not as a lesson on moral development, but as an example of gender (and race) bias in theory development and research.[2] Gender issues are inserted in seemingly genderless topics. For example, despite there being little time to cover prenatal development in her child development course, time is allotted to explain the prenatal development of genital and reproductive organs.[3] This is done to demonstrate that "female" and "male" are not opposites or polar dimensions, that "sex" is not biologically fixed at conception but is a complex series of events that can be altered, and that the designation of people's "sex" varies as a function of the definition. In short, this material is used to challenge the assumption of biological determinism as it pertains to our understanding of gender or even biological sex.

When dealing with the topic of cognition, she addresses gender and emphasizes the topic of math and gender issues. This author begins with a review of the literature that suggests that during adolescence, males on the average perform better than females on many mathematical tasks. Benbow and Stanley's (1980, 1983) research with mathematically talented youths, in which they found that boys scored consistently higher on standardized mathematical achievement tests than girls, is cited, and their conclusion that the differences are biologically based is noted. The use of their research by the popular media and its policy implications are discussed. This is followed by the "however": The author states that there is a large body of research that strongly challenges the "natural ability" explanation. Research is explored that suggests that gender patterns in mathematics performance can be explained by a range of psychosocial or environmental factors, such as parents' expectations for daughters' mathematical performance, math anxiety, teachers' differential attention to female and male students, and the perception of mathematics as a male domain (see Eccles, 1983, 1989; Chipman and Thomas, 1985; Eccles, Adler, and Meece, 1984; Eccles and Jacobs, 1986; Hyde, Fennema, and Lamon, 1990; Hyde, Fennema, Ryan, Frost, and Hopp, 1990; Linn and Hyde, 1989). This discussion leads to very different policy implications than does the genetic position.

These two treatments of the curriculum are quite different in their emphasis, although they are equally valid and, we believe, legitimate, for both have their bases in a significant and substantive literature. Both syllabi are admittedly political in their presentation of culturally based alternative explanatory views. It is obvious that in these curricular treatments, topics are introduced and juxtaposed in ways that guide students' thinking in particular directions. In both presentations, the nontraditional "other," that is, ethnic minorities and women (who by 2075 will constitute the majority of students in the nation) (Quality Education for Minorities, 1990), and culture-based theories associated with their development, are taken from the periphery and given equal status with those of dominant societal groups and traditional explanatory models. We differ in our privileging of literature. These differences are also apparent in our presentation styles.

Interpretation

An essential part of teaching is interpretation, that is, transforming the theories, research, and events that are the content of our courses into concepts and knowledge of individuals that are meaningful to our students.

Psychology, as a field, characteristically speaks in generalities (e.g., central tendencies, discernible patterns, and stereotypes) about individuals and groups in their absence. Instructors must make the abstract "real," literally, to bring life to this content. In particular, those of us in teacher training programs must transform hypothetical knowledge that students can use when they become teachers; for example, transforming Piaget's "epistemic child" into personal and practical ways of sensitively and appropriately engaging real children.

To do this, instructors must relate, or embed, new information in students' existing knowledge, constructing "bridges" between the unknown and the known. Not only must characterizations of dominant-group individuals be scrutinized and made "real," so that traditional students may see and know themselves in these generalities, but also characterizations of "nontraditional" students must be scrutinized and made "real" as well. These latter tasks are made infinitely more difficult by the assumptions and the stereotypes used as concept facilitators and descriptors in the field. By contrasting "traditional" individuals and their "standard" behaviors with the nontraditional "other," normative images are posed as polar opposites; that is, "us" versus "them," the positive and the negative, the legitimate and the illegitimate, indeed, the superior versus the inferior. Moreover, in light of Sleeter's (1993) and Haberman and Post's (1992) finding that instruction in multiculturalism often leads "traditional" teachers to reinforce, rather than deconstruct, their views of children of color, particular effort must be made to reconstruct students' existing knowledge about these individuals and groups. For these students, instructors must not only connect the lives, beliefs, and actions of ethnic minorities and women to their existing knowledge base, so that their existence becomes meaningful, but they must also reconfigure students' extant understandings from the alien and negative to that which is legitimate and valued.

In this translation process, our status as members of both traditional and "other" groups facilitates the "bridging" process. In our teaching, we attempt to expose the weaknesses of traditional "logic" in the field—from an insider's position—and to provide substantive examples contrary to the stereotypes—being members of the "other." We therefore talk in terms of the problems inherent in hierarchically ranking individual traits and cultural patterns and the degree to which the stereotypes are valid. To nuance the research and theories constructed about and by the "other" about subaltern groups, we readily draw upon examples from our own lives and the lives of those with whom we are familiar. We thereby attempt not to "reify" the oppressed but to reconstruct "in our own terms" the causal factors, the alternative belief systems, and the previously unfathomable responses to an institutionally hostile environment. The first author, for instance, frequently relates the profound differences in the life outcomes of members of her own family to refute the genetic- and cultural-deficit models, and she chronicles the perceived origins and developmental manifestations of a "negative psychology," said by Ogbu (1991) to characterize the thinking of many caste-like minorities, in one particular relative (e.g., his statement that he does not want to act like "whitey"). And the second author, when addressing socialization processes, talks about the influence her father had in encouraging her as a child to be professionally ambitious and contrasts it to the messages received from her mother. Students are also encouraged to discuss the differential life outcomes and treatments of their sisters and brothers as an opportunity to explore the interaction between ethnic and gender socialization.

In these ways, our intrinsic knowledge of and "privileged" access to our respective "other" has particular value. Because we are able to report our personal experiences and knowledge of individuals whose lives refute as well as support traditional and nontraditional theories, our students are helped to view the perceived differences in the "other" as logical adaptations to often hostile environmental circumstances and institutional practices rather than as deficits inherent in these groups and to develop more nuanced images of disenfranchised populations and of the forces they face. In helping our students to regard racism and sexism as not only mental states but, more important, as institutional realities in these students' lives (Sleeter, 1993), we hope that our students, when they become workers, parents, and teachers, will *not* participate in, and in addition will seek to change, institutional practices that perpetuate extant stratifications.

In our differential content selection and interpretation patterns, we privilege disparate subaltern groups that currently coalesce in the field of culture studies. By doing so, we momentarily mirror larger conflicts on a small scale. We believe this is toward a necessary end. In light of Sleeter's (1993) finding that White teachers and teacher candidates often resist, or only selectively incorporate, aspects of multicultural education that serve to perpetuate extant views that maintain their vested interests, at present "educators of color are much more likely to bring life experiences and viewpoints that critique white supremacy than are white teachers and to engage in activities that challenge various forms of racism" (p. 169).

Thus, our life experiences and "journeys" through the field of psychology have led us to acquire similar perspectives on teaching yet quite differing knowledge bases with which to frame our understanding. We agree that teaching is political, that there is a need to incorporate culturally based views into the classroom, and that the curriculum must be further deconstructed to portray the "real" nontraditional "others." We believe that this is best achieved by assisting students to see the extraordinary institutional and societal forces that act upon them through relating our own unique and privileged knowledge of the "other." As we vary in which "other" we intrinsically best know, we therefore differ in that group that we can make most "real" in our classrooms. We do not assume that we, in fact, ventriloquize for the unique perspective of each subaltern group, but we can convey some of the feelings and societal realities of "otherness" that may be common to membership in these groups. Thus, in our differential privileging, we do not seek to engage in "identity politics" (Watts and Cook, 1991), that is, to appropriate our oppressors' hierarchical ranking among ourselves, but rather to deconstruct racism and sexism so as to reconstruct more real opportunities for subaltern groups. Sleeter (1993) advocates that educators

strongly [work] to reverse policies that propel mainly white people into the profession. . . . What I am suggesting goes beyond interaction patterns in classrooms, role models, or linking home and school cultures. I am suggesting the need to populate the teaching force with people who bring diverse world views and discursive fields of reference, including those that expose, challenge and deconstruct racism rather than tacitly accepting it . . . [and the creation of] multiracial coalitions in which white people participate but do not dominate. (p. 168)

Although it very well may be true that educators from previously disenfranchised groups may be less likely to marginalize minority intellectual discourse (Sleeter, 1993; Gordon, 1990), we cannot forgo or devaluate the political education of teachers from traditional groups, either because of their resistance or by default. As individuals from these groups will continue to constitute an overwhelming majority of the teacher population, every effort must be made to reorganize both their extant views of the "other" and of their privilege and to politicize all teachers to their role in group stratification and the maintenance of the status quo.

A critical multicultural curriculum, which emphasizes anti-racist, anti-sexist change and social reorganization, and utilizes the points of view and experiences of oppressed minorities and working-class women and men as the primary bases for a core curriculum, would constitute a fundamental step in the direction of preparing students for democratic participation in a complex and differential world. (McCarthy, 1993, p. 103)

Conclusion

Teaching is a political act, and true multicultural and feminist education may well be a subversive activity. In denying multicultural perspectives access to the classroom, instructors, by default, fail to present vital contrary evidence to dominant-group theories and beliefs, thereby allowing members of these groups to perpetuate extant stratifications. Conversely, by incorporating culturally based theories and perspectives into the curriculum, teachers deconstruct the canon and the hegemony of traditional worldviews. In making the "other" known, they reconfigure stereotypic and negative understandings of subaltern groups, transforming them into more complex images that incorporate the reality of their oppression by dominant societal institutions. In true multicultural and feminist education, instructors attempt the political act of removing the masks of alleged neutrality to reveal the ethno- and andro-centric biases and further politicizing disenfranchised students to the hegemonic actions of those in power. To fail to do so in all subject areas is to support the politics of the status quo.

Consequently, psychological theories, research, and, yes, our politics must be used in this reconstruction. For as long as instructors are blind to the political nature of their activities and to their direct, and often unwitting, role in perpetuating extant inequalities, they will continue to do so with good conscience and, indeed, with a sense of legitimacy and appropriateness. In variously privileging those subaltern groups, teachers are better able to "make the other real" as a means to deconstruct extant hegemonic views. This privileging should not be regarded as reconstructing a new hierarchical ranking of these groups, for that only will weaken the legitimacy of culture studies and its case. True egalitarian change in society can be effected only through reeducation.

Although certainly not all psychologists hold the same value system or have access to subaltern group knowledge, they hold some value system and students should be made better aware of their perspectives. We hold that there is greater professional integrity in teachers' acknowledging the beliefs that underlie their teaching than in claiming neutrality or blindness to society's hegemonic practices. We believe the greater injustice is to impart to students that the disciplines are indeed neutral and that these culture wars do not exist. The politics of teaching is unavoidable. It is better to be as fully aware as possible of its nature and make decisions accordingly. If we commit ourselves to the profession and to providing a fair and just presentation of the knowledge of the field, then we commit ourselves to political action.

Notes

1. The theme of gender and racial issues in psychology is central to the work and teaching of both of us. One author has greater expertise in areas pertinent to the psychology of race and ethnicity; the other in gender. As a consequence, our courses differ somewhat in the degree to which each is stressed. Nonetheless, our basic philosophies are very similar, so for most of the chapter, when we refer to our classroom experiences and approaches, we use the reference "we" without specifying which author.

2. Lawrence Kohlberg (1964, 1969), an American psychologist, hypothesized a three-stage theory of moral development and devised a scale to assess the individual's level of moral development. Kohlberg found that women and men of color did not score as high in their level of moral reasoning as did white men. However, Kohlberg used only white middle-class males to devise his scale. Females were eliminated because they did not behave as his theory predicted. Thus, Kohlberg formulated a theory and to validate this theory he selected a homogeneous sample that behaved as he predicted it would. Those who behaved differently were judged as less morally developed. Carol Gilligan, a student of Kohlberg, challenged his theory and conclusions (1982). Gilligan engaged in research with women and men and concluded that there are two parallel developmental paths of moral development. One, seemingly favored by males, emphasizes principles of justice and individual rights. The other, which emphasizes caring, relationships, and reciprocity among people, appeared to be favored by females. Research that suggests alternative explanations and ethnic factors (e.g., Collins, 1971; Hare-Mustin and Marecek, 1990) are also noted in this discussion on biases in psychological theory and research.

3. Genetic females have an XX chromosomal pair and genetic males have an XY chromosomal pair. However, for about the first six weeks of gestation, genetic females and genetic males have an identical, undifferentiated sex organ (gonad). If the embryo has a Y chromosome, a gene on the chromosome will release a substance that will begin a series of interuterine events that result in the development of male genital and reproductive organs. In the absence of these events, female genital and reproductive organs develop. Many of the sexual organs in females and males evolve out of the same embryonic tissue. However, events can and do occur, or fail to occur, that cause genital and reproductive variations in both XX and XY chromosomal fetuses. A genetic condition or an interference in the interuterine events dictated by the genetic blueprint may result in persons born with internal or external organs different from their chromosomal sex. The environment the fetus grows in is as important in the development of genitals and reproductive organs as is the genetic contribution. For a more detailed explanation, see Chapter 3 in *Women's realities, women's choices: An introduction to women's studies* (Hunter College Women's Studies Collective, 1995).

References

Apple, M. (1990). *Ideology and curriculum.* New York, NY: Routledge.

Benbow, C. P., and Stanley, J. S. (1980). Sex differences in mathematical ability: Fact or artifact? *Science, 210,* 1262–1264.

Benbow, C. P., and, Stanley, J. S (1983). Sex differences in mathematical ability: More facts. *Science, 222,* 1029–1031.

Bourdieu, P., and Passeron, J. C. (1977). *Reproduction in education, society and culture.* London, England: Sage Publications.

Bowles, S., and Gintis, H. (1976). *Schooling in capitalist society.* New York, NY: Basic Books.

Chipman, S. F., and Thomas, V. G. (1985). Women's participation in mathematics: Outlining the problem. In S. F. Chipman, L. R. Brush, and D. M. Wilson (Eds.), *Women and mathematics* (pp. 1–24). Hillsdale, NJ: Erlbaum.

Collins, R. (1971). *The credential society*. New York, NY: Academic Press.

Collins, R. (1977). Some comparative principles of educational stratification. Reprinted in *Education and society*, pp. 39–60, by K. Dougherty and F. Hammack, Eds., 1990. San Diego, CA: Harcourt Brace Jovanovich.

Dougherty, K., and Hammack, F. (1990). *Education and society: A reader*. San Diego, CA: Harcourt Brace Jovanovich.

D'souza, D. (1991) *Illiberal education: The politics of race and sex on campus*. New York, NY: Free Press.

Eccles, J. S. (1983). Sex differences in mathematics participation. In M. Steinkamp and M. Maehr (Eds.), *Women in science* (pp. 120–130). Greenwich, CT: JAI Press.

Eccles, J. S. (1989). Bringing young women to math and science. In M. Crawford and M. Gentry (Eds.), *Gender and thought* (pp. 44–62). New York, NY: Springer-Verlag.

Eccles, J. S., Adler, T. F., and Meece, J. L. (1984). Sex differences in achievement: A test of alternative theories. *Journal of Personality and Social Psychology, 46,* 26–43.

Eccles, J., and Jacobs, J. E. (1986). Social forces shape math attitudes and performance. *Signs, 11*(21), 367–380.

Ehrhart, J. K., and Sandler, B. R. (1987). *Looking for more than a few good women in traditionally male fields*. Washington, DC: Project on the Status and Education of Women.

Gilligan, C. (1982). *In a different voice*. Cambridge, MA: Harvard University Press. (Republished in 1993 with a new preface).

Gordon, B. M. (1990). The necessity of African-American epistemology for educational theory and practice. *Journal of Education, 172*(3), 88–106.

Gordon, E. W., Miller, F., and Rollock, D. (1990). Coping with communicentric bias in knowledge production in the social sciences. *Educational Researcher, 19*(3), 14–19.

Goslin, D. (1965/1990). The functions of the school in modern society. Reprinted in *Education and society*, pp. 29–38, by K. Dougherty and F. Hammack, Eds., 1990. San Diego, CA: Harcourt Brace Jovanovich.

Greenlee, S. (1969). *The spook who sat by the door*. New York, NY: Bantam.

Haberman, M., and Post, L. (1992). Does direct experience change education students' perceptions of low-income minority children? *Midwestern Educational Researcher, 5*(2), 29–31.

Hale-Bensen, J. (1982). *Black children: Their roots, culture, and learning styles*. Baltimore, MD: Johns Hopkins University Press.

Hare-Mustin, R. T., and Marecek, J. (1990) *Making a difference*. New Haven, CT: Yale University Press.

Hernstein, R., and Murray, C. A. (1994). *The bell curve: Intelligence and class structure in American life*. New York, NY: Free Press.

Hunter College Women's Studies Collective (1995). *Women's realities, women's choices: An introduction to women's studies*. New York, NY: Oxford University Press.

Hyde, J. S., Fennema, E., and Lamon, S. J. (1990a). Gender differences in mathematics performance: A meta-analysis. *Psychological Bulletin, 107,* 139–155.

Hyde, J. S., Fennema, E., Ryan, M., Frost, L. A., and Hopp, C. (1990b). Gender differences in mathematical attitudes and affect: A meta-analysis. *Psychology of Women Quarterly, 14,* 299–324.

Kohlberg, L. (1964). The development of moral character and ideology. In *Review of child development research: Vol. 1,* pp. 383–431, by M. Hoffman and L. Hoffman, Eds. New York, NY: Russell Sage.

Kohlberg, L. (1969). *Stages in the development of moral thought and action.* New York, NY: Holt, Rinehart, and Winston.

Linn, M. C., and Hyde, J. S. (1989). Gender, mathematics and science. *Educational Researcher, 18*(8), 17–27.

McCarthy, C. (1993). After the canon: Knowledge and ideological representation in the multicultural discourse on curricular reform. In C. McCarthy and W. Crichlow (Eds.), *Race identity and representation in education* (pp. 289–305). New York, NY: Routledge.

Meyer, J. (1977). The effect of education as an institution. *American Journal of Sociology, 83,* July, 55–77.

Oakes, J. (1985). *Keeping track: How schools structure inequality.* New Haven, CT: Yale University Press.

Ogbu, J. (1991). Immigrant and involuntary minorities in comparative perspective. In M. Gibson and J. Ogbu (Eds.), *Minority status and schooling: A comparative study of immigrant and involuntary minorities* (pp. 3–36). New York, NY: Garland Publishing.

Parlee, M. B. (1992a). Feminism and Psychology. In S. R. Zalk and J. Gordon-Kelter (Eds.), *Revolutions in knowledge: Feminism in the social sciences* (pp. 101–133). Boulder, CO: Westview Press.

Parlee, M. B. (1992b). On PMS and psychiatric abnormality. *Feminism-&-Psychology, 2,* 105–108.

Quality Education for Minorities (1990, January). *Education that works: An action plan for the education of minorities.* MIT. Cambridge, MA: author.

Roman, L. (1993). White is a color! In C. McCarthy and W. Crichlow (Eds.), *Race, identity and representation in education* (pp. 71–88). New York, NY: Routledge.

Sadker, M., and Sadker, D. (1986). Sexism in the classroom: From grade school to graduate school. *Phi Delta Kappan* (March), 512–513.

Schlesinger, A. M., Jr. (1992). *The disuniting of America.* London, England: Routledge.

Sexton, P. (1969). *The feminized male.* New York, NY: Vintage Books.

Sleeter, C. (1993). How white teachers construct race. In C. McCarthy and W. Crichlow (Eds.), *Race, identity and representation in education* (pp. 157–171). New York, NY: Routledge.

Sleeter, C., and Grant, C. (1988). *Making choices for multicultural education: Five approaches to race, class and gender.* Columbus, OH: Merrill Publishing Company.

Watts, S., and Cook, J. (1991). Racism: Whose liberation? Implications for women's studies. In J. Aaron and S. Walby (Eds.), *Out of the margins: Women's studies in the nineties* (pp. 131–142). London, England: Falmer.

Wilkinson, L. C., and Marrett, C. B. (Eds.) (1985). *Gender influences in classroom interaction.* New York, NY: Academic Press.

Zalk, S. R., and Kelter-Gordon, J. (Eds.) (1992). *Revolutions in knowledge: Feminism in the social sciences.* Boulder, CO: Westview Press.

4

Walking the Talk: On Stage and Behind the Scenes

Julie Kmiec, Faye J. Crosby, and Judith Worell

A central tenet of feminism among academics is that we must change more than the subject matter of our courses. As feminists we pride ourselves on changing the ways in which we teach as well as changing what we teach (Belenky, Clinchy, Goldberger, and Tarule, 1986; Crawford and Marecek, 1989). In the feminist classroom hierarchy is broken down (Caughie and Pearce, 1992; Culley, 1985), as is the distinction between conceptual, abstract knowledge and concrete, personal experience (Cocks, 1985), and students become actively involved with the materials (Cannon, 1990; Higginbotham, 1990). It is possible that feminist professors, even more than other professors, engage in collaborative work with students and that we publish more often than others with both our undergraduate and our graduate students.

This chapter chronicles one such collaboration. Written by an undergraduate student (JK) and two professors (JW and FC), it presents a study of pedagogical ideology and practice among a sample of self-avowed feminists. After describing the study, we turn the spotlight on the intricacies of our own collaboration. We present the play first and then take you backstage.

The point of the study that we present is to document the extent to which feminist professors actually put into practice their (our) ideological commitments, especially when claiming a strong adherence to feminist pedagogy. The data came from a research project conducted by the two professors (JW and FC) on the care and feeding of feminist educators. In analyzing these data with the student (JK), we have asked, in essence: Do feminists "walk the talk?" We then hold the mirror to ourselves and ask:

"And what about us? Do we practice what we study?" Holding the mirror, we notice that we are all three female and all three White. The chapter closes by noting how our gender and our ethnicity have influenced the ways we have approached the data, each other, and ourselves.

Camera, Lights, Action: Watching Feminist Professors Walk the Talk

The revolutionary nature of feminism has not gone unnoticed. How feminist pedagogy can transform college education has, in particular, been a source of great worry to conservative commentators. Observers like Dinesh D'Souza (1991) and Patai and Koertge (1994) have produced volumes of rhetoric in which they link the downfall of Western civilization to the presence of feminists and other liberals on college faculties.

In both the attacks on and the defenses of feminist pedagogy, the assumption is often made of a strong link between attitudes and behaviors. It is assumed that an ideological commitment to the principles of feminist pedagogy results in certain behaviors in the classroom and on the campus. Presumably, the greater the self-conscious adherence to new ways of knowing, the less traditional (e.g., less hierarchical) is the feminist's classroom.

The purpose of our study is to test this assumption. We ask, in effect: Do professors who claim an investment in feminist pedagogy behave in distinctive ways? The research reported here is from a project on female professors of psychology who describe themselves as feminists and who teach in women's colleges, coeducational colleges, and universities in the United States. The main purpose of the project was to understand how the scholars define feminism, how they came to be feminists, and how they sustain their commitment to feminism. The data were collected in 1992 and 1993.

The portion of the data that we analyze here came from both interviews and questionnaires. Our goal was to determine if feminists who claim to be committed to feminist pedagogy actually behave in ways that differ from feminists who make no claim to a well-developed ideology about feminism and teaching. Finding few differences between those who profess a strong commitment and those who, though acknowledging their feminism, claim no special allegiance to feminist pedagogy, we speculate about why this might be.

Methods Used in the Feminist Teachers Project

The Sample.   There are no published lists of self-identified feminists, but there are lists of women who are likely to self-identity as feminists. One such list exists for members of Division 35 (The Psychology of Women) of the American Psychological Association (APA). We used a random sampling procedure described in detail elsewhere (Crosby, Todd, and Worell, in press) and had a 92 percent rate of acceptance of our invitation. Our study included seventy-seven women. Four of our respondents were Black; the rest were White. The average age was two years shy of fifty.

How we developed our protocol and collected the data are described elsewhere (Crosby, Todd, and Worell, in press). Most of the measures for the study were presented as part of a mailed questionnaire, returned by all but one of our participants. Some of the measures were scored from structured interviews, conducted and tape recorded over the telephone.

Instruments: Measures of Ideology. Two interview items tapped the extent to which respondents claimed that their feminism had influenced their pedagogy. The seventh question of the interview was: "Would you say that you make a conscious effort to employ any of your feminist values in your teaching?" Interviewers then probed into how the effort had been made. Coders read the transcripts and divided the answers into two categories: those making a big effort (36 respondents) and those making a small effort (41 respondents).[1] The eighth question was: "Would you say that your goals in any of your classes have been influenced by your feminist values or feminist epistemology? I am asking here about what you aim to achieve in any course more than about techniques." Again, responses were sorted into two groups: the big influence group (n = 34) and the small influence group (n = 43).[2] A composite score, called the engagement score, was derived when coders read through questions 7 and 8 together.[3]

Instruments: Measures of Classroom Methods. Three close-ended questionnaire items assessed classroom techniques with enough specificity to determine if there is a functional relationship between the professor's ideological commitment to feminist pedagogy, on the one hand, and, on the other, what she does in the classroom. First, respondents were asked to indicate which of sixteen activities they try to include in their own teaching. The statements were categorized into five types: those about teaching environment, classroom participation, the breakdown of hierarchy, activism, and feminist process.[4] For each type of activity a sum was calculated by noting how many activities a woman did in her own teaching. We also noted the total number of activities included.

Next came a question about thirteen teaching techniques. These responses were in turn categorized into those that referred to the incorporation of students' personal experiences into the courses; to the breakdown of hierarchy; to the use of collaboration; and to the use of innovative techniques.[5] Scores for each category were again calculated, as was a total score.

The third questionnaire item about classroom experiences asked respondents to review the list of thirteen techniques and indicate "which techniques have been successful for you." The same categorizations were used, yielding four category scores and one total score.

Instruments: Measures of Pedagogical Preoccupations Outside the Classroom. On the assumption that dedicated professors think about teaching issues in their spare time, we assessed how often the respondents performed a number of activities related to teaching. More specifically, we calculated how often they reported discussing issues of pedagogy with colleagues, discussing issues of pedagogy with students, reading about feminist pedagogy, writing about feminist pedagogy, attending workshops on feminist pedagogy, and giving workshops on feminist pedagogy. We summed across six separate questions to calculate scores that could vary, theoretically, between a low of 6 and a high of 26.

Instruments: Measures of Sources of Enjoyment and Challenge. To see if the ideological commitment to feminist pedagogy corresponds to factors that satisfy or dissatisfy professors, we examined three items concerning the sources of pleasure and problems for the participants in our study. In the interview, respondents were asked how they became and remained teachers when many other feminists forgo teaching for other enterprises. Answers were coded for positive themes (e.g., "I've always wanted to be a teacher"); negative themes (e.g., "It was the only job that I could get as a woman with a Ph.D."), and neutral themes (e.g., "That's what one does with a Ph.D. in my areas of psychology"). Respondents could give as many reasons as they wished, and some respondents gave both positive and negative reasons. We examined all reasons to compute a numeric indication of positive motivation. Respondents earned a score of five if they gave only positive reasons; a four if they gave positive and neutral reasons; a three if they gave only neutral reasons or both positive and negative reasons; a two if they gave negative and neutral reasons; and a one if they gave only negative reasons.

Participants were also asked to indicate the amount of pleasure they derived from eighteen different aspects of teaching on a scale of zero to ten. The eighteen items were sorted into ten that dealt with students (e.g., "getting to know students in a personal way") and eight others (e.g., "having the chance to do interesting reading"). From this sorting procedure we derived two scores: a raw score indicating the extent to which the participant derived pleasure from items that involved students and a ratio score in which the amount of pleasure from items involving students was contrasted with the total amount of pleasure from all sources.

Finally, respondents were asked to rate, from zero to ten, how bothersome they found fourteen items that they might have encountered while teaching. Five of the items involved students (e.g., "anger in the classroom between students") and nine did not. Again, raw and ratio scores were derived.

Findings of the Feminist Teachers Project

Preliminary. We looked to see if any of the interview items were sensitive to interviewer effects. We found that the scores for the interview items were not reliably associated with who acted as interviewer.

Classroom Methods. Table 4.1 displays the mean scores of the feminists who did or did not claim to make a big effort to employ their values in their teaching; who did or did not claim to be highly influenced by their feminism; and who were scored as high or low on the composite measure of engagement. Means that differ significantly from each other according to two-tailed t-tests are indicated. As can be readily seen, there is no strong and

TABLE 4.1 Classroom Methods as a Function of Commitment to Feminist Pedagogy: Mean Scores

| | Highest Score Possible | Ideological Commitment to Feminist Pedagogy | | | | | |
| | | *Effort*[a] | | *Influence*[b] | | *Engagement*[c] | |
		Big	Other	Great	Other	Great	Other
Categories of activities							
Environment	2	1.65	1.68	1.70	1.63	1.67	1.84
Participation	3	2.94	2.73*	2.97	2.71*	2.96	2.60**
Hierarchy	5	4.26	3.92	4.03	4.15	4.19	3.78
Activism	3	2.88	2.85	2.85	2.88	2.85	2.90
Feminism	3	2.56	2.36	2.42	2.48	2.38	2.56
Total activities	16	14.39	13.63	14.24	13.76	14.19	13.76
Categories of techniques tried							
Personal	4	3.18	2.68	3.19	2.69	3.12	2.44
Hierarchy	6	4.67	4.06	4.68	4.08	4.67	3.75*
Collaboration	1	.79	.79	.37	.44	.76	.88
Innovation	3	.91	.79	.94	.78	.88	.56
Total techniques	14	9.51	8.32	9.61	8.31*	9.38	7.63*
Categories of successful techniques							
Personal	4	2.74	2.18	2.72	2.23	2.80	1.80
Hierarchy	6	3.76	2.91*	3.50	3.20	3.60	2.73
Collaboration	1	.61	.56	.59	.57	.52	.69
Innovation	3	.68	.62	.69	.61	.52	.44
Total techniques	14	7.88	6.27*	7.50	6.68	7.44	5.67

*$p < .05$.
**$p < .01$.
[a]Thirty-six respondents were coded as making a big effort and forty-one as making a small effort.
[b]Thirty-four respondents were coded as being highly influenced and forty-three as not.
[c]Twenty-eight respondents were coded as being very engaged and twenty as being less engaged.

consistent relationship between an ideological commitment to feminist pedagogy and activities or techniques within the classroom among the professors in our sample. The only measure to show a difference on all three indicators of ideological commitment is participation.

Pedagogical Preoccupations Outside the Classroom. Scores for this measure showed no reliable differences. With the use of one-tailed t-tests, there was no difference between the preoccupation scores of those who claimed to make a big effort (M = 15.2) and those who did not (M = 14.0) or between those who claimed much influence (M = 14.9) and those who did not (M = 14.3). Nor did a one-way Analysis of Variance (ANOVA) show the composite measure scores to vary as a function of engagement (F[4, 68] = 1.24, p > .05).

Sources of Enjoyment and Challenge. There was no association between a commitment to feminist pedagogy and the reasons for becoming and remaining a professor. When we focused on the positive side of the motivation to be a teacher (on a 5-point scale), we saw that those who made a big effort to employ their feminist values (M = 4.2) looked similar to others (M = 4.0). Those who claimed to be very influenced (M = 4.0) looked similar to others (M = 4.1), and those who were very engaged (M = 4.1) resembled those who were not engaged (M = 4.0).[6]

As Table 4.2 shows, the responses concerning pleasures and challenges did not reliably show a distinction between those who espoused a great commitment and those who did not.

TABLE 4.2   Pleasures and Challenges as a Function of Commitment to Feminist Pedagogy

	Ideological Commitment to Feminist Pedagogy					
	Effort[a]		*Influence*[b]		*Engagement*[c]	
	Big (n = 17)	*Other* (n = 23)	*Great* (n = 20)	*Other* (n = 20)	*Great* (n = 23)	*Other* (n = 17)
Pleasure from students						
Raw score	85.94	81.13	87.05	79.30	83.30	83.00
Ratio score	1.70	1.81	1.67	1.84	1.70	1.85
Difficulties with students						
Raw score	12.18	15.70*	15.80	12.60	14.43	13.88
Ratio score	.40	.80	.43	.83	.55	.73

*p < .05.
[a]Thirty-six respondents were coded as making a big effort and forty-one as making a small effort.
[b]Thirty-four respondents were coded as being highly influenced and forty-three as not.
[c]Twenty-eight respondents were coded as being very engaged and twenty as being less engaged.

Interpreting the Findings
of the Feminist Teachers Project

All told, there was a minimal association between attitudes and behaviors among our sample. Women who claimed a self-conscious commitment to feminist pedagogy did not seem to behave very differently from other feminists of the college professors whom we interviewed. Nor did they experience different sources of pleasure and challenge.

How can we explain our findings? Two alternatives spring to mind. First, it may be that rhetoric is not confined to the forces of conservatism. Perhaps feminists are prone to ideological statements, so that those who claim to make a big effort, to be influenced or generally to be engaged in issues of feminist pedagogy, are really only boasting. Maybe, in other words, our participants do not actually act on their feminist claims. Alternatively, it may be that virtually all members of our sample engaged in the behaviors under consideration. Maybe just being a feminist is enough to motivate a professor to teach in nontraditional ways. Perhaps, in other words, our findings can be attributed to the modesty of those who do much without making ideological claims rather than to the boastfulness of those who claim much without doing much. To phrase it differently, perhaps all our participants "walk the talk" whether or not they "talk the talk."

To determine whether modesty or boastfulness was operating, we returned to our data and looked for answers there. We noticed immediately that we had a truncated range of scores. Most of the participants—whether or not they claimed a commitment—had very high scores for all classroom activities and derived a lot of pleasure from their contact with students. The high scores would be consistent with the modesty explanation.

We also checked to see if our respondents gave high-handed pronouncements about what feminists "ought" to do in the classroom. Our questionnaire item that asked participants if they attempt eighteen certain behaviors also asked them which of the items they thought "every feminist teacher ought to do." The kinds of behaviors about which we asked included trying to open the course to divergent points of view; trying to link knowledge and its social implications; taking steps to create a safe environment for all students; and paying attention to issues of power in the classroom. To devise a rough index of pompousness or preachiness, we calculated the number of times any woman identified an item as something that "every feminist teacher ought to do" and did not claim to do the behavior herself. Examining all seventy-six questionnaires, we found that the vast majority of the time, our participants did what they thought every feminist ought to do and also, to a somewhat lesser extent, that they thought every feminist ought to do what they did. Of the seventy-six women evaluating sixteen behaviors, there were 1,006 instances in which there was a complete match between what they thought every feminist teacher should do and what they do; 185 instances in which the respondents reported their own behavior without prescribing it for all feminists; and only 23 instances in which the respondents prescribed a behavior for all feminists but declined to do it themselves. Clearly, these data argue against the hypocrisy explanation of our findings.

Finally, we divided our sample into those who were highly identified as feminists, whether or not they claimed a commitment to feminist pedagogy, and those who sometimes did not label themselves as feminists. The former group included 35 women who, in response to some close-ended questions, selected the option "always" in response to the questions "Do you label yourself as a feminist?" and also "Do your colleagues consider you to be a feminist?" The latter category included 12 women who selected the options "sometimes" or "seldom" for either question. We reasoned that if the former group differed from the latter, we would know that just being identified as a feminist, even without the ideological commitment to feminist pedagogy, would produce changes in people's teaching. When a series of t-tests revealed no differences between the groups on any of the dependent variables we had examined, the hope of conclusive answers evaporated.

Professors of psychology in our sample varied in terms of their avowed involvement in issues of feminist pedagogy. Yet by and large, those who said they were highly committed did not behave differently from others in the sample. They were not more active in the classroom than others, perhaps because all of the sample were very active. Nor did they derive more pleasure from contact with students than did others—once again perhaps because virtually everyone in the sample enjoyed contact with students. The highly committed group also did not manifest more than the modest amount of out-of-classroom preoccupation with pedagogical issues shown by their less ideologically committed sisters.

Further analyses of our data did not conclusively explain the lack of correspondence between attitudes and behavior among our sample of feminist professors. We saw that our participants showed virtually no tendency to proscribe behaviors for others beyond what they did themselves and generally showed a strong devotion to teaching. It would be inconsistent with our observations to see the lack of correspondence between attitudes and behaviors as resulting from boastfulness or empty rhetoric on the part of those participants who claimed a deep commitment to feminist pedagogy. Indeed, our observations lead us to suspect that all feminist professors of psychology are given to behaving in ways that feminist writers have identified as promotive of learning.

Without a contrast group (i.e., professors who do not claim to be feminists), our supposition cannot be conclusively tested. Perhaps all professors of psychology—and not just feminist professors of psychology—behave in the ways the experts have tagged as beneficial to students. To find out whether feminist psychologists differ from others in terms of their teaching will be a task for dedicated future researchers.

Behind the Scenes:
Three Feminists in Search of an Author

Although we leave for future researchers the task of contrasting feminist professors with others, we embrace—with some trepidation—the assignment of reflecting on how our gender and ethnicity have influenced the work we have done. The prime question is: Would we have found the same pattern of results if one, two, or all three of us were male and/or if one, two, or all three of us were people of color?

Dealing in counterfactuals, we propose a positive answer to our query. It seems quite probable that were any of us male and/or non-White, we would have found different patterns in our data. There are three reasons why. First, we might have accessed different samples. Had there been more women of color or males in our sample, their pattern of experiences tapped by our questions might have been very different. Second, we might have created different research instruments. Patterns are nothing more or less than answers to questions, whether explicitly or implicitly stated. Finally, given the context of this research collaboration, where hundreds of miles separated all three authors and where two of the authors have never met face to face or even on the telephone, homogeneity of sex and ethnicity probably allowed us to keep asking questions of the data that we might not otherwise have felt comfortable enough to ask.

In what way would our originating questions have differed if one or both of the principal investigators were male? Probably we would have been less sensitive to the difficulties that face women faculty in colleges and universities. As evidenced by the overwhelmingly female membership of the American Psychological Association's Division on The Psychology of Women, men take less of an interest in feminism than do women. It seems improbable that two men would have delved into as much detail as we did about the perils and pleasures of feminist pedagogy. But if by some chance two male investigators did inquire about feminist pedagogy, they, unlike us, would probably have focused on the special challenges that face male feminists in the classroom. In support of our assertion, we note that when men write about feminism, gender issues, and teaching, they tend to dwell on their own position, a position that they view as somewhat incongruous (Atlas, 1992; Caughie and Pearce, 1992; Bezucha, 1985; Snoek, 1985). Men are, after all, just as self-absorbed as women.

No less influential was the skin pigmentation of the two principal investigators. Educated by the recent analyses of gender and color (e.g., Reid, 1993; Reid and Clayton, 1992), we remained alert to issues of ethnicity (as well as of class and sexual orientation). We included in our interview a broad question that asked the participant to speak directly to issues of how ethnicity, class, and sexual orientation had been part of her experiences as a feminist and a teacher. But our attention to issues of color could certainly have been stronger and more detailed than it was. We placed, for example, the item that spoke directly and explicitly of ethnic issues toward the end of the interview so as not to unduly influence respondents who might be striving to appear politically correct. Although our strategy did permit us to see how many White women and how many women of color spontaneously raised issues of ethnicity, we were naive to imagine that our respondents were not influenced by our silence. That we did not ask about ethnicity until the end of the interview no doubt communicated much to our participants, albeit subliminally.

Indeed, our very conception of feminism, implicit in the way we phrased our questions, was predicated on seeing the struggle for gender equity as ethically uncomplicated. Such is the conception of the White woman, whose fathers, sons, brothers, cousins, and intimate male partners tend also to be White and privileged. Had we been women of color, we might have seen the issues of feminist pedagogy to be more complex and perplexing than we did, and we might have asked more questions about the negative or problematic aspects of self-consciously employing feminist principles in or out of teaching.

The words of one of our respondents, a Black woman who filled both a teaching and an administrative role at a coed college, reminded us of the complexities of feminism. Asked what feminism meant to her, she observed:

> Feminism means many different things to people. Until very recently I did not call myself a feminist, [rejecting] the lay public's idea of what feminism was. In fact, even academic feminism did not include me until the 1980s. Feminism in the United States was pretty monolithic, pretty homogeneous. Even in my attempts to join feminist groups, I remained marginalized. The kind of politics of the wider society follows us wherever we go. . . . And these groups [of different ethnicities] were very, very exclusive in terms of what they considered to be priorities. . . . And so until recently, America did not embrace my experiences. I did not want to do violence to myself by labeling myself by a philosophy that did not include me.

We believe that the gender and ethnic composition of our work team constrained the patterns we found not only by shaping our original research questions but also by influencing how we worked together, asking new questions as we progressed in our data analysis. Specifically, some sections of the data analyses were handled exclusively by two of us, a White young adult college student (JK) and a White middle-aged professor (FC). When the computer printouts revealed virtually no behavioral differences between those who claimed a strong commitment to feminist pedagogy and others, the student dared to suggest that this reflected poorly on the ideologically committed group. "You mean," prodded the professor, "they are full of hot air?" and the student replied, "yes." Thus was born the boastfulness explanation of the first round of findings. In defense of herself and her colleagues, the professor put forward the modesty explanation, and together the student and the professor looked to see which explanation more closely conformed to the data.

Would the student have dared to be as irreverent as she was if the professor were a White man? Quite possibly, the student would not have suggested boastfulness out of loyalty to her gender. And what if the professor were a person of color? The White student has had at least one successful and easygoing collaboration with a professor of color, but circumstances permitted them to work closely together on a day-to-day basis and they were also close in age.

How might the collaboration have proceeded if the student were a person of color interacting with a White professor? Again, we can only speculate that the interactions might have been completely different, for the risk of alienating one's professor might loom especially large to the minority college student (Tatum, 1992). It is hard to imagine that a minority student would not have proceeded much more gingerly than was in fact the case for us.

As it was, the ease that comes from being similar to each other enabled the student and the professors to work well together and to complete all the analyses. The collaboration, though not always smooth, was one in which the student could feel the special sense of accomplishment that accompanies a budding scholar's first publication and in which, therefore, the two professors could pride themselves on having, after all, managed to "walk the talk." Perhaps if we were other than we are we would mistakenly overlook demographic factors, such as homogeneity of gender and color, or overlook contextual factors, such as good computer facilities, and attribute our ability to behave in accordance with our feminist ideology solely to our own individual and collective magnificence. It is quite possibly the truest indication of our postmodern ethnically sensitive feminism that we avoid such dreadful hubris.

Notes

1. Twelve transcripts were coded independently by two coders, who agreed 83 percent of the time.

2. Twelve transcripts were coded independently by two coders, who agreed 75 percent of the time.

3. Coders rated the transcripts according to the length and depth of commitment to issues of feminism in teaching. Respondents who were able to articulate a long and concerted engagement with issues of feminist pedagogy were given a score of 5. Those with a fairly long engagement were given a score of 4. Those whose connection to issues of feminist pedagogy was erratic and/or of middling intensity received a 3. A score of 2 went to those who showed only a little engagement, and 1 meant no engagement. In some of the analyses, we collapsed respondents into two groups: those who were very engaged (scores of 4 or 5) and those who were not very engaged (scores of 1 or 2). Twelve transcripts were coded independently by two coders who agreed 75 percent of the time.

4. Two statements concerned environment (e.g., "takes steps to create a safe environment for all students"); three concerned participation (e.g., "encourages active interaction in the classroom"); five concerned the breakdown of hierarchy (e.g., "acknowledges own biases"); three concerned activism (e.g., "tries to link knowledge and its social implications"); and three concerned explicit feminism (e.g., makes explicit issues of process").

5. Techniques were divided into four types. Four techniques referred to the incorporation of students' personal experiences into the courses (e.g., "have students keep a journal"); six referred to the breakdown of hierarchy (e.g., "give a choice of papers"); one referred to the use of collaboration ("encourage students to do group projects"); and three referred to the use of innovative techniques (e.g., "use role play exercises").

6. Nor did a woman's coded narrative about how she became a teacher bear much relation to how much pleasure she derives from contact with students or how much of a challenge she finds students to be.

References

Atlas, R. (1992, October). As a male feminist. Paper presented at a meeting of the American Association of University Women, Oakland, CA.

Belenky, M. F., Clinchy, B. M., Goldberger, N. R., and Tarule, J. M. (1986). *Women's ways of knowing*. New York, NY: Basic Books.

Bezucha, R. J. (1985). Feminist pedagogy as a subversive activity. In M. Culley and C. Portuges (Eds.), *Gendered subjects: The dynamics of feminist teaching* (pp. 81–95). Boston, MA: Routledge and Kegan Paul.

Cannon, L. W. (1990). Fostering positive race, class, and gender dynamics in the classroom. *Women's Studies Quarterly, 18*, 126–134.

Caughie, P. L., and Pearce, R. (1992). Reading "The dominance of the professor": Gendered teaching, gendered subjects. *National Women's Studies Association Journal, 4*, 187–199.

Cocks, J. (1985). Suspicious pleasures: On teaching feminist theory. In M. Culley and C. Portuges (Eds.), *Gendered subjects: The dynamics of feminist teaching* (pp. 171–182). Boston, MA: Routledge and Kegan Paul.

Crawford, M., and Marecek, J. (1989). Feminist theory, feminist psychology: A bibliography of epistemology, critical analysis, and applications. *Psychology of Women Quarterly, 13,* 477–491.

Crosby, F. J., Todd, J., and Worell, J. (in press). Have feminists abandoned social activism? Voices from the academy. In L. Montada and M. Lerner (Eds.), *Current concerns about justice.* New York, NY: Plenum.

Culley, M. (1985). Anger and authority in the introductory women's studies classroom. In M. Culley and C. Portuges (Eds.), *Gendered subjects: The dynamics of feminist teaching* (pp. 209–217). Boston, MA: Routledge and Kegan Paul.

D'Souza, D. (1991). *Illiberal education: The politics of race and sex on campus.* New York, NY: Free Press.

Higginbotham, E. (1990). Designing an inclusive curriculum: Bringing all women into the core. *Women's Studies Quarterly, 18,* 7–23.

Patai, D., and Koertge, N. (1994). *Professing feminism: Cautionary tales from the strange world of women's studies.* New York, NY: Basic Books.

Reid, P. T. (1993). Poor women in psychological research: Shut up and shut out. *Psychology of Women Quarterly, 17,* 133–150.

Reid, P. T., and Clayton, S. (1992). Racism and sexism at work. *Social Justice Research, 5,* 249–268.

Snoek, D. (1985). A male feminist in a women's classroom. In M. Culley and C. Portuges (Eds.), *Gendered subjects: The dynamics of feminist teaching* (pp. 136–143). Boston, MA: Routledge and Kegan Paul.

Tatum, B. D. (1992). Talking about race, learning about racism: The application of racial identity development theory in the classroom. *Harvard Educational Review, 62,* 1–24.

PART 2

Women's Work: Mothering and Modeling

Mothering may be the world's most rewarding occupation, but it is not the easiest. Most mothers know this. So do some women who are not mothers and some men. How do psychologists understand motherhood? What is known and what is knowable from systematic inquiry into women's parenting experience? What wisdom has accumulated?

Time was when nearly all the ills of any family member were blamed on the woman who gave birth to the person in trouble (Caplan, 1989). When college freshmen took Psychology 101 in the 1950s and 1960s, they learned of the "schizophrenogenic mother." In the fashion of college freshmen, many began to worry that they had one. Some even worried that they might become one.

Times change. During the 1970s, for example, the blatant misogyny of earlier decades gave way to more subtle attacks on women as mothers. Psychologists and others gave a show of sympathy with the presumably stressed-out woman who sought to combine career and motherhood. Yet close scrutiny of the literature revealed that the pretended sympathy was little more than a diversionary tactic used to keep attention away from the real sources of difficulty: sexism and rampant individualism (Crosby, 1991).

Times changed more. As increasing numbers of psychologists have become mothers, the discipline of psychology has shifted its view of motherhood. Mothers are cast less as prime creators and more as mere human beings caught up in the business of sustaining life. Romanticism, which has alternately deified and demonized mothers, has given way to realism.

Realism characterizes the chapters that form this section of the book. Both separately and together, these chapters address three interrelated questions: What are the stresses of motherhood? What circumstances influence the amount of stress? What circumstances influence coping?

To answer these questions, the contributors emphasize resilience more than pathology. In Chapter 5, Elizabeth Sparks describes what she has seen as an African American therapist working with African American women clients. Many of Sparks's clients have internalized myths about what it means to be a good person—and more specifically a good mother—and they feel that they do not live up to the idealizations. Sparks traces the cultural context in which the myths have developed and provides case examples that illustrate how destructive the myths can be. She reflects on ways that her clients, and she herself, can overcome the myths.

Chapter 6, by Karen Fraser Wyche and Debra Lobato, is based on a set of focus group interviews with minority women who have children with special needs. Although therapeutic to the mothers who participated in them, the interviews were primarily intended to provide systematic information to the investigators. Quoting frequently from their respondents, Wyche and Lobato document the great amount of stress faced by the African American and Latina families when one of the children is mentally retarded, and they also show the resilience of the families. What helps the women to cope are social supports. The mothers in their sample are especially likely to rely on their husbands/partners for both emotional and instrumental support. Although we do not wish to make too many claims from one finding in a pilot study, we cannot help but notice that the present findings are inconsistent with common images of the absent minority fathers and of the incompetent female-headed ethnic minority family unit.

Also at odds with the image of the hapless family unit are the fifty respondents in the interview described by Sheryl Olson and Rosario Ceballo in Chapter 7. All of the women interviewed were poor mothers. About half were women of color and half were White women. Despite their extremely reduced economic circumstances, the women showed a range of mothering skills, with many of the women giving their children enriched conditions for social and emotional development. Among African American women, but not among White women, strong social supports went hand in hand with good mothering.

What themes run through the chapters of this section? We see three:

- Mothering is a challenge. Even though it sustains women and provides them with enormous gratification, the job contains a lot of work. Trying to meet unrealistic expectations augments the work.
- Social context influences how the challenge of mothering is met. Although personality factors are important, social circumstances de-

termine a great deal about how the work of mothering is conducted and about what is achieved in the family.

- The task for feminists is to help expand women's ways of meeting the challenge of mothering. One especially promising way to do this is to facilitate an understanding—among scholars and policymakers and among the women themselves—of the contextual factors that influence mothering.

The themes of challenge and resilience, which characterize the findings of this section, also characterize the discovery process itself. All five women in the study have faced adversity. In all of the projects, much has been accomplished with meager economic resources. And throughout, community and identity have been inextricably linked to each other and to the contributors' professional work. All of the authors in this section hope their work is instructive to those whom they study, and they believe that the lives they study are instructive to us all. We think so too.

References

Caplan, P. J. (1989). *Don't blame mother.* New York, NY: Harper and Row.

Crosby, F. J. (1991). *Juggling: The unexpected advantages of combining career and home for women and their families.* New York, NY: Free Press.

5

Overcoming Stereotypes of Mothers in the African American Context

Elizabeth E. Sparks

I am an African American, middle-aged professional woman who has spent the past twenty years thinking about and discussing with others what it means to be an African American woman in this society. Because of the clients with whom I have interacted over the years, I have been particularly interested in what it means to be an African American mother in contemporary America. My viewpoint has undergone changes during this time, and the perspective expressed in this chapter is the culmination of my personal experiences as an African American daughter (who is not a mother), experiences that I have shared with female kin and friends (most of whom are mothers), and from my work as a psychotherapist with African American mothers. We have all struggled to understand what it means to be a woman and mother, both within our own cultural context and as we are perceived by the White-majority culture. Our experiences of motherhood range from feeling strong and empowered because of who we are to feeling overwhelmed, burdened, and unfulfilled.

In this chapter I explore some of the stereotypes of African American women that have been promulgated by the White establishment and which have been internalized by at least some of my clients. In the first part of the chapter, I look at the historical roots of these images of motherhood and outline current stereotypical conceptualizations of African American women. I next present a set of case examples. In them, we see women who are struggling with difficult situations in their lives and whose recovery has been hindered by the internalization of these stereotypical images. In the third section, I discuss the personal journey required to free myself from these controlling images and my work in helping clients overcome the negative impact of this internalization process. Finally, I argue for a new definition of African American motherhood and for rekindling the sense of collectivism that has been so highly valued within the African American community throughout its history.

Stereotypes

African Roots and Transformations During Slavery

The analysis of motherhood that is presented in this chapter incorporates the broader perspective of African American womanhood because of the intricate connection that exists between these two identities for African American women. In traditional African society, reproduction and mothering formed a valued and integral aspect of women's identity (Mbiti, 1969). The tradition involved not only nurturing one's biological offspring but also caring for other, often nonrelated children (Oppong, 1973). Child rearing was thought to be a shared responsibility of the community, and there was a common African practice of fostering children as a means of minimizing what was viewed as a dysfunctional emphasis on individualism within a communal setting (James, 1993; Sudarkasa, 1993). Although enslaved West Africans were unable to replicate traditional family and communal patterns and values in America, some traditions, including the emphasis on the interconnectedness and interdependence between families, appear to have been adapted as a means of coping with slavery's highly destructive system of exploitation and oppression (Gutman, 1976).

African American slave women played an integral role in the maintenance and survival of the family. However, the control of motherhood (reproduction) and mothering (caretaking) was ultimately held by the White slave master. African American female slaves were generally not seen as women at all, but as beasts whose reproductive capacities (as well as their physical labor) were used to produce commodities for someone else's benefit (Fox-Genovese, 1988; Greene, 1994). In some instances, women were able to establish solid relationships with male partners and to provide caretaking for their children. Slave narratives provide stories of women who stole food and clothing from their White masters in order to supplement the meager provisions allocated for their children and stories of women who made valiant attempts to keep their children with them (Shaw, 1994). However, there was a darker side to this struggle between African American slave women and their White masters for the control of motherhood, which sometimes resulted in drastic measures being used by the slave women to influence the fate of their offspring. Documents written by slave owners during this era indicate that there were high rates of infant mortality, including deaths by natural causes and those that were the result of infanticide (Shaw, 1994). Some documents also indicate the use of self-induced abortions as a means of controlling reproduction.

Despite the attempts made by women to provide consistent caretaking for their children, slave owners' disregard for the sanctity and unity of the family often led to instability (James, 1993; Greene, 1994). It was against the law for African American slaves to marry; however, documents in counties throughout the South indicate that many couples who had been informally married and living together during slavery had their marriages legalized and registered after emancipation (Billingsley, 1992). Both official documents and slave narratives suggest that slaves created patterns of family life that were functionally integrative and that did more than prevent the destruction of personality. Family life also created the conditions out of which came African American pride, identity, culture, and community (Billingsley, 1992).

The conditions of slavery made it necessary for mothers and fathers to be psychologically prepared, and their children socialized, for possible separation. This led to a conceptualization of "mother" that was collective. The term "mother" was used to refer to birthmothers and any other adult slave woman who provided basic caretaking for the child. Thus, the African tradition of fostering was adapted to meet the needs of the enslaved community in America, and the practice of "othermothering" played a critical role in child rearing (James, 1993). This tradition of women-centered units being primarily responsible for the nurturing and rearing of children has continued in the African American community since the times of slavery. It reflects both a continuation of West African cultural values and functional adaptations to race and gender oppression faced by African Americans in this society (Tanner, 1974; Stack, 1974; Sudarkasa, 1981).

What is most important about these years in slavery, and the period of time immediately following emancipation, is the way in which African Americans developed their own socially constructed definition of family. This definition included those adults (whether birth parents, relatives, or fictive kin) who accepted responsibility for the nurturance and socialization of children and who shared strong feelings of loyalty and trust. The work of contemporary scholars such as Carol Stack (1974) and Joyce Aschenbrenner (1975) show that these patterns of cooperation have been a very important factor in the survival of African American families in cities as well as in rural areas throughout America. During slavery, othermothers cared for children orphaned by sale or death of their parents and children conceived through rape whose mothers were unable to bond with them. In more contemporary times, othermothers support children born into extreme poverty or to alcoholic or drug-addicted mothers, children of young mothers, as well as children who for other reasons cannot remain with their birthmothers (Young, 1970; Dougherty, 1978).

Although there is little discussion in the literature about the quality of the relationships between birthmothers and othermothers, the interactions are described as cooperative and seem to reflect the importance of women working together collectively to raise children successfully under oppressive conditions (Collins, 1990). Cross-residential or transresidential cooperation among African Americans was, and continues to be, an important factor in rearing children, providing financial support in times of need, caring for aged family members, and providing shelter for various kinfolk who need it from time to time. Thus, many contemporary mothers rely on women-centered communities as their basis for support in caring for their children (Sudarkasa, 1993).

Stereotypical Images from Slavery to the Civil Rights Era

In addition to supporting each other and caring for their partners and children under severe conditions of racism, sexism, and oppression, African American women have also had to struggle to counteract negative stereotypes promulgated by the White-majority culture since the time of slavery (hooks, 1981; Greene, 1994). A stereotype is defined as a belief about a group of people that gives insufficient attention to individual differences among members of that group (Brislin, 1993). In situations where these stereotypes are negative, pervasive, and have existed for many generations, they become part of the culture into which children are socialized and reflect prejudicial feelings about this group. Throughout the history of this country, the White-majority culture has created negative stereotypes about African American women as mothers, and these stereotypes have been used to legitimize their oppression (Collins, 1990).

In her sociopolitical analysis of race, class, and gender bias in America and its impact on African American women, Patricia Hill Collins identifies stereotypes that seem to have penetrated the consciousness of African American women today. Collins's thesis represents a bringing together of sociological research, ideas of Black feminist theorists, her own experiences as an African American woman, and experiences of other women she has encountered in many different arenas. She examines the complexity of ideas that exist in both scholarly and everyday life and formulates a perspective that helps us understand the experiences of African American women as they attempt to find an authentic "voice" in the current social, political, and economic climate (Collins, 1990). In identifying these stereotypical images, Collins utilizes observations taken from African American literature, historical documents, the media, and research. She highlights the controlling nature of these stereotypical images and describes how each has contributed to the oppression and subjugation of African American women. Two of these images, "Mammy" and "Jezebel," were developed during slavery. Three others evolved later.

The stereotypical Mammy was portrayed as the faithful, obedient domestic servant who loved, nurtured, and cared for White children without any thought or attention to her own needs or to those of her family (Collins, 1990). This image not only characterized African American women as having exceptional nurturing and caretaking skills, but it also promoted the belief that she preferred to care for White children, even if this meant neglecting her own. Thus, the Mammy image was one that provided support for White superiority while it characterized African American women as both understanding and accepting of their subordinate place in society. The Mammy image buttressed the ideology of the cult of true womanhood, in which sexuality and fertility are severed. "Good" White mothers were expected to deny their female sexuality and to devote their attention to the moral development of their offspring. In contrast, Mammy was an asexual, surrogate African American mother who handled the more basic child care needs for White children (Collins, 1990). This image was used to justify the economic exploitation of African American women both as slaves and later as domestic workers (Gilkes, 1994).

In the Jezebel stereotype, African American women were portrayed as being sexually aggressive and responsible for their own sexual victimization. This image was created by Whites as a way of justifying the widespread sexual assaults on African American women by White males that occurred during slavery (Davis, 1981; hooks, 1981; White, 1985). By their acceptance of the Jezebel stereotype, the White establishment was able to rationalize using African American women as "breeders" for the financial gain of slaveholders. This stereotype has continued to be applied to African American women even in more modern times, as evidenced by the fact that White males who were accused of raping African American women received no legal sanctions in courts in many southern states from the time of emancipation through more than two-thirds of the twentieth century (White, 1985). In a similar way, the Jezebel stereotype was reflected in the treatment received by African American domestic workers in White homes during the early 1900s. According to narratives from women who were domestics during that time period, African American women often risked sexual harassment and victimization by White male employers. As one woman remarked in 1912: "I believe that nearly all White men take, and expect to take, undue liberties with their colored female servants—not only the fathers, but in many cases the sons also. Those servants who rebel against such familiarity must either leave or expect a mightily hard time, if they stay" (quoted in Mann, 1990, p. 148).

Although the Jezebel stereotype is not directly focused on mothers, as is the Mammy stereotype, it has affected the perception of African American mothers within the larger White-majority culture because of the complex, often contradictory, connection between sexuality and motherhood that exists in this society. Although children are conceived through sexual activity, the prevailing notion of motherhood is of one that is relatively asexual, with "good mothers" expected to have rigid control over their sexuality. As a result, women are often seen as being either a "Madonna," who is a devoted, asexual mother figure, or as a "Whore," whose maternal feelings and instincts are thought to be minimal at best. The Jezebel stereotypical image portrays African American women as having excessive sexual appetites; therefore, it follows that these women could not possibly be good mothers because of their preoccupation with sexuality. During slavery, this stereotype contributed to the rationalizations used by the White establishment to legitimize separating slave children from their mothers, as these women were believed to have little, if any, commitment to mothering the children who resulted from their sexual activity. Although the Jezebel stereotype may have freed African American women from the rigid, puritanical attitudes toward sexuality that affected the lives of most White women of that day, it ultimately made them vulnerable to sexual assault and held them responsible for their own sexual victimization and for the removal of their children.

The third stereotypical image, the "Matriarch," was constructed by the White establishment during the 1960s. She is an African American woman who has failed to fulfill her traditional "womanly" role by working outside the home and who is so negative and critical toward her male partner (or spouse) that he is unwilling to live with her (Collins, 1990). This stereotype presents African American women as bad mothers, since, according to this stereotype, their work outside of the home forces them to neglect their children, and their critical, negative interaction with the children's father causes him to abandon the family. Although the Matriarch image does present African American women as strong and powerful maternal figures, in opposition to the then prevailing cultural image of White women as being weak, passive, and submissive, it is nonetheless used as a means of controlling African American women.

The Matriarch stereotype allows the White establishment to blame African American women for the success or failure of their children and for the economic circumstances of African American families (Collins, 1990; Greene, 1994). White scholars, journalists, and policymakers have claimed that the African American family structure is the main cause of the high rates of crime, unemployment, school dropouts, teenage pregnancies, drug abuse, and disaffection among young people in the inner cities (Moynihan,

1967). This perspective, although challenged by many researchers of color (e.g., Billingsley, 1968; Hill, 1972; McAdoo, 1981), is an extremely difficult myth to overcome because many in this country, including some African Americans, believe the stereotype and accept it as truth (Sudarkasa, 1988).

Current Stereotypical Images

The fourth image is that of the "Welfare Mother," which labels the fertility of women who are not White and middle class as unnecessary and even dangerous to the values of this country (Collins, 1990). Unlike the Matriarch, who was seen as too aggressive, the Welfare Mother is not aggressive enough. She is seen as too lazy to work and as having repetitive pregnancies in order to collect more money from the state. She is portrayed as a mother who does not appropriately socialize her children to accept the societal values and normative behaviors surrounding the work ethic, thereby causing her family to remain in poverty. The Jezebel image can be seen underneath the Welfare Mother stereotype, since the latter is also seen as being sexually promiscuous and having little emotional connection to her offspring, who result from her heightened sexual activity. As with the other stereotypical images of African American women, the Welfare Mother image allows the White-majority culture to blame the victims for their own oppression and victimization and shifts the focus away from the institutional and structural factors that perpetuate poverty.

The final stereotypical image is that of the "Superwoman." Unlike the earlier stereotypes, which were constructed by the White establishment to justify its exploitative behavior toward African American women, the Superwoman image has been perpetuated by the African American community and is embraced by many as being an "idealized" image of motherhood. The Superwoman image requires that African American women sacrifice their own needs for those of their children and families, while being committed to maintaining the economic viability of their families by working and contributing to the advancement of the African American community as a whole through their participation in service work. Michele Wallace (1991) describes the Superwoman as follows:

> [She is a woman] of inordinate strength, with an ability for tolerating an unusual amount of misery and heavy, distasteful work. This woman does not have the same fears, weaknesses, and insecurities as other women, but believes herself to be and is, in fact, stronger emotionally than most men. Less of a woman in that she is less "feminine" and helpless, she is really more of a woman in that she is the embodiment of Mother Earth, the quintessential mother with infinite sexual, life-giving, and nurturing reserves. In other words, she is a Superwoman. (p. 107)

The Superwoman image is deceptive because it builds on the efforts that African American women have made through the years to oppose negative stereotypes prevalent in the White-majority culture, particularly the Matriarch and Welfare Mother images. Because it appears to be positive and to represent the strengths of African American motherhood, it is one that many African American women have internalized (Boyd-Franklin, 1991; Greene, 1994). In the 1980s the Superwoman image was expanded to include another criterion—she must also be a highly educated, professional woman. This newer image has been labeled the "Super/Essence woman," after the popular magazine geared toward professional African American women (Edwards, 1992). The Super/Essence woman is expected to be a supportive, and at times submissive, partner to her spouse, a devoted mother who is actively involved in her children's lives, while also being aggressive, competent, and career-focused in her professional life. She must be able to create and maintain a viable marriage, while also being prepared to care for herself and her children alone if necessary.

This stereotype has a strong influence on mothering and on the mother-daughter relationship for African American women. Mothers strive to equip their daughters with the skills necessary to meet these expectations, making every effort to ensure that their daughters have the stability and emotional strength to overcome whatever obstacles are in their way (Collins, 1990).

With the Super/Essence woman image held up as an ideal, life for African American women can become a gauntlet race. Some succeed, but there are many casualties. The "wounded" are those women who make up the 42.8 percent (1988 figures) of Black female heads of households who live at or below the poverty level (Mullings, 1994). They are the mothers of the 70.1 percent of Black children who are living in families with incomes less than twice the poverty level (Edelman, 1985). These women head families that constitute what has been called the "underclass," which refers to those individuals who live in persistent poverty and who have "dropped out" of the struggle to attain economic stability and security. Many of these women living in poverty are young. Statistics indicate that the African American female head of household has become younger over the past forty years, which compounds the difficulties that these women and their children face. In 1980, figures indicated that 1 in 8 female-headed African American families were headed by women under twenty-five years of age (Smith, 1988). Among this number, three-fourths of these young women have never been married. They tend to be women from low-income families whose incomes are depressed even further as they form their own families out of wedlock (Smith, 1988). Clearly, teen mothers are quite disadvantaged in their capacity to attain the Super/Essence woman ideal. For those who have internalized the image, the result can be depression and guilt.

The Internalization of Stereotypes

Case Examples

Claudine.   Claudine is a 35-year-old African American woman who is the single parent for her two boys, ages 8 and 6. She was married to, and lived with, the boys' father for seven years, during which time he was physically and emotionally abusive to her. When Claudine left her husband, she had a high school education but no specific job-related skills. She applied for and received Aid to Families with Dependent Children (AFDC) and began living in an inner-city apartment near her mother and sisters. Once her children were in school all day, Claudine requested job training through the Welfare Department. She hoped to be able to find a job that would provide her with a livable income so that she would no longer need AFDC. Claudine was referred to a program that trained women to work as instrument technicians, preparing surgical kits for hospitals. She faithfully attended the training, and at graduation she received an award for being the most consistent and conscientious trainee in the program.

For six months after completing the training, Claudine applied for jobs in local hospitals. Although she received a few interviews, she was not hired. From time to time, Claudine found temporary work (usually during the Christmas season) in a local department store. However, she could never seriously consider taking a full-time position and terminating her AFDC benefits because the minimum-wage salary that she could earn would not be sufficient to compensate for the benefits she would lose. In addition to the stipend, Claudine's AFDC benefits included subsidized housing, Medicaid coverage for herself and the children, and food stamps.

Claudine is in therapy because one of her sons developed severe behavior problems following the parental separation. She actively participates in his treatment and in supportive sessions for herself. In her individual sessions, Claudine expresses frustration with her life. She very much wants to establish a "better life" for her children, and she blames herself for not being able to figure out a way to work and take care of her family. Although she does not want to return to her abusive husband, she sometimes wonders whether she caused him to be abusive, often blaming herself for some "defect" that made her a "failure" as a wife and mother.

Claudine's life situation reflects at least two of the prevailing stereotypes of African American women—that of the Matriarch and that of the Welfare Mother. She is a single head of household and feels personally responsible for the plight of her family and for the failure of her marriage. In many ways, Claudine has internalized these stereotypical images, which contributes to her feelings of worthlessness, guilt, and depression.

Annette.   Annette is a 22-year-old African American young woman who has been in treatment since she was 14 years old. She was raised by her mother in a single-parent household and has a history of physical and sexual abuse. At age 15, Annette ran away from her mother and went to live with a family friend (she was Annette's fictive aunt). While in her aunt's home, she was raped, which resulted in her being placed in a Department of Social Services (DSS) foster home. Annette became pregnant during her senior year in high school and decided to keep her child. This disrupted her foster placement, and after the baby's birth, she (and her child) went to live with a biological aunt. Annette, with the help of an adult female cousin, was able to adequately parent the child for the first two years. She completed high school and was admitted to a small two-year college in the area. Annette's situation is complicated by the regulations of the social services system, which made her ineligible for AFDC benefits because she was still considered a foster child under the jurisdiction of DSS. The financial support Annette received from DSS was not sufficient to care for herself and her child, and the agency refused to provide support for the child since she was technically not in foster care. Although Annette's therapist attempted to advocate, she was unsuccessful. Eventually, Annette no longer had the financial resources or the emotional energy to continue both attending college and adequately parenting her child. After a great deal of deliberation, Annette released custody of the child to her cousin. She is currently attempting to complete her college education and is employed as a temporary worker.

In Annette's case, we see internalization of the Super/Essence woman image by a young, single mother who has had a problematic life history. Her decision to attend college was based on a firm belief that as an African American woman, she was expected to educate herself so that she could obtain a professional-level job in order to adequately care for herself and her child. Annette's early history and life experiences undoubtedly complicate her situation; however, she has continued to feel totally responsible for her plight. Annette faced tremendous stress, both emotionally and physically, when she tried to parent her daughter and attend college at the same time, but she frequently comments that other African American women have been able to do these things successfully. She blames herself (and feels that others also blame her) for this perceived failure. Annette gives little credence to the financial hardships she faced being unemployed and receiving a small stipend from the DSS and to the contradictions in the social services system that contributed to the problems she faced. The internalization of the Super/Essence woman stereotype is certainly not the only factor responsible for Annette's distress; however, it has contributed to her self-perception and expectations in a way that is detrimental.

Darlene. Darlene is a 35-year-old African American mother of four children. The children have two different fathers, and she has little consistent contact with either man. Darlene lost custody of her children two years prior to her entering treatment because of her chronic alcoholism and neglect. The children are placed with Darlene's mother, who altered her retirement plans in order to care for them. Darlene's relationship with her mother is strained, although they try to cooperate in the caretaking of the children. Darlene hopes to have her children returned to her care and custody some day, but she has been unable to consistently follow through with treatment for her alcoholism. She seems to have also internalized the Matriarch and Super/Essence woman images and blames herself for her situation. She suffers from depression, low self-esteem, and a sense of failure about her inability to appropriately take care of her children. Darlene believes that she has had every opportunity to "make it" in life and feels that she is solely responsible for her failure to be a strong, resilient woman who could overcome all of the obstacles inherent in the society in order to adequately care for herself and her children.

Problems with the Image

The Super/Essence woman stereotype, like the other negative stereotypes of African American women, attributes total responsibility for the status of one's life situation to the individual, while ignoring the prevailing sociopolitical conditions that have a negative impact on women's lives. In a society where almost 30 percent of all African American families live under oppressive conditions that threaten their survival, such as pervasive poverty, joblessness, drugs, and violence, the Super/Essence woman image can be used by the White establishment to once again blame African American women for their own (and their family's) plight. Those African American women who have been able to embody the Super/Essence woman image have been written about in many different sources, and their self-sacrifice, struggle, and commitment to family and to the broader community should not be discredited (Gilkes, 1994; Collins, 1990; Greene, 1990). However, maintaining this strength in the face of oppression and poverty is quite costly, and many African American mothers have not been able to successfully overcome these barriers (Collins, 1990).

The often difficult nature of motherhood within the African American cultural context explains the range that is found in women's reactions to motherhood and the ambivalence that many feel about mothering (Collins, 1990). In a unique way, some contemporary African American mothers are like the voices heard in slave narratives and the slave mothers portrayed in

Toni Morrison's book *Beloved,* whose losses are so deep and pervasive that they are driven to desperate acts. African American women living in poverty are often overwhelmed by the task of caring for children, and they may experience motherhood as a challenge that they have no hope of winning. Some women may simply give up and let go of the attempt to nurture and provide for their children. They are the victims of the structural conditions of racism and discrimination that limit their access to adequate resources to care for themselves and their children and victims of the depression and hopelessness experienced as a result of their internalization of the stereotypes. African American women like the ones described in the above case examples represent those who have been unable to reach the stereotypical, idealized image of the Super/Essence woman. Even within the African American cultural context, their voices have seldom been recorded or heard (Weems, 1993).

The silence that has surrounded these African American mothers who are "not so sturdy bridges" for their children is a reaction within this community against the negative stereotypes that are prevalent in the White-majority culture. Some, however, have begun to speak out about this issue and to call for a deeper understanding of the complex experience of African American motherhood (Bell-Scott, Guy-Sheftall, Jones-Royster, Sims-Wood, DeCosta-Willis, and Fultz, 1991; Wade-Gayles, 1984; Weems, 1993). They suggest that it is critical that we not romanticize the struggles of African American mothers by failing to acknowledge and understand fully the psychological and physical costs to their survival (Greene, 1990). The mothers in the case examples would be considered failures in their attempts to achieve the Super/Essence woman ideal, and their internalization of the stereotype has contributed to their feelings of depression, guilt, and self-blame. In the treatment process, it is essential to find a way to counteract these stereotypes, while helping the women construct a more comprehensive understanding of the experience of African American motherhood in order to facilitate positive growth and empowerment.

Counteracting Stereotypical Images

In clinical work with clients like Claudine, Annette, and Darlene, I try to find a way to effectively counteract their internalization of stereotypical images. Most often this is done by providing information about the controlling nature of these stereotypes and explanations of how they have been used to blame African American women for their condition in life and for the plight of their families and the community. I have done most of my clinical work with low-income African American women who are struggling with economic and personal hardships and who are parenting alone.

Therefore, I also inform them of the systemic and institutional forces that contribute to their continuing poverty and limited access to resources.

To be able to work with African American women in this way, I first had to struggle to counteract my own internalization of the Super/Essence woman stereotype. I was socialized to believe that this was an ideal image for an African American woman, and I began my professional career thinking that I would "have it all" by the time I was 35 years old—a husband, beautiful children, and a successful, exciting career. I knew that women sometimes were not able to achieve all of these things, but I felt that I had been taught how to effectively handle the stress involved and therefore would be one of the "successful" ones. I quickly learned that this was an almost impossible task. The amount of time involved in establishing and maintaining a successful professional career interfered with developing relationships, and I could never figure out when I would have the time to absent myself from work long enough to have a child. Gradually, I began to realize that all women (including African American women) must make choices about their lives and that often something had to be put "on hold." As I came to terms with this insight, I also realized that African American women (including myself) have been attempting to reach a mythical image, one that is not possible to achieve in reality. I began to understand that the sociopolitical forces that keep many of my African American clients in poverty also drive me to work extra hard to develop a professional career. I realize that I have purchased my professional success at a high price.

After gaining this personal perspective on the stereotypical nature of the Super/Essence woman image, I was ready to utilize my experiences to help clients better understand their lives. I decided to use the psychotherapeutic relationship to help strengthen their "psychological armor." This term describes the behavioral and cognitive skills used by African Americans and other persons of color to decrease their psychological vulnerability in encounters where there is a potential for racism (Faulkner, 1983; Greene, 1993). African American mothers socialize their daughters in such a way that they can make psychological sense out of the racist and sexist messages that they receive on a routine basis in this society, thereby creating a psychological barrier that protects one's self-esteem and identity.

Many of my clients have grown up in dysfunctional families where they have been deprived of an effective racial socialization process. Since they have not received the type of training that would prepare them to confront institutional barriers and negative stereotypes in an adaptive manner, my clients are especially vulnerable to the effects of racism. I see my job as helping them overcome the inadequate training they received, while strengthening their adaptive strategies for coping with racism.

Within the context of the therapeutic relationship, I engage with the client in a form of racial socialization. The therapy sessions are an opportunity for us to discuss appropriate responses to situations reflecting institutional racism that occur within a woman's life and to develop strategies for self-advocacy. The racial socialization process also involves my understanding of, and empathy for, the experiences of racism and sexism that occur in my clients' lives, and I provide emotional support for the feelings of anger and impotence that result from their attempts to overcome these barriers.

To see psychotherapy as the building of this psychological armor represents a culture-specific approach to treatment. In the more traditional models of psychodynamic psychotherapy, an individual's difficulties in functioning are thought to be the result of intrapsychic conflicts and anxiety that is not effectively being controlled because the client has poor coping skills or is using inappropriate defenses. Effective psychotherapy with African American clients requires that the therapist identify *both* the internal and external sources of stress and not just assume that the problem has an internal locus of etiology. The internal sources of stress are treated in much the same way as they would be in nonminority clients. There is a recognition, however, that the external sources of stress can exacerbate any internal conflicts that may be present. In working with African American mothers, the therapist must find a way to challenge the internalization of stereotypical images that can contribute to the client's feelings of frustration, anger, and helplessness. The therapeutic focus can then move beyond self-blame and feelings of helplessness toward helping the client envision ways to effectively maneuver around these barriers. In addition to psychological armoring, another adaptive strategy that is often observed in African Americans is "cultural paranoia" (Grier and Cobbs, 1968). Therapists working with African American clients need to understand that these behaviors, and the complex attitudes that accompany them, are necessary for survival in this society and should not conclude that their presence in the clinical picture is evidence of psychopathology.

The Need for a New Definition of Motherhood

In many instances, the clinical interventions that I provide for my African American female clients are helpful in facilitating their ability to understand the internalization of negative stereotypes and the mythical nature of the Super/Essence woman image. More than this is needed, however, to overcome the impact that these controlling images have on the psychological well-being of African American women. The Super/Essence woman stereotype must be challenged as an idealized image of African American motherhood. It does not acknowledge the negative impact that racism and discrimination have on the lives of African Americans or how these factors can inhibit a woman's ability to effectively care for her children. What is called for is a redefinition of motherhood: one that not only takes into account the strengths and resilience of African American women but also incorporates the sociopolitical and economic issues that act as barriers to success.

Prior to the civil rights movement of the 1960s there was an understanding in the African American community that poverty was directly attributable to the racist, discriminatory practices of the larger society. The changes in discriminatory laws and social policies that resulted from this movement have been accompanied by the attribution of complete personal responsibility for one's success or failure in life. Some segments of the African American community, along with the White-majority culture, seem to believe that equal opportunity exists for all, and they cite intraindividual deficits as the only causal factor involved when someone is chronically unemployed and living in pervasive poverty. This attribution of individual responsibility for success and failure in life underlies the Super/Essence woman stereotype.

The belief in intraindividual causality is only one thesis that has been proposed to explain chronic poverty. A related theory, the cultural-deficiency model, assumes that the African American culture holds a value system that is characterized by low aspirations and accepts female-headed families as normative (Corcoran, Duncan, Gurin, and Gurin, 1985). It attributes poverty to the disintegration of the traditional male-dominated family structure, embracing the notion that welfare creates disincentives to work and incentives to have children out of wedlock (Moynihan, 1967). From this perspective, the African American culture is seen as maladaptive and creating thought processes within individuals that cause the continuation of poverty in the Black community (Zinn, 1990). This cultural-deficiency model is reflected in the stereotypes of the Matriarch and the Welfare Mother.

The structural model challenges this perspective and provides an alternative explanation of the existence of chronic poverty. It focuses on the socioeconomic conditions and institutional forces that work to keep ethnic-minority groups in poverty (Zinn, 1990; Wilson, 1987). Within this model, attention is drawn away from psychological and cultural issues and is focused on the social structures that allocate economic and social rewards (Zinn, 1990). The structural model explains such conditions as the prevalence of female-headed households in the African American community as being the result of poverty, not the cause of it. Researchers cite such statistics as the decline in the male-female ratio that occurs by ages 25 to 44 and attribute causality to early mortality (1 in 10 African American males dies before age 20), high levels of incarceration (1 in 4 African American males are either in prison or on parole), and the number of African Americans who marry outside of their ethnic group (Jenkins, 1994). They also suggest that the chronic joblessness experienced by many African American men contributes to the problem of female-headed families, since men who are unable to obtain consistent employment are unlikely to marry their partners (Wilson, 1987).

Utilizing this model, we can now begin to see how an African American woman's difficulties in caring for herself and her children are not solely the result of intrapersonal deficits but have roots in the socioeconomic conditions that limit access to employment, the amount of income she can earn even if employed, and the likelihood that she will be able to establish and maintain a viable marital partnership with an African American male. With clients who are low-income mothers living on welfare, I often discuss the structural model and use examples from their own lives to illustrate the fact that the conditions under which many African American women (and men) live are extremely vulnerable to economic change. The client is then able to understand that as an African American mother living in poverty, she is being hampered in her efforts to rise out of this condition even when she follows all of the "rules" of the society. When she is able to work, she is the lowest paid among all employed individuals. If she is unable to find a job, which will most likely be the case if she resides in the inner city, the welfare benefits she receives will keep her at or below poverty level. And even if she longs for the traditionally female role of homemaker and nurturer of children, she is unlikely to have a male partner who is in a position to adequately provide for the family and with whom she can share the challenge of survival.

As a clinician, I am particularly concerned with African American women's internalization of the stereotypical images described above, since this can have a powerful negative effect on their psychological well-being (Greene, 1994; Jenkins, 1993). When women have internalized the Super/Essence woman stereotype, they often feel that they have somehow failed to attend appropriately to all of their burdens or to solve all of their family members' problems. These clients rarely wonder whether their responsibilities are too extensive or if their expectations of themselves are unrealistic. They express the fear that coming to therapy means that they are "weak" or "couldn't take it" and believe that it is "indulgent" to spend time talking about their own personal concerns (Childs, 1990; Jenkins, 1994; Greene, 1992). These women not only blame themselves for their inability to function, but they may also harbor attitudes and beliefs that interfere with their ability to seek and sustain important support and validation from other women (Greene, 1994). The conditions that exist today in the African American community highlight the need to return to women-centered communities that care for children—in much the same way that they were needed during slavery. Yet, the Super/Essence woman image hinders the development of this sense of community.

The current idealized image of African American motherhood (the Super/Essence woman), buttressed by the negative stereotypes of poor African American mothers in the White-majority culture (the Matriarch and Welfare Mother), creates a dilemma for most women and makes it difficult for many to succeed. Both low-income and professional women must struggle to deal with the controlling nature of each of these stereotypes, and their internalization contributes to feelings of guilt and shame, which complicate the treatment process. Further, the attribution of total individual responsibility for success or failure that underlies each of the stereotypes makes it difficult for African American women to join together across social class lines to form a collective sisterhood. Challenging the existing Super/Essence woman image and creating a new definition of African American motherhood should help to counteract the internalization of these stereotypes and to enhance cooperation and collective support for mothering. Although this new definition acknowledges the negative effects of institutional racism and other sociopolitical factors on the lives of African Americans, I am not suggesting that there should be no attribution of personal responsibility, since there is always a component of individual agency under even the most oppressive conditions. However, there is an interaction between these systemic forces and individual skills that must be taken into account if we are to truly understand the complexities of African American motherhood.

With the new definition that I am suggesting, it should be possible for African American mothers to overcome the arbitrary class divisions that have kept them apart and women would realize that we are all adversely affected by the sociopolitical and institutional conditions in society. This perspective should also help reduce the tendency to blame one segment of the community for its own victimization, thereby contributing to a more cooperative social climate. Communities of women (as birthmothers, othermothers, and community othermothers) could provide support and caring for each other while working together to nurture African American children in this hostile environment. This definition challenges us to remember, and to put into practice once again, the patterns of collectivism, mutual support, and interdependency that have been highly valued in the African American community throughout its history. These values helped African American families survive the most brutal years of our history in America. They can also effectively lead us through this modern-day maze of social ills.

References

Aschenbrenner, J. (1975). *Black families in Chicago*. Prospect Heights, IL: Waveland Press.

Bell-Scott, P., Guy-Sheftall, B., Jones-Royster, J., Sims-Wood, J., DeCosta-Willis, M., and Fultz, L. P. (Eds.) (1991). *Double stitch*. New York, NY: HarperCollins.

Billingsley, A. (1968). *Black families in White America*. Englewood Cliffs, NJ: Prentice-Hall.

Billingsley, A. (1992). *Climbing Jacob's ladder*. New York, NY: Simon and Schuster.

Boyd-Franklin, N. (1991). Recurrent themes in the treatment of African American women in group therapy. *Women and Therapy, 11*(2), 25–40.

Brislin, R. (1993) *Understanding culture's influence on behavior*. New York, NY: Harcourt Brace Jovanovich.

Childs, E. K. (1990). Therapy, feminist ethic, and the community of color with particular emphasis on the treatment of Black women. In H. Lerman and N. Porter (Eds.), *Feminist Ethics in Psychotherapy* (pp. 195–203). New York, NY: Springer.

Collins, P. H. (1990). *Black feminist thought*. Boston, MA: Unwin Hyman.

Corcoran, M., Duncan, G. J., Gurin, G., and Gurin, P. (1985). Myth and reality: The causes and persistence of poverty. *Journal of Policy Analysis and Management, 4*(4), 516–536.

Davis, A. (1981). *Women, race and class*. New York, NY: Vintage.

Dougherty, M. C. (1978). *Becoming a woman in rural Black culture*. New York, NY: Holt, Rinehart and Winston.

Edelman, M. W. (1985). The sea is so wide and my boat is so small: Problems facing Black children today. In H. McAdoo and J. McAdoo (Eds.), *Black children: Social, educational and parental environments*. Newbury Park, CA: Sage.

Edwards, A. (1992). *Children of the dream: The psychology of Black success*. New York, NY: Doubleday.

Faulkner, J. (1983). Women in interracial relationships. *Women and Therapy, 2,* 193–203.

Fox-Genovese, E. (1988). *Within the plantation household: Black and White women of the old south*. Chapel Hill, NC: University of North Carolina Press.

Gilkes, C. T. (1994). "If it wasn't for the women . . . ": African American women, community work, and social change. In M. B. Zinn and B. Thorton Dill (Eds.), *Women of color in U.S. society*. Philadelphia, PA: Temple University Press.

Greene, B. (1990). What has gone before: The legacy of racism and sexism in the lives of Black mothers and daughters. *Women and Therapy, 9*(1–3), 207–230.

Greene, B. (1992). Black feminist psychotherapy. In E. Wright (Ed.), *Feminism and psychoanalysis*. Oxford, England: Blackwell.

Greene, B. (1993). Psychotherapy with African American women: Integrating feminist and psychodynamic models. *Journal of Training and Practice in Professional Psychology, 7*(1), 49–66.

Greene, B. (1994). Diversity and difference: The issue of race in feminist therapy. In M. Mirkin (Ed.), *Women in context: Toward a feminist reconstruction of psychotherapy*. New York, NY: Guilford.

Grier, W. H., and Cobbs, P. (1968). *Black rage*. New York, NY: Basic Books.

Gutman, H. G. (1976). *The Black family in slavery and freedom: 1750–1925*. New York, NY: Vintage Books.

Hill, R. B. (1972). *The strengths of Black families*. New York, NY: Emerson Hall.

hooks, b. (1981). *Black women and feminism*. Boston, MA: South End Press.

James, S. M. (1993). Mothering: A possible black feminist link to social transformation? In S. M. James and A.P.A. Busia (Eds.), *Theorizing Black feminisms: The visionary pragmatism of Black women* (pp. 44–54). New York, NY: Routledge.

Jenkins, L. (1994). African-American identity and its social context. In E. P. Salett and D. R. Koslow (Eds.), *Race, ethnicity and self: Identity in multicultural perspective* (pp. 63–88). Washington, DC: National Multicultural Institute.

Jenkins, Y. (1993). African American women: Ethnocultural variables and dissonant expectations. In J. L. Chin, V. De La Cancela, and Y. Jenkins (Eds.), *Diversity in psychotherapy: The politics of race, ethnicity and gender* (pp. 117–136). Westport, CT: Praeger.

Mann, S. A. (1990). Slavery, sharecropping, and sexual inequality. In M. R. Malson, E. Mudimbe-Boyi, J. F. O'Barr, and M. Wyer (Eds.), *Black women in America* (pp. 133–157). Chicago, IL: University of Chicago Press.

Mbiti, J. (1969). *African religions and philosophies.* New York, NY: Anchor.

McAdoo, H. P. (1981). *Black Families.* Beverly Hills, CA: Sage.

Moynihan, D. P. (1967). The Negro family: The case for national action. In L. Rainwater and W. L. Yancy (Eds.), *The Moynihan report and the politics of controversy* (pp. 39–132). Cambridge, MA: MIT Press.

Mullings, L. (1994). Images, ideology, and women of color. In M. B. Zinn and B. T. Dill (Eds.), *Women of color in U.S. society.* Philadelphia, PA: Temple University Press.

Oppong, C. (1973). *Growing up in Dagbon.* Tema, Ghana: Ghana Publishing Corporation.

Shaw, S. (1994). Mothering under slavery in the antebellum south. In E. N. Glenn, Chang, G., and Forcey, L. R. (Eds.), *Mothering: Ideology, experience and agency* (pp. 237–258). New York, NY: Routledge.

Smith, J. P. (1988). Poverty and the family. In G. Sandefur and M. Tienda (Eds.), *Divided opportunities: Minorities, poverty and social policy* (pp. 141–172). New York, NY: Plenum.

Stack, C. B. (1974). *All our kin: Strategies for survival in a Black community.* New York, NY: Harper and Row.

Sudarkasa, N. (1981). Interpreting the African heritage in Afro-American family organization. In H. P. McAdoo (Ed.), *Black families* (pp. 37–53). Beverly Hills, CA: Sage.

Sudarkasa, N. (1988). Interpreting the African heritage in Afro-American family organization. In H. P. McAdoo (Ed.), *Black families* (2d ed., pp. 27–43). Newbury Park, CA: Sage.

Sudarkasa, N. (1993). Female-headed African American households: Some neglected dimensions. In H. P. McAdoo (Ed.), *Family ethnicity: Strength in diversity* (pp. 81–89). Newbury Park, CA: Sage.

Tanner, N. (1974). Matrifocality in Indonesia and Africa and among Black Americans. In M. Z. Rosaldo and L. Lamphere (Eds.), *Women, culture, and society* (pp. 129–156). Stanford, CA: Stanford University Press.

Wade-Gayles, G. (1984, Fall). The truth of our mother's lives: Mother-daughter relationships in Black women's fiction. *Sage: A Scholarly Journal on Black Women,* 1, 8.

Wallace, M. (1991). *Black macho and the myth of the superwoman.* New York, NY: Verso Press.

Weems, R. J. (1993). *I asked for intimacy: Stories of blessings, betrayals, and birthings.* San Diego, CA: Lura Media.

White, D. G. (1985). *Ar'n't I a woman? Female slaves in the plantation south.* New York, NY: W. W. Norton.

Wilson, J. (1987). *The truly disadvantaged: The inner city, the underclass and public policy.* Chicago, IL: University of Chicago Press.

Young, V. H. (1970). Family and childhood in a southern Negro community. *American Psychologist, 72,* 269–288.

Zinn, M. B. (1990). Family, race, and poverty in the eighties. In M. R. Malson, E. Mudimbe-Boyi, J. F. O'Barr, and M. Wyer (Eds.), *Black women in America.* Chicago, IL: University of Chicago Press.

6

Minority Mothers: Stress and Coping When Your Child Is in Special Education

Karen Fraser Wyche and Debra Lobato

This chapter presents preliminary findings from an ongoing investigation of parenting in African American and Latina mothers of children with mental retardation. This broad study examines the relationship of social context factors, variables of stress as defined by the women, and levels of social support experienced by these women as they attempt to address their children's special needs. The discussion in this chapter highlights issues of informal and formal social support as presented by mothers who participated in focus group interviews. We examine what these mothers tell us about their social networks and examine their utilization of social supports in their parenting under especially stressful conditions. No one can deny that minority women have a great deal of stress in their lives (see chapters in this volume by S. Olson and R. Ceballo and E. Sparks). The mothers in this study have a particular type of stress related to their parenting role. Outcomes are to evaluate how social supports are utilized and evaluated across groups, how social supports are differentiated within groups, how the environmental situation or context influences social supports, and how cultural values mediate these differences.

Our initial plan was to use the data from these and other focus groups in progress to apply for funding to study the instrumental and affective components of social supports as they relate to psychological functioning and parenting within minority women. Later in this chapter we will discuss how the findings of these focus groups have made us rethink our initial research study. We are now in the process of redefining our research questions to incorporate what we have learned from the mothers in our focus groups.

The structure of our chapter will be to discuss the choice of our research topic, the characteristics of our research collaboration between an African American and a White woman psychologist, methodological issues in the study of minority women in general and specific issues relating to the study of minority mothers of children who are mild to moderately retarded, some findings from our focus groups, and the process by which we are reevaluating our initial research questions based on the information provided by these mothers.

Why Study Social Supports?

The first author, an African American woman, has had a long-standing interest in studying issues relating to minority women. As a researcher and clinician she witnessed the role that social supports can play in the lives of women. Furthermore, social supports have been a part of her own life, both personal and professional. She has always chosen to study something that she can identify with personally and has some knowledge about but which has not been fully examined in the literature. For a long time she has been interested in the generalizability of social supports across contexts and cultural groups. These ideas came from the clients she saw in her practice and the students she taught, especially those who attended a predominantly minority college in New York City of which she was a faculty member. When she became a faculty member at a predominately White university, she noticed how the lack of social supports for minority students influenced their adjustment to the institution.

An opportunity to study the interaction of culture, ecological influences, and social supports became available in summer 1993. The National Institutes of Health (NIH) issued a call for proposals for research on minority families who have children with handicapping conditions. It appeared a good opportunity to combine her interest in mental health issues of minority women with her ideas regarding social supports within specific contexts.

She needed a collaborator who had expertise with special needs children. Such a collaborator also needed to share the same enthusiasm for the study of minority women, believe in culturally sensitive research, and, finally, be a reliable and nice person. She called the women in her professional social support network, who suggested Dr. Debra Lobato. At that time, Debra was working as a clinical psychologist and associate professor within a university medical center. Her work involved evaluating and treating children with developmental problems and their families.

Debra is a second-generation White descendant of immigrants from Spain, was raised in New York, and is married to a Latino. Although she is not a Latina, her family life experience and professional circumstances combined to foster particular interest in working with Hispanic families. For many years Debra was the only Spanish-speaking licensed psychologist in the state of Rhode Island. Increasingly, she became an important resource for many of the Latino families and children in need of developmental and mental health services. She witnessed, on a case-by-case basis, how the experience of raising a child with mental retardation could be affected by mothers' English proficiency, social support, economic and educational resources, acculturation, and assumptions regarding mental retardation and child rearing. When approached by Karen to study minority families of children with special needs, many personal and professional ambitions coalesced.

This is how the collaboration between Karen Wyche and Debra Lobato began. When we first met we realized that our similarities greatly outweighed our differences, that we shared the same values and goals in working with minority families, and that we had built our careers on advocacy and service to minority families. We wrote the NIH grant and did not get funded, but we continued to forge ahead, knowing that some day our ship would come in and we would be ready.

Collaborative Research as a Social Support Process

We have a wonderful collaboration and often laugh at the irony that the minority woman can talk only to the English-speaking woman and that the White woman can speak to both African Americans and Latinas. As a pair we can relate and speak comfortably with a wider group of women than either of us could address alone. Our type of collaboration and topic of investigation require that we support each other and that we struggle to be sensitive researchers, striving to identify the culturally valid questions and problems to investigate. Neither of us alone is able to do this task. Our collaboration has helped us to learn from each other and, in doing so, to become better researchers. We each have become a validity check for the other's realities, forcing reevaluations of our research goals and questions. Debra has instilled in Karen a better understanding of the issues of children with developmental disabilities and their families. Debra has prompted sensitivity to the politics of language and labeling within this field. Karen can claim responsibility for rekindling Debra's interest in ethnographic methods and literature. Karen has succeeded in shifting Debra's focus on families as emanating from their social and cultural context rather than from the characteristics of their children.

Our collaboration is a model of interethnic cooperation for the research participants as well as for the graduate students serving as research assistants. Karen's graduate research assistant is a White woman, whereas Debra's graduate assistant is a bilingual Latina. Our students tell us that they have come to recognize the important role that people of all ethnicities can play in conducting such research through seeing how the different perspectives that we bring to the research process add to the value and richness of our work. Both of the research assistants state that witnessing a successful collaboration of two researchers from different ethnic backgrounds is an educational, liberating, and empowering experience. Thus at all levels of this project, interracial and cross-cultural cooperation occur as we pursue a common task. With our students we share our vulnerabilities and struggles with the research process of participant recruitment, equipment failures, and endless searches for money. We remind each other of the value of our goals and efforts. One sees the guiding light when the other succumbs to feelings of despair. We exchange literature, resources, and feelings of exaltation as well as defeat. This is the nature of social support.

We share a feminist view of research that has been strengthened by the focus groups we have conducted. That is, we believe that to study minority women and their families we need to respect what they tell us about their lives and then check this against our hypotheses about what we think about their lives. Our view is that gender, race, and ethnicity are universal experiences but that the ways in which these attributes are experienced depends on class and contextual variables of meanings assigned to these concepts. This is the view that frames our research agenda and the lens through which we view our participants.

Methodological Issues

What are the methodological issues in studying minority women? The research on minority women excludes minority women who are normative and segregates findings on nonprivileged groups from findings about women in general (Wyche, 1993). Comparisons of minority women to White women or comparisons of lower-status women to higher-status women lead to incorrect conclusions (Comas-Diaz and Greene, 1994; Yoder and Kahn, 1993). Findings of significant differences between these groups are interpreted to imply that the difference is exclusive, and the overlap between groups and the variability within groups are ignored. Race and ethnicity are often treated as equivalent proxies for culture (Osborne and Feit, 1992; Trimble, 1991). Consequently the functional aspects of culture are minimally considered or overlooked (Morawska, 1990). This narrow view of culture ignores within-group diversity and understanding of the cultural processes and how they influence behavior (Wyche, 1993).

In our attempt to understand stress and coping in mothers of children with mild to moderate retardation, we were aware that this literature has emphasized models of cognitive aspects of coping and the microenvironments in which families live (Blacher, 1993; Crnic, Friedrich, and Greenberg, 1983). With a few recent exceptions (Weisner, Beizer, and Stolze, 1991; Heller, Markwardt, Rowitz, and Farber, 1994), this literature ignores cultural influences on family adaptation and functioning. We wished to focus on the dynamic reciprocal process between people and their environment. For this reason we knew that our study needed to be able to assess subjective cultural features. These cultural features that can be exhibited in social roles and personal values could help us to understand that family functioning is not homogeneous and that social context factors can become important in delineating differences between groups. We wanted to make sure that our research extended beyond the examination of status or categorical variables to a culturally sensitive examination of family adaptation to a child with a significant disability. By studying African American and Latina mothers we sought to understand how cultural norms, values, and behaviors were interpreted. Without measuring or assessing cultural dimensions, comparisons between these two cultural groups would not tell if culture plays a role. Nor would it be possible to make distinctions between cultural variables and psychological processes (Betancourt and Lopez, 1993).

We recognize the importance of appreciating that our participants' experiences are not universal experiences of African American and Latina mothers. We need to be aware of class differences and how these differences relate in a larger context. We also understand that these mothers could be mistrusting of the research process even though we are trying to be sensitive to them and to conduct a study that integrates issues of ethnicity and gender. We understand that methods relying on paper-and-pencil tasks alone could alienate women whose cultures value a strong oral tradition and the process of interpersonal communication. In all cases, we listened first to personal histories and experiences before giving the paper-and-pencil measures. In addition, we chose to provide ample refreshments and to schedule the group at an accessible neighborhood agency with a well-integrated, multiethnic staff and a history of community service. For that reason we decided that both qualitative as well as quantitative measures would be needed if we were to generate data that would be both reliable and valid. These types of assessments would enable us to focus on women in real contexts and to examine the social-structural variables that influence behavior.

In our design, we use the grounded-theory approach (Glaser, 1978) wherein the researcher first develops conceptual categories from the data and then makes new observations to clarify and elaborate these categories.

By doing this we could develop concepts and tentative hypotheses from the data generated from the focus groups. We judged that an analytical induction method (i.e., a top-down method of the researcher-generated hypotheses to be tested) would be inappropriate since little information exists regarding the interplay of gender, race, and culture in raising a handicapped child in the United States. Therefore, we let our participants tell us what was important rather than us developing the categories of importance.

Social Support Literature

The literature on social supports is a gendered literature. It is seen as women's work. It is a type of human capital. As such, it is open to analytic questions such as, How and for what reasons do women negotiate for help? Whom do they negotiate with? What are the affective and instrumental components? How appropriate are the resources desired? What are the characteristics of the resulting social network? All of these behaviors can be viewed as a type of social intelligence.

The literature on social supports has tested the buffering hypothesis (Cohen and Willis, 1985). The predominant research finding is that social supports reduce stress (Anderson, 1991; Caspi, Bolger, and Eckenrode, 1987; Neighbors, Jackson, Bowman, and Gurin, 1983; Brown and Gary, 1985). This research has been concerned more with types of stress than with stress in relation to gender, ethnicity, and/or class. When minority women have been studied, the primary focus has been on correlational studies of single-parent and/or low-income women (Wyche, 1993). This focus segregates these women into a group that is often viewed as deviant from White women. Findings of these studies indicate that social supports function as protective factors, with African American women having larger social support networks than White women (Brown and Gary, 1985). These networks are utilized for economic as well as emotional support.

Effective parenting appears related to social networks (Stevens and Duffield, 1986), especially when a grandmother or another adult partner is involved (Brown and Gary, 1985; Lewis, 1989; Stevens, 1988; Stevens and Duffield, 1986; Thompson and Ensminger, 1989). Traditionally, social networks, especially kinship, have played a key role in the lives of immigrants and minorities. We know little about women who vary by socioeconomic status. This omission fails to provide information as to how stress, racism, discrimination, and/or sexism, which are not under self-control but are common to African American and Latina women regardless of class, are handled. Our goal was to address this problem by studying African American and Latina women within a particular context (having a child with mild to moderate retardation who was enrolled in elementary special education classes) as a way to assess commonalities and uniqueness regarding how life is negotiated and family functioning preserved or disrupted. This context of life is not manipulated and is not class bound. We then had to decide how to study this situation.

Unfortunately, most studies of families with children with mental retardation and disabilities use survey instruments. These methods are selected because of experimental judgments about what variables are important (Stoneman and Berman, 1993). This approach does not allow researchers to understand fully how culture influences mentally retarded children's impact on family functioning. However, some survey instruments are very helpful in generating information that can be used as a follow-up to interviews. Widely used are measures of formal social supports (Sarason, Levine, Basham, and Sarason, 1983) and informal support (Antonucci and Israel, 1986). Unfortunately, many researchers select only a few items from these measures and then generalize to all levels of social support. As a member of her Institutional Review Board, the first author routinely sees examples of this. One example of this method is asking, "With whom do you spend most of your free time? Family, friends, or alone?" This range of responses is restricted and fails to distinguish others who might be in the network and the quality of the relationship. Asking forced-choice (yes or no) information is common (e.g., "Are you satisfied with spending your time this way?"). Similarly, questions that yield numerical responses are popular, such as, "How many close friends do you have?" All of these examples, taken from studies that come before the Institutional Review Board, are typical of the current trend of asking a few questions relating to social supports and then making the assumption that the response generated is a template to understanding social supports in the population under investigation. The assumption is always that more is better. More people in one's social network yield more social support and therefore this situation is better.

Among nonminority families of children with developmental delays, informal supports (e.g., family and friends) have a stronger influence on parental well-being than formal supports (e.g., professionals, support groups, institutions) (Dunst, Trivette and Cross, 1986; Heller, Markwardt, Rowitz, and Farber, 1994). Although formal and informal support reduces stress in nonminority families, the type of support available may be perceived differently across different cultural groups. For example, in one study (Heller et al., 1994) among Hispanic families, support from relatives was associated with less caregiving burden, whereas professional support and services were associated with more burden. Hispanic families reported difficulties obtaining information on their family members and participating in parent groups.

Many considerations led to our adoption of both qualitative (in-depth, open-ended interviews) and quantitative (written/translated questionnaires) measures. As noted before, we could not be sure if our researcher-driven hypotheses about social supports in this population were correct. We wanted our methods to reflect the interpersonal contact many of the women might value and require in order to participate sincerely in the phases of the process. For our pilot work we chose to conduct focus groups, led together. These focus groups became a way to have mothers imbue their values, behavior, and cultural norms and to discuss openly material that is not obtained or is difficult to talk about via a structured interview or questionnaire. Our intention was to capture information that may not be gained from quantitative assessment alone. We wondered if because of the stressful situation of these mothers in parenting these special needs children, their social supports would be elaborate in type and structure. There is an assumption in the literature that social supports are cross-situationally specific rather than situationally specific, although it has been well documented in behavioral assessment that behaviors are situationally specific (Mischel, 1968, 1977). Therefore, our goal was to use the focus groups to test this information and to generate new hypotheses. We wanted to extend the notion of behavioral consistency, or lack thereof, in terms of contemporary environmental influences toward an understanding of social supports, not by sampling behaviors deemed relevant by us but by asking these mothers what is relevant. Rather than interview women individually regarding social support, we chose the social context of the focus group (i.e., mothers with children with mental retardation) to explore both the content and process of social support.

Focus Groups of African American and Latina Mothers

We recruited a sample of African American and Latina women from three sources: a local school system's department of special education, a community social service agency, and the interdisciplinary child evaluation team of the local university hospital. Letters in English and Spanish were sent home with the children asking for study participants. Each mother had to have a child in special education classes in public elementary school. The primary handicapping condition of the child was to be mild to moderate retardation; however, many of the children had more than one diagnosis. The data reported here are from 10 Latina women (all Spanish speaking) and 6 African American women (recruitment is still ongoing). There were separate groups for African Americans and Latinas. Mothers were paid twenty-five dollars for their participation in a focus group, which lasted about one and one-half hours. The focus groups were co-led by Karen and Debra for African American mothers and Debra for Latina mothers. For the Latina mothers group, which was held in Spanish, Karen and her research assistant remained on the periphery, operating recording equipment and watching two younger children who accompanied two mothers. Because we are both experienced clinicians, the group process was not dominated by any mother. All mothers participated fully and were mutually supportive of each other. After the focus groups, mothers filled out questionnaires on demographic information (see Table 6.1) and some survey instruments that are being piloted. The majority of these women lived with their husbands or partners and had young children. The Latinas were slightly older, poorer, had fewer children, and were less educated than the African American mothers. Most Latinas were born outside of the United States.

All groups were audiotaped and videotaped. Results presented below are taken from the verbatim transcripts. Although we asked about many aspects of parenting their children, the data here refer only to mothers' assessment of their stress in parenting and their social supports as a way of handling that stress. As we have discussed before, our goal was to look at cultural influences and to understand what these mothers could tell us about their social supports within this context.

How the Mothers Described Their Stress

Mothers (10 Latinas and 6 African Americans) provided vivid accounts of the stress they experience in parenting their children. As mentioned before, many of the children had multiple diagnoses, of which attention deficit and disruptive behavior disorder were the most common. The effects of these multiple problems are seen in the mother's descriptions of her child. These mothers had both male and female children, although males predominated. Neither ethnicity nor number of children appeared to make any difference.

TABLE 6.1 Demographic Characteristics of Mothers

	African American (n = 6)	*Latina (n = 10)*
Age	29.6 years	33.5 years
Marital status		
married/partner	67%	60%
Born in the United States	100%	11%
Age of children		
1–5	50%	50%
6–12	50%	50%
Income		
Poor	60%	100%
Lower/middle	40%	0%
Years of education (mean)	11.0	9.0
Household size (mean)	4.3	4.6
Number of children (mean)	3.2	3.0

Mothers gave striking accounts about their *inability to control* their children and how it made them feel:

> Susan (African American): "My son [age five] is hyper from the time he gets up in the morning. I give him his medication, when he goes to school, when he comes home he's just, it's . . . sometimes I get to the point where I don't know what to do. That's my only child, it's the only child I have."

Exhaustion. This was a common experience that mothers shared with us. It took the form of never feeling that they could leave their child alone for fear that something would happen. This fear was not unrealistic, for many described situations where their children were in danger because they could not follow directions and as a result would leave home unattended, get in fights, or be disruptive in public places. Mothers responded to this behavior by trying to focus the child's attention on various things. But these attempts were usually very unsuccessful:

> Joan (African American): "We are unable to keep him [age eleven] concentrated on one thing for any length of time. Trying to keep him on one thing and he is just aggravating everybody that's around. I mean he has energy, I don't know where it comes from. The whole house is totally exhausted. He is really active and just aggravating to one's brains. They [three of her children] never get tired. Never, I'm so happy if they doze off for ten minutes, it's like a day of sleep. Then they're ready to go. Energy after a ten minute nap. I'm totally exhausted, totally drained."

Fears. Multiple fears about the children were the common stressors:

> Lillian (Latina, speaking to her own mother): "Ay, Mom, I think he has something wrong, something wrong, something which is not normal, because he is not like the other children are. My mother said, no girl, it is you who sees him that way. But I said, no Mom, he has something wrong and I am watching him and I am always observing his behavior and I am sure he has a problem."

This mother was correct that something was terribly wrong. Many other mothers recognized the problem when their children got to school. It was more common for the Latina mothers to view the problem as an illness rather than a permanent disability. Consequently, they looked to doctors and teachers as a source of cure for the child. They tended to view the child's disruptive behavior as stemming from his or her illness and beyond the boundaries of their parenting. Despite their frustration, for many of these mothers there was little appreciation of how their interactions with the child would have any effect on the child's behavior.

Other fears were related to school situations, that is, what would happen to the child in school:

> Judy (African American): "My daughter [age seven] is very difficult. The medication doesn't work at all. It's like she doesn't want to hear nothing no one tells her, she wants to be in control. Nobody likes her. She don't pay attention to nothing the teacher says. Every day I get a bad feeling that she is coming home with a bad report."

Stress relating to school was constant. It took the form of the teacher being unable to control the child, requests for the child to be transferred to another school, lack of communication regarding the child's progress, and mothers feeling that they were blamed by the school for their child's behavior and condition. Mothers felt that the school should be a resource to them and wondered why teachers did not seem trained to help their children. Multiple school placements were common.

Self-Blame. Another stress experienced by all of the mothers was self-blame. Faced with a situation beyond their control, they began to wonder why this was happening to them and their child:

> Maria (Latina, daughter age seven): "After listening to the doctor, we were frightened and her father started to spoil her. I do not know if her problems are due to that . . . now with so many children, they are all fighting each other. She cannot be with other children, even with the children who live downstairs, my neighbors, they are always fighting. And for almost no reason she has a tantrum and I say, Oh my God, because she gets furious and I throw cold water on her face to calm her down. After this, she starts crying. I start to wonder what is the reason for all this, I cannot explain all this to myself."

Other mothers make comparisons to themselves as children while continuing to wonder why this is happening to them.

> Susan (African American): "He is going into first grade and he cannot read. I get so frustrated, it's like my God, what did I do wrong? I wasn't like that when I was in school, his father wasn't either. So where did I go wrong? Am I doing something wrong, or what? Did somebody put a curse on me?"

These vivid descriptions are samples of the types of stress experienced by these mothers. The commonalities among them were striking. As they talked abut these very painful experiences we began to see how surprised, and at the same time relieved, each was that her story was similar to other women's. Their support for each other's situations was very encouraging.

Do Social Supports Buffer the Stress?

To answer this question we probed for social support characteristics. This was very easy to do because during the group session mothers had begun to feel a sense of comfort with each other and shared anguish. We needed only to ask them to tell us who helps them with these situations of fear, self-blame, exhaustion, and child care for them to speak at great length. Since there were more Latina mothers, we saw the most variability in that group. Many of them felt that they could depend on family members for instrumental and emotional support. Only a few indicated they felt they could not depend on family members; for some, family members were significant sources of stress and abuse. These women relied primarily on their other children. One woman with older children said:

> Luz (Latina): "All my family live in New York. I am here with my kids, by myself. I don't have friends here. I live with my kids and try to do the best for them and things like that."

African American mothers indicated more isolation from family members. But since there were only six African American mothers, we need more women to see if this is really a difference. Some mothers reported that many family members (e.g., uncles, grandparents) viewed their children as being just plain "bad" and in need of firm discipline. Thus, rather than seek instrumental support from extended family, mothers avoid this situation for the child:

> Edna (African American): "My brother says he will take him for the weekend and I said, no you are not. He says when I bring him back he'll be all right. I say the child does not need a beating. He is hyperactive. He will not hurt anyone but himself. It's just the noise and the things he is doing."

Although some women were single mothers, the majority of women in both groups had husbands, partners, or brothers as a major source of support. This finding is very important, for the social support literature has not indicated that males are part of this process and has not examined their role. It is also important in that the role of the father in minority families has often been conceptualized as synonymous with "absent." Here, in a very stressful environmental situation, males are actively participating in parenting.

Clemencia (Latina): "I do not have problems [with help] because I am not working and after he arrives from school I am always home with him and when I leave my husband stays with him."

However, as this mother continues, we see how this partnership in parenting exacts a price from the couple's relationship:

Clemencia (continues): "Sometimes we want to go out as a couple alone, going to the movies or something. It is not possible. So, we rent a movie."

Or as another mother states:

Norma (Latina): "My husband helps. When I have to go out he comes with me and we bring all five children."

Mothers expressed sympathy and gratitude for what their husbands or partners were doing for them:

Joan (African American): "My kid's father helps me 200 percent with the kids. They got him as crazy as they got me."

Alice (African American): "My daughter's father is not the boy's [the special needs child's] father. Sometimes he can be a pain in the butt, but I don't think most men will put up with half of the stuff that he does. He's there and supports me and the household stuff. Half the time I wonder how the hell he puts up with it because they are not his kids."

Sisters and aunts were the females most often mentioned as helpful. The type of help they offered related to emotional support, such as listening, and behavioral support, such as child care. The mothers of these women were not mentioned; if they helped it was very reluctantly.

Marsha (African American): "Sometime I call-up my mom and ask can he stay over. No she says, he's too difficult. . . . I don't think she understands what I'm going through. Sometimes she will keep him, like I can bring him over on Friday night and pick him up Saturday (morning). It's like he is too difficult."

Leticia (African American): "My mother says just leave her alone, she will get over it. I can't depend on her, on anybody."

The role of grandmother has been given much attention in the social support literature. Grandmothers have been actively involved in parenting in minority families (Wilson, 1986) and have been reported as being the second most active caregiver (Pearson, Hunter, Ensminger, and Kellam, 1990). But for these mothers who have a child with mild to moderate retardation, the pattern seems not to hold.

Older children have been conscripted into the helping role, as is common in families. What was interesting here is that the older children are depended upon more so than other adults outside the family. This finding differs from the social support literature, which describes how kin and extended kin are major sources of help in time of need.

How Does Religion Function as a Social Support?

Ethnic minority families hold religious views that may serve to buffer stress. Glidden (1993) raises the question of the relationship between religious behaviors and cognitive coping success of families with a child who is developmentally delayed. Mothers who score high on measures of religion report religion as serving as a buffer or coping mechanism against stress (Friedrich, Cohen, and Wilturner, 1988; Fewell, 1986). Religious parents may be more likely to perceive their child with mental retardation as an opportunity or challenge from God than a caretaking burden (Weisner, Beizer, and Stolze 1991).

This literature has not fully explored ethnicity as a variable. We do not know how ethnic minority families who have children with handicapping conditions utilize religion. Is prayer used as an effective coping method? Is intrinsic religiousness associated with empathy and responsibility in parenting a special needs child? The literature on African American families of nonspecial-needs children emphasizes that church attendance serves as a social support network (Taylor, Chatters, Tucker, and Lewis, 1990) and is viewed as important across class (Spencer, 1990). In a recent comparison of Hispanic and non-Hispanic families with a mentally retarded member (Heller et al., 1994), most Hispanics believed that taking care of the person was a religious duty that brought unique meaning to their lives. Because religion could be an important aspect of understanding coping among the mothers in our group, we asked, "Does religion help you?" Our participants' responses seemed to indicate that religion helps, but the feelings were not as strong as we had thought they would be. Across all groups, only one mother was adamant.

> Ava (African American): "I put my faith in the Lord. Prayer works, prayer changes things, I pray, my kids will pray for you if you tell them that you are sick or something."

Other mothers talked about faith, prayer, and their belief in God.

Carmen (Latina): "I do believe in God, yes. I know He exists. But I am
... like I go to church, sometimes, not always. I beg Him a lot, but
I do not think that ... I have faith. I think that my faith helps me
in ... because I never thought I would be able to reach this point
with the boy."

Hortensia (Latina): "I have to live with this [the child's limitations] and
sometimes I feel full of problems and sometimes I take a deep
breath and say my Lord, help me to continue my life."

More depressing for us was the mother who said:

Rose (African American): "Nothing, nothing works."

Conclusion

We learned many things from the focus groups of mothers. We learned that
our assumptions about social support in this population were incorrect:
The extended kin, especially grandmothers, were not as helpful as the literature on minority families has indicated, and fathers and male partners
were very helpful. There were more similarities than differences between
women, even though one group was African American and one group was
Latina and Spanish speaking. Perhaps the particular environmental context
accounts for that difference: A situation that is chronic, unchangeable, or
beyond one's control changes the nature of the social support. We saw the
bonding of the women in the group. Each group cried and laughed together
and shared painful and personal experiences with women they did not
know. A leader emerged from each group, who shared her secrets for navi-
gating the medical or school system and who was viewed as a model to em-
ulate by others.

We are necessarily cautious in our conclusions because of the small number of women we are discussing. We are continuing to recruit mothers for
focus groups and are especially interested in having a group of English-
speaking Latinas to look at acculturation effects.

Without the grounded-theory approach and the resulting methodology,
we never would have gotten the rich information that the mothers discussed. Because these mothers have told us what they feel and think, we
now realize that our research questions must be changed to incorporate the
new information and our research design must be altered. We have certainly
learned more from them than we have given back.

References

Anderson, J. M. (1991). Stress and burnout among nurses: A social network approach. Special Issue: Handbook on job stress. *Journal of Social Behavior and Personality, 6,* 251–272.

Antonucci, T. C., and Israel, B. A. (1986). Veridicality of social support: A comparison of principal and network members' responses. *Journal of Consulting and Clinical Psychology, 54,* 432–437.

Betancourt, H., and Lopez, S. R. (1993). The study of culture, ethnicity, and race in American psychology. *American Psychologist, 48,* 629–637.

Blacher, J. (1993). Siblings and out of home placements. In Z. Stoneman and P. W. Berman (Eds.), *The effects of mental retardation, disability, and illness on sibling relationships: Research issues and challenges* (pp. 245–262). Baltimore, MD: Paul Brooks Publishing.

Brown, D. R., and Gary, L. (1985). Social support network differentials among married and non-married Black females. *Psychology of Women Quarterly, 9,* 229–241.

Caspi, A., Bolger, N., and Eckenrode, J. (1987). Linking person and context in the daily stress process. *Journal of Personality and Social Psychology, 52,* 184–195.

Cohen, S., and Willis, T. A. (1985). Stress, social support, and the buffering hypothesis. *Psychological Bulletin, 98,* 310–357.

Comas-Diaz, L., and Greene, B. (Eds.) (1994). *Women of color: Integrating ethnic and gender identities in psychotherapy.* New York, NY: Guilford Press.

Crnic, K. E., Friedrich, W. N., and Greenberg, M. T. (1983). Adaptation of families with mentally retarded children: A model of stress, coping, and family ecology. *American Journal of Mental Deficiency, 88,* 125–138.

Dunst, C. J., Trivette, C. M., and Cross, A. H. (1986). Mediating influences of social support: Personal, family, and child outcomes. *American Journal of Mental Deficiency, 90,* 403–417.

Fewell, R. R. (1986). Support from religious organizations and personal beliefs. In R. R. Fewell and P. F. Vadasay (Eds.), *Families of handicapped children: Needs and supports across the life span* (pp. 296–316). Austin, TX: Pro-Ed.

Friedrich, W. N., Cohen, D. S., and Wilturner, L. T. (1988). Specific beliefs as moderator variables in material coping with mental retardation. *Journal of Children's Health Care, 17,* 40–44.

Glaser, B. G. (1978). *Theoretical sensitivity.* Mill Valley, CA: Sociology Press.

Glidden, L. M. (1993). What do we not know about families with children who have developmental disabilities: Questionnaire on Resources and Stress as a case study. *American Journal on Mental Retardation, 97,* 481–495.

Heller, T., Markwardt, R., Rowitz, L., and Farber, B. (1994). Adaptation of Hispanic families to a member with mental retardation. *American Journal on Mental Retardation, 99,* 289–300.

Lewis, E. A. (1989). Role strain in African American women: The efficacy of support networks. *Journal of Black Studies, 20,* 155–169.

Mischel, W. (1968). *Personality and assessment.* New York, NY: Wiley.

Mischel, W. (1977). On the future of personality research. *American Psychologist, 32,* 246–254.

Morawska, E. (1990). The sociology and historiography of immigration. In V. Yane-Moisughlin (Ed.), *Immigration reconsidered: History, sociology and politics* (pp. 187–238). New York, NY: Oxford University Press.

Neighbors, H. W., Jackson, J. S., Bowman, P. J., and Gurin, G. (1983). Stress, coping and Black mental health: Preliminary findings from a national study. *Prevention in Human Services, 2,* 5–29.

Osborne, N. G., and Feit, M. D. (1992). The use of racism in medical research. *Journal of the American Medical Association, 267,* 275–279.

Pearson, J. L., Hunter, A. G., Ensminger, M. E., and Kellam, S. G. (1990). Black grandmothers in multigenerational households: Diversity in family structure and parenting involvement in the Woodlawn community. *Child Development, 61,* 434–442.

Sarason, I. G., Levine, H. M., Basham, R. B., and Sarason, B. R. (1983). Assessing social support: The social support questionnaire. *Journal of Personality and Social Psychology, 4,* 127–139.

Spencer, M. B. (1990). Development of minority children: An introduction. *Child Development, 61,* 267–269.

Stevens, J. H. (1988). Social support, locus of control, and parenting in three low-income groups of mothers: Black teenagers, Black adults, and White adults. *Child Development, 59,* 635–642.

Stevens, J. H., and Duffield, B. N. (1986). Age and parenting skill among Black women: The efficacy of support networks. *Journal of Black Studies, 20,* 155–169.

Stoneman, Z., and Berman, P. W. (Eds.), (1993). *The effects of mental retardation, disability, and illness on sibling relationships: research issues and challenges.* Baltimore, MD: Paul Brooks Publishing.

Taylor, R. J., Chatters, L. M., Tucker, M. B., and Lewis, F. (1990). Development in research on Black families: A decade review. *Journal of Marriage and the Family, 52,* 993–1014.

Thompson, M. S., and Ensminger, M. E. (1989). Psychological well-being among mothers with school age children: Evolving family structures. *Social Forces, 67,* 715–732.

Trimble, J. E. (1991). Ethnic specification, validation, prospects and the future of drug use research. *International Journal of Addictions, 25,* 149–170.

Weisner, T. S., Beizer, L., and Stolze, L. (1991). Religion and families of children with developmental disabilities. *American Journal on Mental Retardation, 95,* 647–662.

Wilson, M. N. (1986). Perceived parental activity of mothers, fathers, and grandmothers in three-generational Black families. *Journal of Black Psychology, 12,* 43–59.

Wyche, K. F. (1993). Psychology and African American women: Findings from applied research. *Applied and Preventive Psychology, 2,* 115–121.

Yoder, J. D., and Kahn, A. S. (1993). Working toward an inclusive psychology of women. *American Psychologist, 48,* 846–850.

7

Emotional Well-Being and
Parenting Behavior Among
Low-Income Single Mothers:
Social Support and Ethnicity
as Contexts of Adjustment

Sheryl L. Olson and Rosario E. Ceballo

Recent decades have witnessed a dramatic upsurge in the number of American women who are raising young children alone and in poverty. Nearly one-quarter of all American children under the age of six live in poverty. This represents an increase, relative to 1979, of over 50 percent (U.S. Bureau of the Census, 1992). The majority of these families are headed by single women (National Center for Children in Poverty, 1993). Although this demographic trend has been nationwide, nonwhite families are highly overrepresented among the poor. For example, approximately two-thirds of all African American families are headed by women with dependent children, and of these families, two-thirds live in poverty (U.S. Bureau of the Census, 1992).

The strains of combining poverty and lone parenthood are potentially overwhelming. Single parents at any notch on the socioeconomic ladder report higher rates of life stress than their married counterparts (McLanahan, Wedemeyer, and Adelberg, 1981; Weinraub and Wolf, 1983), but those who are poor face a host of acute and chronic stressors that are usually unknown to their wealthier counterparts (Makovsky, 1982; Simons, Beaman, Conger, and Chao, 1993).

Small wonder, then, that the co-occurrence of poverty and single parenthood places women at extremely high risk for problems of depression and of poor physical health (Belle, 1982a and 1982b, 1990; Guttentag, Salisin, and Belle, 1980; Hall, Williams, and Greenberg, 1985; McAdoo, 1986; McGrath, Keita, Strickland, and Russo, 1990; Pearlin and Johnson, 1977). For example, in her study of forty-three low-income mothers and their children, Belle found that half of her sample scored in the depressed range on a symptom checklist and that the group mean score for depression rivaled that of individuals who had recently experienced the death of their spouse (Belle, 1982a). And in a community survey of mental health service utilization, Guttentag, Salisin, and Belle (1980) found that the risk of mental health problems was highest among poor single mothers of young children.

Nor is it surprising that maternal stress and depression have been linked to irritable and harsh parenting in many previous reports (e.g., see Downey and Coyne, 1990). For example, highly stressed or depressed mothers were more likely than others to use hostile, dominating styles with their children (Longfellow, Zelkowitz, and Saunders, 1982). Children's bids for attention, help, or even food tended to be ignored or punished. Relative to other women, these mothers rarely praised or showed affection to their children.

What is surprising is that many poor single mothers manage to keep up their spirits and provide stable, loving environments for their children. How do these women stave off depression and remain in good health? Over a ten-year period, first in Maine and then in Michigan, one of us (SO) has pursued this issue (Olson and Banyard, 1993; Olson, Kieschnick, Banyard, and Ceballo, 1994). Since 1990 one of the graduate students who has taken a lead role in this work is Rosario Ceballo (RC), junior author of this chapter. Together with a team of competent and enthusiastic graduate and undergraduate students, we conducted an in-depth study with fifty single low-income women and their children. Based on our own experiences and our readings of related research, we agreed that social supports might be extremely important in helping low-income single mothers cope with the many sources of strain in their lives. We also expected that the experiences of Black mothers and White mothers might vary.

This chapter describes in detail some (but not all) aspects of the study we have conducted. The chapter closes with reflections of a more personal nature, first by Sheryl Olson and then by Rosie Ceballo. We have taken inspirations from the resilience and creativity of those we study and hope that our work can eventually help, in some small measure, to improve the lives of families like those whom we have studied.

Background

We are not the first to be interested in the coping of low-income single mothers. Unfortunately, until recently the research has been limited. For example, prior to the late 1970s, there were numerous reports contrasting children of single parents (almost invariably women) with those living in two-parent families. A common conclusion was that children in single-parent households were developmentally disadvantaged, presumably because of the sheer absence of a father in the home (e.g., see review by Gongla and Thompson, 1987). Group differences in family SES were often uncontrolled, and single-parent families were frequently drawn from highly selective samples, resulting in a biased and misleading body of literature (Blechman, 1982; Herzog and Sudia, 1968; Sprey, 1967). It is likely that social policy decisions have been shaped by similar biases.

More recent studies have shown that children who grow up in mother-only families are at elevated risk for a broad range of adverse developmental outcomes and that economic hardship plays an important role in accounting for these relationships (McLanahan and Booth, 1989; McLoyd, 1990). However, these studies tell us little about the range of variability within at-risk families. A growing body of research has shown that low-income families vary widely in effectiveness and that the ways in which they differ from one another can be clearly identified (Clark, 1983; Garmezy, 1991; Werner and Smith, 1992). For example, in their famous longitudinal study, Werner and Smith (1977, 1989, 1992) examined an entire cohort of children born in 1955 on the island of Kauai. Children in the study were from ethnically diverse families and experienced high rates of poverty. After careful monitoring of these individuals over four decades, Werner was able to identify factors associated with competent functioning among children who had experienced poverty and other associated risk factors. Such "protective" factors ranged from the individual to the community level, but family characteristics were prominent: Competent at-risk children tended to have parents who provided ample emotional support, set clear and consistent rules, maintained a stable and cohesive home, and showed respect for their children's individuality. Clearly, there is much to learn from examining variability within high-risk groups.

Research on low-income single parents and their children has often been embedded in studies of either poverty *or* single-parent families. We felt that it was important to identify issues and themes specific to this growing subpopulation, however. Thus, we identified women who were coping well emotionally and in their maternal roles, despite having such stressful lives. What characteristics of their backgrounds or current life situations differentiated them from women who felt dysphoric and powerless?

In this chapter, we examine relationships between social network support and adjustment among low-income, single mothers of young children. Social networks are potential lifelines for impoverished, single-parent families. The availability of social support has been associated with psychological well-being in Black and White single mothers (Colletta and Lee,

1983; McAdoo, 1986; Zur-Szpiro and Longfellow, 1982) and with individual differences in their parenting experiences and competencies (Colletta, 1979; Crittenden, 1985; Simons et al., 1993; Stevens, 1988). However, the mere presence of social relationships does not ensure reductions in life stress. One key distinction is between the quantity of regular social contacts and their perceived quality (House and Kahn, 1985; Milardo, 1987). Satisfaction with the quality of support has been related to positive mental health among single mothers (Colletta, 1979; Olson et al., 1994; Wilcox, 1986) and among others under stress (Cohen and Wills, 1985). Extensive social ties, however, have often been associated with high levels of stress and distress (Belle, 1982a; Wilcox, 1986). This is especially true when one's network ties involve heavy reliance upon relatives. Kin networks provide material support and assistance with childcare, necessities for the survival of poor, single-parent families. However, these ties exact many different costs as well, including interference with one's parenting roles and personal life, reciprocal demands for help, heightened interpersonal conflict, and the vicarious pain of witnessing relatives and friends experience misfortune (Belle, 1982a; Chase-Lansdale, Brooks-Gunn, and Zamsky, 1994; Colletta, 1979; Milardo, 1987; Riley and Eckenrode, 1986; Stack, 1974; Weiss, 1979; Wilcox, 1981).

Moreover, there are many different ways in which single mothers can derive support from others. Some help, such as baby-sitting or household assistance, is practical or "instrumental." Other sources of help, such as having someone to confide in, or having a mentor who can give advice when appropriate, are more emotionally toned than instrumental. Not all dimensions of support have been related to positive adjustments among single mothers (McLoyd, 1990). Thus, in the current study, distinctions were made between many different dimensions of support, and within each dimension, between the amount of support given and women's subjective evaluations of how helpful that support was.

We have also highlighted the role of ethnicity as a potentially important context for understanding women's social network ties. Prior research has suggested that ethnicity may be a powerful moderator of women's postdivorce adjustment. For example, relative to Euro-American women, African American single mothers have shown less emotional distress, fewer adjustment difficulties, and greater satisfaction with their parental roles (Gove and Shin, 1989; Kitson and Holmes, 1992; Menaghan and Lieberman, 1986). We wished to go beyond simple comparisons of ethnically different groups by identifying aspects of support related to superior adjustment among African American and Euro-American single mothers. This is a step in the direction of explaining how ethnicity may serve as a context for adjustment among highly stressed women.

In summary, we posed three main research questions. First, how much variability is there among our samples of White and Black single mothers in terms of emotional coping and effective parenting? Second, what specific aspects of social network support were most highly related to positive emotional adjustment and to supportive and involved child caregiving among these women? Finally, are relationships between social network support and positive adjustment differentially patterned for African American and Euro-American women?

Methods of the Study

Participants

We recruited families through preschool programs serving those with low incomes in Washtenaw County, Michigan. Fliers requesting participation in the study were sent home with children. These fliers briefly described the project, promised payment for participation, and listed a name and phone number to call. When potential participants phoned us, we conducted an initial telephone screening interview and invited only mothers over the age of twenty who had been single for at least one year and had no immediate plans to marry or remarry. The latter restriction was to avoid confounding families in the acute stages of divorce or remarriage adjustment with those who had achieved more stable adaptations to single-parent life.

The participants were fifty single mothers and their preschool-age children. Women ranged in age from 22 to 45 years, with an average age of 32. Their children were 21 boys and 29 girls who had ranged in age from 3 to 6.5 years of age. Twenty-one mothers described themselves as White, 21 as African American, 7 as a blend of races, and 1 as Asian American. As a group, the women were fairly well educated: All but 3 had completed high school, 28 had attended some college, 9 were college graduates, and 7 had completed some graduate school. Twenty-three mothers had never been married, 24 had been married once, 2 had been married twice, and 1, three times. Women had spent an average of 5.5 years as single parents (range = 2–19 years). The majority of families (60 percent) had incomes below $10,000 per year; the remainder had incomes below $20,000 per year.

Some sense of the daily lives of our participants can be gleaned from a few examples. S. J., a 31-year old unemployed mother of two boys who lived on less than $10,000/year, wrote:

> At this time I have two children who are 5 and 3 years of age. They are at the age where there is constant battles between the two of them [describes recent sibling fights in detail]. The children feel quite angry if they cannot buy toys at the store. A common complaint I hear is "Mommy you never get us anything." Their father and stepmother buy them things on a regular basis. . . . C., the old-

est child, seems to be an angry youngster. He will get quite upset with me for discipline measures that are taken. The other main area of stress is with the job search. It is really difficult to obtain a job that will cover all expenses and also be conducive to spending time with the children.

Similarly, Z. T., an employed mother of one son who earned less than $11,000/year, said: "Everyday I worry about bills, childcare, job, car, family in Florida, losing home, losing my child." And, R. N., an employed mother of three girls and one boy who earned less than $10,000/year, described recent daily stresses she experienced: "The kids attacked me with problems when I walked in the door after an exhausting day at work . . . I felt like running away to the wilds and never returning." She also described how she felt during a weekend "day off": "It's the weekend again. My day alone and as usual I have a million things to do when all I want to do is sleep . . . I feel completely overwhelmed."

Procedures

Each family was paid fifty dollars for participating in the study. Families were observed and interviewed in their homes by trained research assistants. The research staff included five undergraduate and graduate women. Two assistants visited each home together on two occasions, approximately two weeks apart. Each visit lasted about three hours. Whenever possible, one interviewer was a White woman and one was a woman of color. The junior author (RC) visited about half of the families.

During the first session, we gave each woman a brief overview of the project, explained that this was exploratory research and that we wanted to learn from them, and asked her to sign consent forms for herself and her child. One assistant gathered background information about the family and then administered the preschool version of the Home Observation for the Measurement of the Environment (Bradley and Caldwell, 1979), which aims to assess the cognitive and emotional home environment for the child. The mother was then left alone to complete the Beck Depression Inventory (BDI) (Beck, Ward, Mendelson, Mock, and Erlbaugh, 1961). Meanwhile, the other assistant established rapport with the child, took note of toys and other sources of cognitive stimulation available to the child, and administered standardized tests. Mother and child then came back together, and we videotaped them performing several interactive tasks.

Between the first and second visits, women kept a journal record of daily stresses they experienced (see Olson and Banyard, 1993). During the second home visit, women were asked to complete a second Beck Depression Inventory, the Social Network Form (Weinraub and Wolf, 1983), a child behavior checklist, and a short stressful events checklist. The Social Network Form, described below, allowed us to gauge various aspects of social support in order to assess its role in emotional health and parenting competence among our participants.

Measures

Some of the information we gathered, such as the videotaped interactions, is still being analyzed and will be reported elsewhere. Here we describe only the measures that were used in the present data analyses.

Home Observation for the Measurement of the Environment (HOME). During the first visit we administered a revised version of the HOME scale that has been shown to have good test-retest reliability (Bradley and Caldwell, 1979). HOME involved both observation and question-asking by one of the two assistants, who then filled out the eight subscales, shown in the HOME scale section of Table 7.1. A full description of the subscales can be found in Caldwell and Bradley (1984), but here is a brief description of each scale:

Learning Stimulation: the extent to which the parent structures the environment to facilitate specific cognitive skills (e.g., learning shapes, building a vocabulary)

Language Stimulation: the extent to which the parent models and encourages competent verbal expression

Physical Environment: the extent to which the home environment and its immediate surroundings are safe, clean, organized, and uncrowded

Warmth and Acceptance: the parent demonstrates praise, affection, and emotional responsiveness to child and is proud of child's accomplishments

Academic Stimulation: the parent encourages the development of preacademic skills (e.g., numbers, words)

Modeling: the parent makes appropriate maturity demands and demonstrates patience and tolerance toward the child

Variety in Experience: the parent provides stimulating outings and encourages individual expression and autonomy

Acceptance: infrequent use of power-assertive discipline (e.g., physical punishment, physical restraint) or emotional derogation of child.

TABLE 7.1   Means and Standard Deviations (SDS) for Study Variables for Single Mothers

	African American			White		
Background Variables	*M*	*SD*	*Range*	*M*	*SD*	*Range*
	Background Variables					
Age	31.05	5.70	22–45	31.20	4.56	23–39
Age at birth of first child	22.50	3.18	18–29	23.90	3.43	19–30
Ever wed	1.65	0.49	1–2	1.28	0.46	1–2
Time as single parent	7.45	4.82	2–19	4.00	2.49	1–11
Number of children in home	4.25	2.24	1–8	3.04	0.97	1–5
Number of males in home	1.45	1.57	0–6	1.14	0.85	0–3
Income	1.30	0.47	10–20	1.52	0.51	10–20
	Social Support					
Total contacts	53.92	31.83	6–120	91.95	42.62	29–161
Emotional support						
Amount	80.67	16.59	53–99	78.86	17.19	45–99
Satisfaction	6.63	2.09	3–10	6.86	2.31	3–10
Parenting support						
Amount	44.99	14.90	13–79	39.76	12.84	17–60
Satisfaction	7.00	2.26	2–10	6.05	1.79	3–9
Child care support						
Amount	27.50	25.59	0–50	36.52	24.71	0–55
Satisfaction						
Household support						
Amount	2.59	4.54	0–15	1.57	2.89	0–10
Satisfaction	5.05	3.47	1–10	3.57	2.71	1–9
Emergency support	5.19	2.93	1–10	4.19	2.23	1–9
Availability of friend	5.89	2.28	3–10	4.57	2.68	1–10
	Coping Scales					
Emotional stress	4.26	0.93	2–5	3.05	1.07	1–5
Child care stress	4.16	1.30	1–5	3.67	1.28	1–5
Beck Depression Inventory	9.37	5.94	0–20	12.14	7.48	1–28
	HOME Scale					
Learning	8.10	1.37	6–10	8.19	1.66	4–10
Language	6.50	0.61	5–7	6.48	0.81	4–7
Physical environment	6.30	1.26	3–7	6.71	0.72	4–7
Warmth	5.80	1.36	3–7	6.24	1.18	2–7
Academic	4.50	0.69	3–5	4.67	0.48	4–5
Modeling	3.25	1.25	1–5	4.00	0.89	2–5
Variety	6.25	1.37	2–8	7.10	1.18	3–8
Acceptance	3.55	1.32	2–8	3.19	1.33	0–4

Social Network Form. Our measure of social support was the Social Network Form (SNF), developed by Weinraub and Wolf (1983). This questionnaire, administered in the form of a structured interview, covers different dimensions of actual and perceived support. First, extensiveness of social contacts is calculated from the number of monthly contacts with the four friends and/or relatives mothers reported seeing most frequently. How frequently the mother obtained "informal" support from friends and/or relatives and "formal" support from organizations such as churches or parenting groups yields a measure of emotional support. Parenting support is the extent to which women valued parenting beliefs of friends and relatives in their networks and also valued support from organizations. Practical help with child care and housework is defined in terms of the number of hours of help obtained on a weekly basis. Women also rated, on ten-point scales, the availability of support in the event of an emergency and the availability of support from adult friends. Finally, feelings of satisfaction with emotional, parenting, child care, and household supports were rated separately on ten-point scales ("1"= never satisfied, "10" = always satisfied with quality of support).

Self Ratings of Copings. Women rated their ability to cope with child care and emotional stressors on separate five-point scales developed by Weinraub and Wolf (1983). Scale points ranged from 0 ("rarely in control") to 5 ("almost always in control").

Beck Depression Inventory. The Beck Depression Inventory (BDI) (Beck et al., 1961), a standard twenty-one-item self-report measure of depressive symptoms, was also administered. Symptoms of dysphoria were rated on three-point scales, with higher levels indicating greater symptoms severity. To achieve the most reliable index of dysphoria, women's BDI scores were obtained twice, then averaged across visits.

Results

How Much Variability Is There?

As you can see in the upper portion of Table 7.1, African American and Euro-American women did not differ significantly in relation to their age, household income, or age at the time of their first child's birth. However, African American mothers had spent more years as single parents, were more likely to have never wed, and had larger families than their Euro-American counterparts.

Table 7.1 also shows the range of scores. As can be seen from the table, there was strong individual variability in actual and perceived support, self-rated coping, and parenting competence among both groups. Some of the participants functioned very well in terms of their own emotional health and in terms of the environments they provided to their children. There were few group differences in relation to actual and perceived social support. Only the extensiveness of social contact differed significantly between ethnic groups, with African American mothers reporting more extensive network ties than their Euro-American counterparts. In relation to self-ratings of coping and depression, Black and White mothers did not differ in their ratings of ability to cope with child care stressors or in the number of depressive symptoms they endorsed on the BDI. However, Black mothers felt more confidence in coping with emotional stressors than White mothers, and this difference was highly significant. Finally, there were few group differences in parenting behavior on the HOME scale, with the exceptions that White mothers tended to provide somewhat greater encouragement of mature behavior (modeling), and greater variety in daily stimulation, than did Black mothers.

Who Enjoys Strong Social Support?

There were many significant correlations between background characteristics and social network ties among the White and Black mothers in our study. African American mothers who had the most extensive social network ties tended to be unemployed ($r = .56$, $p < .01$), less highly educated than others ($r = -.57$, $p < .01$), and had relatively large families ($r = .52$, $p < .01$). This pattern may also account for the fact that mothers with large families reported having more household help available than with smaller families ($r = .62$, $p < .001$) (indeed, older children were frequently mentioned as household helpers). Older African American mothers reported having higher levels of emotional support ($r = .54$, $p < .01$), parenting support ($r = .58$, $p < .01$), and household support ($r = .47$, $p < .05$) than younger mothers but less availability of support in the event of an emergency ($r = -.43$, $p < .05$). Finally, women who become mothers at relatively young ages felt more satisfied with the quality of their child care supports than those who became mothers at later ages ($r = .53$, $p < .01$).

Relationships between background characteristics and support were patterned similarly for Euro-American women. Women who reported greater availability of support from friends tended to have large families ($r = .58$, $p < .01$), less education ($r = -.65$, $p < .001$), and were relatively young when their first child was born ($r = .65$, $p < .01$). Conversely, women who became mothers at relatively late ages reported lower levels of satisfaction with their household supports ($r = -.58$, $p < .01$) and less availability of support from friends ($r = -.65$, $p < .001$) than those who made this transition at earlier ages. Finally, women who enjoyed more parenting support than others tended to be older ($r = .45, p < .05$), formerly married ($r = .46, p < .05$), and currently employed ($r = .43, p < .05$).

Background Correlates of Adjustment

Because women varied strongly in the nature of their backgrounds, we also computed correlations between those demographic characteristics and measures of emotional adjustment and parenting behavior. Within each domain of adjustment, correlations were computed separately for African American and Euro-American women.

Emotional Adjustment. Several different family background characteristics were related to African American women's scores on the coping and symptom indices. Women who felt effective in coping with emotional stress tended to have fewer male children than others ($r = -.37, p < .05$), were employed outside the home ($r = .46, p < .05$), and had been married prior to becoming a single parent ($r = .38, p < .05$). Ex-spouses' education (in years) was also associated with high self-perceived efficacy in coping with child care and emotional stressors ($r = .59, p < .01$). Finally, women with the lowest levels of depression had spent the greatest number of years as single parents ($r = -.41, p < .05$).

In contrast with results for African American mothers, background characteristics were mostly unrelated to self-ratings of coping among Euro-American women. Only one relationship emerged: Women who had been married prior to becoming parents reported higher feelings of efficacy in handling child stressors than those who had never been married ($r = .51, p < .05$).

Parenting Behavior. Family background characteristics were related to variations in parenting behavior among African American mothers. Women who had previously been married tended to provide greater learning stimulation ($r = .42, p < .05$) and greater warmth and acceptance ($r = .58, p < .01$) to their children than never-married women. Those who had reported higher annual incomes tended to provide greater warmth and acceptance ($r = .42, p < .05$), greater use of nonpunitive discipline ($r = .42, p < .05$), and a more adequate physical home environment ($r = .37, p < .05$) than others. Older mothers tended to engage in higher levels of warm, accepting caregiving behavior than younger mothers ($r = .42, p < .05$). Finally, women who had relatively few children were able to provide more adequate physical home environments than those who had many children ($r = .42, p < .05$).

Among Euro-American women, age was also positively correlated with ability to provide learning stimulation ($r = .45, p < .05$) and nonpunitive discipline ($r = .36, p < .05$) to their children. In addition, use of nonpunitive discipline was associated with prior married status ($r = .58$, $p < .01$) and with present employment outside the home ($r = .38$, $p < .05$). Mothers who frequently modeled and encouraged mature behavior tended to have more years of education ($r = .49$, $p < .05$) and smaller family sizes ($r = .46$, $p < .05$) than others. Finally, as with the African American women, adequacy of the physical home environment was associated with higher amounts of annual income ($r = .43$, $p < .05$) and with smaller family sizes ($r = .62$, $p < .01$).

Emotional Well-Being and Social Support

One main research question focused on relationships between emotional well-being and support. We expected that women who had higher levels of perceived and actual support would possess more positive emotional outlooks than those who felt dissatisfied with their support resources. This expectation was generally confirmed, but patterns of relationships between support and adjustment differed somewhat for African American and Euro-American women.

Among African American women, perceptions of personal efficacy were consistently related to the quality and perceived quality of social support resources. Those who felt most effective in their ability to manage child caregiving stresses reported having greater amounts of potential emergency assistance ($r = .77$, $p < .001$), greater feelings of satisfaction with the quality of their child care supports ($r = .62$, $p < .01$), and greater availability of close friendships ($r = .52$, $p < .01$) than women who felt less effective in their maternal roles. It was interesting to find that women who reported having the most household help (in hours per week) tended to feel less effective in coping with child care than others ($r = -.40$, $p < .05$).

Women who felt highly effective in coping with emotional stress reported higher levels of emotional support ($r = .39$, $p < .05$), greater satisfaction with the quality of their emotional supports ($r = .42$, $p < .05$), more hours of child care assistance ($r = .53$, $p < .01$), ample emergency support ($r = .35$, $p < .05$), and greater availability of adult friendships ($r = .40$, $p < .05$) than others. Similarly, those who reported the lowest levels of depression tended to feel more satisfied with the quality of their emotional and parenting supports than others ($rs = -.86$ and $-.51$, $ps < .001$ and $.01$ respectively).

Many of the same social support variables that predicted coping with child care among African American women also related to Euro-American women's feelings: satisfaction with emotional and child care supports ($rs = .53$ and $.57$, $ps < .01$ respectively) and availability of support in the event of an emergency ($r = .39$, $p < .05$). However, there were relatively few relationships between emotional adjustment and support. Women who received the highest amount of household help tended to feel most effective in handling emotional stress ($r = .44$, $p < .05$). Similarly, women who felt satisfied with the quality of their parenting supports tended to experience the lowest levels of depression ($r = -.44$, $p < .05$).

Parenting Competence and Social Support

Our other main research question focused on relationships between child caregiving behavior and social support. Because of previous research, we expected that women who showed the highest levels of positive involvement with their children would experience high levels of supportive assistance from others. This expectation was only partially confirmed.

As predicted, quality of caregiving competence was related to many different aspects of African American women's support networks. Women who provided relatively frequent learning and academic stimulation to their children tended to perceive that they had better emergency resources ($r = .50$, $p < .01$) and greater availability of adult friends ($r = .42$, $p < .05$), though fewer hours of household supports ($r = -.39$, $p < .05$), than others.

Women who were warm and accepting toward their children tended to report high satisfaction with the quality of their household supports ($r = .68$, $p < .001$) and higher levels of actual household support ($r = .41$, $p < .05$) than others. Finally, women who frequently used nonpunitive discipline reported higher levels of emergency support ($r = .46$, $p < .05$), greater satisfaction with their household supports ($r = .44$, $p < .05$), greater satisfaction with the quality of their child care supports ($r = .56$, $p < .01$), and greater access to support from friends ($r = .38$, $p < .05$) than those who were relatively punitive.

However, relationships between maternal support and quality of caregiving were patterned quite differently for Euro-American women than for African American women. Those who provided frequent cognitive stimulation to their children reported more hours of household help ($r = .40$, $p < .05$) but less availability of support from friends ($r = -.40$, $p < .05$) than others. An unexpected finding was that women who frequently modeled mature behavior for their children reported fewer total social contacts ($r = -.59$, $p < .01$) and less availability of support from friends ($r = -.58$, $p < .01$) than others. Similarly, women who used nonpunitive discipline with their children tended to feel less satisfied with the quality of their emotional supports than others ($r = -.43$, $p < .05$).

Summary and Conclusion

We asked initially: Within our group of lone parents living on meager incomes, what factors are associated with positive emotional health and with supportive parenting? Our findings gave us many answers to this query, some expected and some surprising. First, variability in women's backgrounds was clearly associated with differences in their personal adjustment and parenting behavior. Women who felt least capable of coping effectively with their life situations, and who were observed to be less optimal in their parent-child interactions, tended to be young, unemployed, and never married and with larger family sizes and lower incomes than others. It was interesting to find that this subgroup of women also had the most potential support available but expressed less satisfaction than others with the quality of these supports.

As expected, women's perceptions of emotional well-being and coping efficacy also were related to qualities of their support networks, but in somewhat different ways for African American and Euro-American single mothers. Women who felt most confident in handling child care and emotional stressors tended to perceive that they had ample support in the event of an emergency and felt highly satisfied with the quality of their child care and parenting supports. However, availability of adult friends was a unique correlate of perceived coping efficacy and emotional well-being among African American women. Why was this the case? Group comparisons eliminated the most obvious explanation: African American and Euro-American women did not differ in relation to the number of friends in their lives or in the sheer number of individuals who were considered emotionally supportive. Qualitative studies of the nature of friendship ties among these two groups of women would enrich our understanding of this interesting issue.

Finally, quality of child caregiving was associated with perceptions of social support, but in strikingly different ways for African American and Euro-American women. African American women who provided stimulating and nurturing environments for their children reported that they had ample access to friends and to emergency support and felt satisfied with the quality of their household supports. These findings converged with previous research (Colletta, 1979; Hashima and Amato, 1994; McLoyd, 1990; Zur-Szpiro and Longfellow, 1982) in suggesting that among highly stressed individuals, optimal child caregiving is most likely to occur in the context of enriched support. However, for Euro-American women, relationships between support network variables and aspects of child caregiving were relatively few in number and in unexpected directions. Generally, women who perceived that they had good parenting and emotional supports, relatively large numbers of social contacts, and ample access to adult friends tended to engage in *less* optimal child caregiving than others. We were startled by this finding. Initially, we wondered whether these correlations were statistical artifacts; for example, did they reflect the operation of unspecified demographic variables? However, controlling for all relevant variables (age, education, prior marital status, current family size) in partial correlation analyses did not alter the original relationships. Thus, we speculate that some women with dense social networks may invest less in their mother-child relationships than those with more restrictive networks. If this is indeed true, it is unclear why it would pertain to Euro-American and not to African American single mothers. In further research, it would be important to examine how ethnicity affects ways in which highly stressed women balance different role relationships.

Our study had several noteworthy limitations. Dividing the sample by ethnicity produced fairly small subgroups, which potentially limits the generalizability of our findings. Furthermore, although our measure of parenting behavior was psychometrically sound, it provided only a bird's-eye view of the home environment, and one that was based primarily on maternal report. Planned analyses of videotaped parent-child interactions may reveal an entirely different picture of parenting behavior under the strains of poverty. Finally, because of the correlational nature of our study, we cannot assume that there are causal connections between support variables and women's adjustment. For example, one could argue that emotionally distressed women actually possess fewer adequate support resources than others or that these women tend to see their worlds in a negative light that is highly colored by feelings of distress. This issue is important for understanding relationships between support and adjustment among highly stressed individuals, and it has implications for the types of supportive interventions that may be optimal for these women. In further research, it would be critical to examine these issues longitudinally and with larger samples of women.

To conclude: Single mothers in poverty are often portrayed as a homogeneous group, perhaps in part because they have been contrasted with more advantaged groups of women. However, we found strong variability in the background characteristics and current life circumstances of women in our study. These sources of diversity were important for understanding differences between women in personal adjustment and in parenting behavior. In particular, ethnic background was one factor that consistently affected the nature of relationships between social network support, emotional well-being, and quality of child caregiving. Ignoring the dimension of ethnicity would have obscured many of these findings. Thus, in further research it is important to consider how ethnicity affects the nature of social network support by examining women's perceptions of their support relationships in greater detail and over extended periods of time and by including key support figures as research informants.

Personal Reflections

SO: Combining motherhood with a demanding career has been the greatest challenge of my life. Being economically advantaged and part of a stable, supportive marriage, I am simply in awe of women who must parent alone and with few material resources. I feel offended by media images of poor single parents (almost invariably women) as "symptoms" of societal decay and by research reports that simply contrast economically advantaged and disadvantaged groups on measures of adjustment, thereby supporting stereotyped, negative overgeneralizations. However, I do not pretend to understand the worlds of women in my studies, because my own life situations are so different. My history of privilege may blind me to important aspects of their experience.

I began looking at the lives of single mothers living in poverty nine years ago, when I held a faculty position at the University of Maine. As a child and family clinical psychologist with strong developmental leanings, one of my charges at the time was to develop a mental health consultation service for regional Head Start preschools. Together with a small army of clinical psychology practicum students, we were able to provide consultation services to over 400 children and families each year. All families had annual incomes below federally designated poverty lines, and about three-fourths were headed by women. Their economic hardships were chronic and often severe—for example, some families had to survive the bitter Maine winters in unheated, ramshackle houses. This experience gave me a rich window into the lives of poor single mothers and their children. I was extremely impressed by the variability among these families, particularly that so many mothers managed to provide stable and supportive homes for themselves and their children despite the many powerful barriers in their lives. I do not intend to imply that these resilient women were somehow superhuman, merely that they seemed determined to make the best out of an inherently difficult situation. Especially because this subgroup of women has been underresearched in psychology and vilified in media reports, I wanted to know more about the stresses and supports in their lives from their own points of view and about features of their past and present lives that appeared to make a difference in their personal and maternal adjustment. Women have been very open in sharing their experiences with us and have given us many insights into the nature of strength under conditions of chronic adversity. Our most important insight has been that such strength is contextual in that it is deeply rooted in both past and present supportive relationships.

RC: When I arrived at college, I initially presumed that psychological research involved only rats in sterile university labs. When I learned otherwise, I was immediately drawn to research endeavors that could investigate the lives of poor children and families. As a Hispanic woman from a working-class background, I seek to apply the skills and knowledge I have gained in my schooling to investigate sources of strength and resilience within families living under conditions of relentless economic hardship.

My work with Sheryl Olson is, in part, based on a shared approach to research that rejects the theoretical framework of deficiency that has traditionally been used to study African American families, especially female-headed ones. It is especially important to me that we strove in every aspect of the research endeavor to be respectful of the participants, who traveled to a university setting to tell us about their experiences. For example, we did not solely confine our assessments to standardized, empirical measures: We also explored mothers' reflections of their own experiences as provided in their own words. What I remember as most salient about my many visits to these mothers' homes was their creative coping responses to difficult situations, their ability to joke about the obstacles stacked against them, and their steady determination to make the best of their situations for themselves and their children. I also do not mean to imply that they were superwomen, but there is a quality of richness in many families that deserves our respect. I believe that part of my responsibility as a member of an elite, mostly White academic institution is to promote respectful and serious study of people whose lives in impoverished and crime-stricken communities are as distant as can be from the lives of those who work in ivory-tower universities.

References

Beck, A. T., Ward, S. H., Mendelson, M., Mock, J., and Erlbaugh, J. (1961). An inventory for measuring depression. *Archives of General Psychiatry, 4,* 561–571.

Belle, D. (1982a). *Lives in stress: Woman and depression.* Beverly Hills, CA: Sage.

Belle, D.(1982b). Social ties and social support. In D. Belle (Ed.), *Lives in stress: Women and depression* (pp. 133–144). Beverly Hills, CA: Sage.

Belle, D.(1990). Poverty and women's mental health. *American Psychologist, 45,* 385–389.

Blechman, E. (1982). Are children with one parent at risk? A methodological critique. *Journal of Marriage and the Family, 44,* 179–195.

Bradley, R. H., and Caldwell, B. M. (1979). Home Observation for the Measurement of the Environment: A revision of the preschool scale. *American Journal of Mental Deficiency, 84,* 234–244.

Caldwell, B. M., and Bradley, B. M. (1984). *HOME Administration Manual* (Rev. ed.). Little Rock, AR: University of Arkansas.

Chase-Lansdale, P. L., Brooks-Gunn, J., and Zamsky, E. S. (1994). Young African-American multigenerational families in poverty: Quality of mothering and grandmothering. *Child Development, 65,* 373–393.

Clark, R. M. (1983). *Family life and school achievement: Why poor Black children succeed or fail.* Chicago, IL: University of Chicago Press.

Cohen, S., and Wills, T. A. (1985). Stress, social support, and the buffering hypothesis. *Psychological Bulletin, 98,* 310–357.

Colletta, N. D. (1979). Support systems after divorce: Incidence and impact. *Journal of Marriage and the Family, 41,* 837–846.

Colletta, N. D., and Lee, D. (1983). The impact of support for Black adolescent mothers. *Journal of Family Issues, 4,* 127–143.

Crittenden, P. M. (1985). Social networks, quality of childrearing, and child development. *Child Development, 56,* 1299–1313.

Downey, G., and Coyne, J. C. (1990). Children of depressed parents: An integrative review. *Psychological Bulletin, 108*(1), 50–76.

Garmezy, N. (1991). Resiliency and vulnerability to adverse outcomes associated with poverty. In T. Thompson and S. C. Hupp (Eds.), *Saving children at risk: Poverty and disabilities* (pp. 45–60). Newbury Park, CA: Sage.

Gongla, P. A., and Thompson, E. H. (1987). Single parent families. In M. B. Sussman and S. K. Steinmetz (Eds.), *Handbook of marriage and the family* (pp. 397–419). New York, NY: Plenum Press.

Gove, W. R., and Shin, H. (1989). The psychological well-being of divorced and widowed men and women: An empirical study. *Journal of Family Issues, 10,* 122–144.

Guttentag, M., Salisin, S., and Belle, D. (1980). *The mental health of women.* New York, NY: Academic Press.

Hall, L. A., Williams, C. A., and Greenberg, R. S. (1985). Supports, stressors, and depressive symptoms in low-income mothers of young children. *American Journal of Public Health, 75,* 518–522.

Hashima, P. Y., and Amato, P. R. (1994). Poverty, social support, and parental behavior. *Child Development, 65,* 394–403.

Herzog, E., and Sudia, C. (1968). Fatherless homes: A review of research. *Children, 15,* 177–182.

House, J. S., and Kahn, R. L. (1985). Measures and concepts of social support. In S. Cohen and L. Syme (Eds.), *Social support and health* (pp. 83–105). New York, NY: Academic Press.

Kitson, G., and Holmes, W. M. (1992). *Portrait of divorce: Adjustment to marital breakdown.* New York, NY: Guilford Press.

Longfellow, C., Zelkowitz, P., and Saunders, E. (1982). The quality of mother-child relationships (1982). In D. Belle (Ed.), *Lives in stress: Women and depression* (pp. 163–176). Beverly Hills, CA: Sage.

Makovsky, V. P. (1982). Sources of stress: Events or conditions? In D. Belle (Ed.), *Lives in stress: Women and depression* (pp. 35–53). Beverly Hills, CA: Sage.

McAdoo, H. (1986). Strategies used by black single mothers against stress. In M. Simms and J. Malveaux (Eds.), *Slipping through the cracks: The status of black women* (pp. 153–166). New Brunswick, NJ: Transaction Books.

McGrath, E., Keita, G. P., Strickland, B. R., and Russo, N. F. (1990). *Women and depression: Risk factors and treatment issues.* Washington, DC: American Psychological Association.

McLanahan, S., and Booth, K. (1989). Mother only families: Problems, prospects, and politics. *Journal of Marriage and the Family, 51,* 557–580.

McLanahan, S., Wedemeyer, N., and Adelberg, N. (1981). Network structure, social support, and psychological well-being in the single-parent family. *Journal of Marriage and the Family, 43,* 601–612.

McLoyd, V. (1990). The impact of economic hardship on black families and children: Psychological distress, parenting, and socioeconomic development. *Child Development, 61,* 311–346.

Menaghan, E. G., and Lieberman, M. A. (1986). Changes in depression following divorce: A panel study. *Journal of Marriage and the Family, 48,* 299–328.

Milardo, R. (1987). Changes in social networks of women and men following divorce: A review. *Journal of Family Issues, 8,* 78–96.

National Center for Children in Poverty (1993). *Five million children: A statistical profile of our poorest young citizens: 1993 Update.* New York, NY: Columbia University, School of Public Health.

Olson, S. L., and Banyard, V. (1993). "Stop the world so I can get off for a while": Sources of daily stress in the lives of low-income single mothers of young children. *Family Relations, 42,* 50–56.

Olson, S. L., Kieschnick, E., Banyard, V., and Ceballo, R. (1994). Socioenvironmental and individual correlates of psychological adjustment in low-income single mothers. *American Journal of Orthopsychiatry, 64,* 17–31.

Pearlin, L., and Johnson, M. (1977). Marital status, life-strains, and depression. *American Sociological Review, 42,* 704–715.

Riley, D., and Eckenrode, J. (1986). Social ties: Subgroup differences in costs and benefits. *Journal of Personality and Social Psychology, 51,* 770–778.

Simons, R. L., Beaman, J., Conger, R., and Chao, W. (1993). Stress, support, and antisocial behavior trait as determinants of emotional well-being and parenting practices among single mothers. *Journal of Marriage and the Family, 55,* 385–398.

Sprey, J. (1967). The study of single parenthood: Some methodological considerations. *Family Coordinator, 16,* 29–34.

Stack, C. (1974). *All our kin: Strategies for survival in a black community.* New York, NY: Harper and Row.

Stevens, J. H. (1988). Social support, locus of control, and parenting in three low-income groups of mothers: Black teenagers, black adults, and white adults. *Child Development, 59,* 635–642.

U.S. Bureau of the Census (1992). Poverty in the United States, 1992. *Current Population Reports,* series P-60, no. 185. Washington, DC: U.S. Government Printing Office.

Weinraub, M., and Wolf, B. (1983). Effects of stress and social supports on mother-child interactions in single and two-parent families. *Child Development, 54,* 1297–1311.

Weiss, R. (1979). *Going it alone: The family life and social situation of the single parent.* New York, NY: Basic Books.

Werner, E. E., and Smith, R. S. (1977). *Kauai's children come of age.* Honolulu, HI: University of Hawaii Press.

Werner, E. E., and Smith, R. S. (1989). *Vulnerable but invincible: A longitudinal study of resilient children and youth.* New York, NY: Adams-Bannister.

Werner, E. E., and Smith, R. S.(1992). *Overcoming the odds: High risk children from birth to adulthood.* Ithaca, NY: Cornell University Press.

Wilcox, B. L. (1981). Social support in adjusting to marital disruption: A network analysis. In B. H. Gottlieb (Ed.), *Social networks and social support* (pp. 97–115). Beverly Hills, CA: Sage.

Wilcox, B. L.(1986). Stress, coping, and the social milieu of divorced women. In S. E. Hobfoll (Ed.), *Stress, social support, and women* (pp. 203–225). New York, NY: Hemisphere.

Zur-Szpiro, S., and Longfellow, C. (1982). Fathers' support to mothers and children. In D. Belle (Ed.), *Lives in stress: Women and depression* (pp. 145–153). Beverly Hills, CA: Sage.

PART 3

Gender, Culture,
and Values

In this section intraethnic diversity is examined. Ethnic identity becomes a tool for studying women and men who are similar and different in ethnicity from our authors. The authors of Part 3 raise important issues. What are the questions that can be asked by studying diversity within groups? How does being self-identified as an ethnic woman shape the ways in which these questions are conceptualized as well as the way in which they are asked? What are the ethnocentric values that the researcher brings to the process? What happens when one is a White woman and thus an "outsider" in studying ethnic minority people? The chapters in this section relate in various ways to these issues.

In Chapter 8, Sandra Schwartz Tangri is interested in the puzzles of group membership and identity. Hers is a personal narrative in teasing out these issues and providing us with several dilemmas. She begins by outlining a research problem: She and her colleagues have struggled to adapt a study designed for White women to include African American and New Zealand women (the Women's Life Paths Studies). Tangri points out quite clearly that cross-cultural research cannot use a standardized approach to comparing participants. The cultural context shapes the research process.

Following from this are Tangri's thoughts regarding the categories of gender, ethnicity, and race, which set up multiple dilemmas concerning the ways in which people are labeled and studied in society. What do these categories mean? How are they used? How do they influence people on individual, family, and group levels? Tangri addresses these questions by examining her Jewish identity—what being Jewish means to her in her personal life and in the social context of teaching in a historically Black college. She shares her insights as the cross hairs of ethnicity, gender, feminism, and various forms of racism sharpen her focus on the connection between what she does and who she is.

Mary Brabeck continues the theme of ethnic identity. In Chapter 9 she wonders about the variations in the social construction of personhood and how that is related to one's community, ethnic, gender, or cultural group. How is the relational self distinguished among those factors? The combining of theoretical conceptualizations of feminist scholars who argue that women are more relational than men and psychological theories that challenge the ethnocentric views of self as individualistic and autonomous sets the stage for Brabeck's work. Brabeck's study on Guatemalan youths indicates that they have a concept of moral self that is more communal and relational than that of American youth. Her consciousness of her role as "the other" in this culture caused her to challenge some of her assumptions about the centrality of the autonomous self and the limits of her own thinking—her ethnocentrism.

Chapter 10 is a collaboration between Guadalupe Gutierrez and Donna Nagata. They address questions of ethnic identity, worldview, and acculturation among minority individuals by presenting two specific research studies conducted independently. The authors show how rich data can emerge in studying intraethnic diversity. They focus on gender, acculturative influences, and intergenerational dynamics in ethnic communities. Their approach to these issues varies. Nagata's research explores the effects of the Japanese American internment of World War II upon the adult offspring of former internees. She is interested in factors that may be linked to differences in acculturation among different generations of Japanese Americans. Nagata's research details vividly how family communication, gender, geographic residence, and acculturation generate a picture of diversity within the Japanese American community and the extent to which current perceptions are linked to the past.

Guadalupe Gutierrez's research is with Mexican Americans. She explores the complex interplay of acculturation and gender in the worldviews of Mexican Americans residing in Chicago and Detroit. Women were found to have a greater orientation toward autonomy than men. Acculturation influenced attitudes. Those who were more Anglo in behaviors were more likely to value individualism over collectivism.

In Chapter 11, Amy Dabul and Nancy Felipe Russo explore achievement attributions. They present a new model of achievement that moves away from individualistic assumptions. This model reflects a multilevel approach to achievement that reflects diverse cultural identities in varying contexts. Dabul and Russo discuss how their own gender and ethnicity have contributed to this work. They describe their collaboration (between a graduate student, Dabul, and faculty member, Russo), in which they extend attribution theory research to include the interpersonal side of achievement, as a mutually beneficial learning experience.

What themes run throughout the chapters of this section? We see three:

- Diversity can be studied within multiple contexts to provide information within groups and between groups. This is a move away from traditional thinking in psychology, which has relied heavily on comparisons between groups. These comparisons most often compare ethnic and racial minorities to Whites.
- Ethnic identity can be studied in various contexts that are influenced by language, nativity, social class, marital status, and age. Historical antecedents become important in these studies and are often ignored.
- Feminist researchers work collaboratively with their students and colleagues. This collaborative process is one in which learning is mutual. Feminist researchers constantly monitor their research—the value assumptions they make and their own limitations as researchers.

These chapters help us to understand better the role of ethnicity, gender, and culture in the psychological experience. All of these women have been involved in blazing trails to develop empirical work with a multicultural emphasis. This has not been without cost to them, for psychology still is more comfortable with between-group comparisons rather than understanding within-group differences. How cultural patterns and norms influence behaviors is not an easy research topic. These women bring integrity to the study of such questions and a commitment to furthering scholarship.

8

Living with Anomalies: Sojourns of a White American Jew

Sandra Schwartz Tangri

The invitation to contribute to this volume could not have come at a better time, as the cross hairs of ethnicity, gender, feminism, and various forms of racism have increasingly sharpened my focus on the connection between what I do and who I am. The paradox is that despite my internal perception that what I do flows very directly from who I am, these perceptions are clearly seen by some as anomalous.

I am a White woman and teach at Howard University, a historically Black College. As a highly educated daughter of Jewish immigrants, one of whom was a Yiddish poet and wallpaper-hanger, and neither of whom finished high school, I have always been intrigued by ethnicity. I have long puzzled over whether the negative aspects of group membership such as outgroup hatred can be rent from the positive aspects. More recently, I have come to question the very nature of group membership and wondered how it is that we can know what group membership means to women in a number of cultural contexts.

The puzzles of group membership and identity form the meat of this chapter. My exposition proceeds through a set of five dilemmas that assume prominence in my work and in my life. The dilemmas range from the abstract to the personal. The first concerns comparability: How can we as researchers faithfully record the experiences of distinct groups without making it impossible to compare the realities of one group with the realities of other groups? Closely related is the dilemma of context: How can we preserve meanings across different cultural contexts? The third dilemma centers around the question, Should we eliminate categories? The dilemmas of comparability and context presume that there are such entities as cultural and/or ethnic groups, but some social commentators propose that ethnic groupings are, theoretically, avoidable. I come down on the side of ethnic diversity and against ethnic assimilation, which provokes for me a fourth dilemma: How can ethnic groups appreciate themselves without derogating each other? In the fifth and most personal dilemma, issues of appreciation surface again, and picking up threads from previous sections, I wonder: How do I wish to be appreciated?

The First Dilemma:
How Can We Compare Across Groups?

I remember when in the early 1970s feminists patiently explained why psychology of women (POW) was not just (or even primarily) the study of sex differences. One of the arguments was that women have experiences that are unique (though not universal) to them as women, both because of sexism and because of biology (menstruation, pregnancy, birth, lactation). Although we always knew that not all women became mothers, feminists ignored other differences among women. Now we acknowledge that groups of women have different experiences related to their ethnicity, their social class, their disability, their age, and so on.

At the time of these feminist stirrings, I began the Role-Innovators' study, later entitled University of Michigan Women's Life Paths Study (UM-WLPS). Included in my study were 200 women drawn from a larger project entitled the Michigan Student Study, or MSS (Gurin, 1971). One-third of the respondents were Role-Innovators (going into male-dominated occupations), one-third were Traditionals (going into female-dominated occupations), and one-third were Moderates (going into occupations having intermediate sex ratios). The women in the study were about to graduate from college, and the data that I used from the MSS questionnaire plus additional data that I collected focused on their occupational aspirations. I was particularly interested in discovering the predictors of nontraditional career choices. This focus was motivated by the desire to challenge then-current negative stereotypes of "career women," constraining assumptions about "appropriate" occupations for women, and sex-role traditions in general. My research was one of several doctoral dissertations and other studies to come out of the Michigan Student Study headed by Gerald Gurin and Theodore Newcomb.

I completed my doctorate in 1969 and followed my husband to North Carolina with our two-month-old son. To keep me from going crazy, my advisers, Patricia Gurin and Joseph Veroff, suggested I apply for a postdoctorate fellowship to do a follow-up study. Funding from the Labor Department came through in 1970, and I began the second wave of data collection. These data, on 150 women from the original sample, were never published by themselves.

In 1981, I was re-energized by the interest of two graduate students, Sharon Rae Jenkins (then at Boston University) and Jan Hitchcock (at Harvard), and Dr. Josephine Ruggiero (of the Sociology Department at Providence College), all of whom had encountered the first two waves in the archives of the Henry A. Murray Center at Radcliffe College. Together we collaborated on developing another questionnaire and finding, contacting, and collecting data from as many of the women as possible. This wave consisted of 117 women. Each of us contributed to the funding of the costs, and each gave a lot of free labor. Funding included dissertation grants to the two students and grants from the Murray Center and Providence College.

The 1981 questionnaire covered in rich detail many aspects of these women's lives, including complete educational and work history, marital and childbirth history, experiences with sex discrimination, mentoring, their satisfaction with various areas of their lives, household composition and division of labor, attitudes toward and participation in the women's movement, and, most important, their continuing aspirations and picture of their future lives.

I was also in a job transition in 1981, going from The Urban Institute to Howard University. I spent part of my first sabbatical on home ground at the University of Michigan, where I met with Abigail Stewart, who was enthusiastic about the idea of launching a fourth wave of the UM-WLPS. The idea of launching a parallel longitudinal study of Howard University alumnae was also born there, and Abby promised to help write the proposal and act as co–principal investigator of the Michigan piece.

I returned to Howard University and asked Martha Mednick and Veronica Thomas to work on the proposal with me. We first got funding from Howard University for pilot studies, so we went through many versions of the questionnaire to adapt the 1981 UM-WLPS questionnaire to this new population. We expanded the questionnaire from one to three parts, adding many new topics that represented the various interests of all of us involved. Eventually, we wrote a proposal to the National Institutes of Mental Health (NIMH) for the two parallel studies (Howard University and University of Michigan). The first submission was turned down. While we waited to hear from NIMH on our revised proposal, I spent six months in New Zealand on a Fulbright Senior Research Fellowship. There I met and worked with Judith Pringle, of the Labour and Management Studies Department, and Julie Park, of the Anthropology Department, both at Auckland University, who became interested in working together on a New Zealand Women's Life Paths Study.

Thus, the Howard University questionnaire was the prototype for the 1991 Women's Life Paths Study for Auckland University and the University of Michigan. Expanding the study and the sample beyond the original sample of mostly White middle-class Americans (who were alumnae of the University of Michigan) enhanced the value of the research immeasurably. As my associates and I have noted elsewhere:

> If we draw conclusions about adult development in women that are based on a single cohort, we would mistake the specifics of their historical experience for generalities; as applicable to women born at any time. If we did the same based on the women in a single culture, we would mistake the specific impact of their culture for generalities applicable to women everywhere. And yet, to know what is common to women of a certain age we have to look across cohorts and across cultures. (Pringle, Park, and Tangri, in preparation.)

To look for generalities across samples meant we had to ask comparable questions. But asking comparable questions created problems. Some of the problems could, in theory at least, be solved. Others could not, and were indeed fundamental epistemological and methodological paradoxes. Pragmatic problems arose as a result of the constraints of working in several sites. The Howard questionnaire was developed before the 1991 Michigan questionnaire because we obtained early funding from Howard University to do the pilot studies. Attempts to then adapt the Howard version of items for the Michigan study sometimes created noncomparability with earlier waves of Michigan data. When this happened, we had to choose between comparability across samples and comparability across waves within a sample; we chose the latter.

Consider in this regard our questions about childhood experiences in one's family. Pilot study participants in the Howard University study were quick to point out how some of the questions from the earlier University of Michigan study did not fit their lives. For instance, the item asking for a description of the family of origin was felt by the African American women to not describe the extended families they grew up in and was expanded to allow fuller descriptions of this history. The item "why did your mother work?" did not make any sense to these women. Everyone did; it was not a matter of choice. Conversely, the importance of the father's ability to work continuously was an issue (Pringle, Park, and Tangri, in preparation; Thomas, Tangri, and Mednick, 1992). Also in response to the discussions in these pilot groups we added items about spirituality and friendship.

More issues arose when we moved the study to distant shores. In the United States we asked both African American and White women the significance to them of the civil rights movement and the women's movement. In New Zealand this question was changed to an open-ended item that yielded comments on the Maori land movement, World War II (New Zealand had sent more men to fight in World War II in proportion to their population than any other country), the Springbok Tour protest (against the New Zealand tour of the South African rugby team in 1981), as well as the women's movement.

Similarly, some of the additions that were created in the New Zealand study were ones that I wished we had included in the American studies. To the Howard University measures of role quality the NZ-WLPS added the role of community member and asked what that community was. When asking New Zealanders what important needs were met in their major relationships, we added "sharing traditions"—an especially important dimension for the non-Pakeha (non-White) women. Unfortunately, these developments took place months after the Howard University questionnaire was printed.

Although some of the issues of comparability might have been solved with more money or a more flexible schedule, some of the issues proved more intractable. To have valid information for the comparisons across groups, we had to make every survey instrument maximally appropriate to each population. Yet questions that suit one group can be ill-fitting for another.

Other questions of comparability concern sampling. Because few women in New Zealand go directly from school to university, and they typically get their first degrees well past adolescence, the sample was defined by age cohort rather than by graduation cohort to create a sample more nearly comparable to that in the United States.

To restrict the study to women of designated graduation years would have distorted the New Zealand sample. Comparison with the U.S. samples, though appearing to be exact, would in fact be spurious. This simple point, namely, that keeping questionnaires, samples, and so on "standardized" in cross-cultural research distorts and masks differences. This problem became crucial as we reflected on our research process, and it was probably the most important learning to result from the project (Pringle, Park, and Tangri, in preparation). To include a reasonable number of educated women from the Maori, Asian, and Pacific island populations, we included not just women who got B.A. degrees but also those who got Teacher and registered nurse certificates.

Other issues arose concerning the research process. Our goal was to make all participants in the studies (including the time-consuming pilot studies) equally motivated and interested. To do so, we had to adjust to cultural context and notice different interactional styles. For peoples with strong oral traditions (the Maori, Island Polynesians, and African Americans), well-founded suspicion of researchers, or inexperience with "intimate questions about painful experiences," the prospects of getting them to complete a lengthy questionnaire by simply leaving it with them was dim. Besides, we wanted their substantive input on improving the questionnaire, not just their answers to the questions. Therefore, we devised a small-group format, in which food and a token of appreciation were provided, that allowed women to complete the questionnaire in the presence of other women participants and the researchers (who could help with any distress experienced). This created a more social, supportive, and reflective occasion. Although we did something similar with the focus groups at Howard University, we did not think of it primarily as an accommodation to cultural styles (although we were aware of this issue) but as a necessary part of piloting the questionnaire and getting the feedback we needed. The meal and "koha" (a gift, in this case of petrol or book tokens) in New Zealand, as well as the refreshments and twenty dollars to the Howard University women, were intended both to express our appreciation and to reduce the perception that researchers are only out to exploit these populations for purposes unrelated to the interests and needs of those they studied. No such gifts were given to the White women in the University of Michigan study.

The Second Dilemma: How Do We Respect Context?

Grappling with issues of comparability made my colleagues and me think about the influences of context. Making comparisons across time and space will always be fraught with epistemological problems. We know that many events have different psychological significance in different cultural contexts, but there are few guidelines for figuring out how to assess different meanings.

The dilemma of contexts has also manifested itself outside of the Women's Life Paths Studies conducted at the University of Michigan, at Howard University, and at Auckland University. In a prize-winning study, my student Askhari Hodari (1994) concluded, as others have, that in studying Black women, one cannot separate the consequences of racism from the consequences of sexism because experientially they are intertwined—just as the identities are intertwined—and because the sexism that Black women experience is different in many ways from the sexism that White women experience. In addition, the racism that Black women experience is different in many ways from the racism that Black men experience. If the things that

Black women would identify as racist sexism and the things they would identify as sexist racism turn out to be the same sorts of things, then the studies of sexism and of racism are inseparable, and they are inseparable for everybody.

Context also renders class a problematic concept in our very heterogeneous society and is too often discussed with race. To paraphrase Hull, Bell-Scott, and Smith (1982), "all the whites are rich and powerful, all the poor are people of color, but some of us are both/neither." My White father supported his family by housepainting until the lead in the paint made him sick; he then supported us by hanging wallpaper. It was demanding physical labor, and he took pride in his skill. I could smell the sweat on him after a day's work.

The standard social scientific measures of class use a combination of how much income one earns, how many years of education one has, and the status of one's occupation. Most analysts think that because counting dollars and years of education constitutes a ratio scale, the resulting numbers have invariant meaning across the board: across ethnic groups, across social contexts of all kinds. Yet we all know that an annual income of $50,000 means different things in a White context than in a Black context. And a moment's reflection is all that is needed to realize that the same occupation may have different status values in different communities. Being a Pullman Porter was a highly regarded accomplishment in many Black communities up to the 1950s; for women, being a schoolteacher has had different status values in the White and Black communities. Class becomes even more complicated if we think in terms of community standing. I remember talking with Dr. Leanor Johnson (who is African American) about our respective fathers' work and their standing in their communities. They were both in manual occupations—skilled trades, they are called. But that occupation was not what defined their status in their respective communities. It was the work they did for their communities, for which they received little or no payment, that was important.

The Third Dilemma: Should We Use Categories at All?

To worry about how to measure variables in different ethnic groups is to presume that different ethnic groups exist. This is like assuming that different genders and even different sexes exist. That we think and perceive in categories does not mean that these mirror a concrete reality or that the categories are immutable. But they do have consequences (see Dilemma Four).

Sex and race are terms for biological categories (which is not to say they are simple), whereas gender and ethnicity are terms for cultural categories.

Gender is a cultural category based as much on patriarchy as on sex. And although many of us would argue that human society would be better off without gender distinctions (or with the distinctions distributed without regard to sex), sex as a biological variable (or set of variables) is unlikely to disappear. Unlike some other living organisms, we humans reproduce sexually. Nevertheless, we may still question whether two categories is an adequate representation of the variation even in this variable. There will be more on this below.

Ethnicity is a category based in part on race and history and is maintained in part by prejudice. Although race could theoretically disappear through interbreeding and ethnicity could disappear through assimilation, most of us would argue that the human race is better off because of the diversity of races and ethnicities it exhibits.

To those who worry that the category "women" will dissolve in a mass of subcategories (by race, ethnicity, age, class, and so on), we have only to notice that calling attention to gender did not make the category "human" disappear. Introducing Psychology of Women (POW) did not render general psychology meaningless; it made it more precise. Introducing and accounting for the varieties of women's experiences does not leave the Psychology of Women meaningless, only more precise. This increasing particularity does not diminish the usefulness of thinking about women as women; nor does it diminish the authority with which we can make political claims for and about women. Instead, those claims will be more targeted and more precise because of this particularity.

And suppose the cultural categories were redistributed without regard to the biological categories, which are not all that clear-cut anyway (Marks, 1995; Molnar, 1991). Suppose gender were redistributed without regard to sex, and ethnicity without regard to race.

In the *Washington Post* (January 30, 1994) I read about David Henry Hwang, author of *M. Butterfly* and director of the movie *Golden Gate*. Mr. Hwang was asked how he would feel "if the racial differences that have given him so much material to play with were wiped out in a couple of centuries by a surge in miscegenation." He replied,

> I know there are a lot of people who feel that there would be something lost in ... the distinctions that human beings feel they need to make. It just seems to me that they should be based on something a little more interesting than skin color and facial features. And so if we all look vaguely alike and we form different cultures and different divisions based on something that's a little less arbitrary, I think that's probably a good thing. (Playwrite, 1994)

Maybe Mr. Hwang is onto something. Maybe we could all become a new version of Anzaldua's (1987) "new Mestiza." John Buggs, my former boss at the U.S. Civil Rights Commission and the first African American to be executive director of that agency, believed that race hatred would end only when race was obliterated by sufficient intermarriage. For a feminist vision of a utopia in which ethnicity is only distantly related to race and gender only distantly related to sex, read *The Fifth Sacred Thing* by Starhawk (1993). For a real-world example of gender divorced from sex, consider the use of "butch" and "femme" concepts among lesbians. For an example of ethnicity divorced from race, consider that there are Jews of many races.

My first lecture on gender usually begins with this question to the students: "How many sexes are there?" Eventually, they come to understand that the answer to many of my questions, including this one, is "it depends." It depends on how you define sex (chromosomes? gonads? genitals? hormones?) or race (skin color? eyelids? blood type? height?). Are these constructs (race, sex) essentialist? We can use them that way, if it is useful to do so. Sometimes it is, as when we want to talk about women's health and what a national health plan must include to give women what they need. This does not mean that all women's health statuses or needs are the same, unaffected by other statuses such as poverty, conditions of employment, and so on. It does mean that in some arenas biological sex (an essentialist category) is a useful variable and explains a lot of variance. And sometimes this is not because of how women are treated as a social category. That many women have babies, that only women get pregnant, and that only those who have babies know what it feels like gives us something important to say about the health care needs of mothers.

The same can be said for race. As an essentialist category it is useful in identifying which persons could most benefit from Tay-Sachs or sickle-cell screening (Jews and African Americans respectively) and which persons should be careful of how much cow's milk they give their children (most peoples other than Anglo-Saxons).

The problem, I believe, is not that we have categories but that there are too few categories (certainly for gender) and they carry different value and power (for race and gender). The competition for value and power sets up the next dilemma.

The Fourth Dilemma: How Can Groups Love Themselves Without Hating Others?

We have all had occasion to notice a tendency among some people to see themselves as part of one tribe and to dislike people who belong to other tribes. Sex and race as well as gender and ethnicity are easy to notice and thus, perhaps, easy to use as dividers. As someone who does not favor total ethnic assimilation, the puzzle for me is how to honor one's own group without dishonoring other groups.

You have only to read the daily papers to see how fiercely people can cling to their own ethnicity and how deeply they can react against other ethnicities. The same day that the *Washington Post* carried the article about Mr. Hwang, it carried pieces about ethnic slaughter or conflict going on in Armenia, Bosnia (between Croats, Muslims, and Serbs), the Congo (between Laris, Niboleks, and Aubevillois), southern Mexico (between Mayans and government troops), Somalia, and South Africa (between Afrikaners and Zulus on the one hand and other South Africans on the other). These examples are not exhaustive. No mention was made that day, although it might have been, of the genocide of Hutus by Tutsis in Rwanda. Nor was there any talk in the *Washington Post* that day, though there might have been, of swastikas painted on synagogues in Germany, of the resurgence of that deep ethnic hatred that has dominated so much of Europe's and America's experience of the twentieth century. I refer to anti-Semitism. Certainly, anti-Semitism has been a major force in the lives of many Jews throughout the world, and without a doubt it played a role in making me the person and the scholar I am.

As a child, I knew that being Jewish meant being different. California of the 1940s and 1950s was not a land of unbounded tolerance racially or politically (see Chernin, 1983). But my parents were able to make that difference, my working-class Jewish identity, a source of pride. From the age of nine or ten until I finished high school, I went to a Jewish school three afternoons a week after regular school to learn to read, write, and speak Yiddish better. (Yiddish had been my first language but suffered the indignity of disuse after I entered public school because my parents wanted to be sure I was competent in English.) I also began an acquaintance with Yiddish literature, learned a little Hebrew, and learned a lot of history. Associated with this school was a children's chorus, drama class/theater company, and modern dance classes. That's where I learned to read music, learned what the Stanislavsky method of acting means, learned what a plié is, and learned how and why we do these things. Standards were high. Teachers were professionals, credentialed by higher-level professionals. There was a lot to learn. I didn't learn all of it very well, but the important material stuck, especially the self-respect. This is not every Jewish kid's experience, but I recommend it highly to any child from a minority culture.

The husband of a cousin told me that his parents had given him the same choice I'd been given when I found I couldn't do everything I was supposed to: I could drop Jewish School, or I could drop piano lessons. I dropped the piano lessons, he dropped Jewish School. He wishes now he'd dropped the piano instead. But he wanted to fit in. He lived in a community where he was the only Jewish kid and the only "progressive" on the block, maybe in the school. It was hard.

I don't take credit for making a hard choice. My parents made sure that I wasn't the "only" anything. They created a community of like-minded families around us. Together they supported the school, the drama, dance, and chorus. They clearly understood that "it takes a whole village to raise a child" (African folk saying). In truth, although I loved Jewish school, I think I chose what I thought would make my parents happier.

If I took for granted my family's ability to instill ethnic pride when I was young, I have recently wondered at their gift for being clearly proud about our own tradition while simultaneously honoring others. In 1993 my late father turned ninety, and my brother and I gave him a big party. To my father's party came my ex-husband, who is from India and who wanted very much to help honor Dad. Shanti Tangri captured an important quality of what being Jewish meant to Dad.

[He] has shown that to love, honor and cherish your own is not to despise others. He has loved his family, his community, his country, his world, his heritage, his beloved language Yiddish and Jewish culture. He nurtured all of them, worked hard and honestly for them and fought for them. His respect and appreciation for other cultures and peoples is an extension of his love for his own. Diversity, to him, has meant richness, not divisiveness, inclusion not exclusion. All around the world, at this time, there are perhaps 150 major ethnic, religious, linguistic or nationalistic conflicts that are tearing people apart in every continent. If they would only listen to Chaim Schwartz! (Tangri, 1993)

Shanti's view of my father mirrored my own. At the nintieth birthday party, I too spoke. Here is what I said about the kind of a father he was to me.

I got more than love from my father. I got my most important values and the basis for my politics from him. I got my sense of place, of belonging to an historic stream of thinkers and "tooers" [activists], and the confidence to be my own person, from him. . . . His passionate commitment to the idea of social justice planted in me the seeds of my feminism. His unquenchable interest in the social world and how it works is reflected in my decision to study Social Psychology. His incurable optimism that we human beings can shape and improve the world we live in contribute to my choice of social problems to study. He was, among other things, a teacher—and so am I. He has passed on to me, and to my son Neil, our love of Yiddish. And perhaps what is most valuable to me is his deep understanding that it's OK to be different: To be a Lefty when the country veers right (even when it meant possible deportation by the House UnAmerican Activities Committee); to be proud of one's own, minority culture when everyone else wants you to assimilate.

So, how am I as a Jew and an offspring of Chaim Schwartz, to understand statements by a professor at Howard University and some other African American intellectuals in which they expressed that although they condemn the anti-Semitism and other prejudices expressed by some students at Howard (including a Law School student and the university's student president), they do not condemn the speaker? I do not for a minute believe that the faculty, administration, or student body at my university are more anti-Semitic than any comparable White institution. But from people at Howard University, I expect more, not less, vigilance against racism, more vigorous defense of minority groups' rights, and greater sensitivity to feelings about racial aspersions. These expectations may be unrealistic, but I was hurt and angry that the then president of the university and other faculty and students responded to these exhibitions of hate so late with so little. I told a colleague at Howard University that I believe there would have been large, public protests by students and faculty if a racist speaker had made comparable speeches about African Americans at Brandeis University. He thought I was perhaps right but that that would be expecting too much in the way of political consciousness at Howard University.

Why should that be? What, if anything, does that imply about our Afrocentric curriculum? And what does it say about teaching tolerance and global responsibility in times of scarcity? How can we teach our students and ourselves to think constructively about difference and conflict? How can we, in the competition for a place in the sun that real and artificial scarcity promotes, allow ourselves to be the pawns in a divide-and-conquer game? This applies as much to Jewish racism as to Black anti-Semitism.

For me, but not for all Jews, tolerance has been part and parcel of being Jewish. As a child I didn't recognize the difference between being Jewish and being progressive. It just made sense. I assumed that any people who had themselves suffered from such long-standing and recently horrific oppression, would be opposed to the oppression of others. Of course, I know now that it doesn't always work out that way. And being at Howard University has exposed me to both Black anti-Semitism/anti-White feelings and what I would call progressive Black pride. I hate the anti-Semitism and savor the Black pride. I feel that because I am well grounded in my own ethnic identity, and grew up in a multiethnic neighborhood, I can appreciate and enjoy most cultural expressions of other ethnic groups.

This is one part of the answer to the question of how to separate racial and ethnic pride from bigotry and prejudice. Another part is reducing ignorance. It is necessary but not sufficient to have a generally open and accepting attitude toward individuals who are different from ourselves. We have a lot to learn from each other about what those differences are and how they play out in various arenas, from the personal to the professional to the political. I learn a lot about Afrocentric perspectives from my students. I get pretty angry with certain kinds of ignorance: One colleague at the Commission on Civil Rights thought there wasn't any Yiddish literature because "Yiddish isn't a written language." Another acquaintance countered my sorrow at the loss of Yiddish speakers from the world (from as-similation as well as genocide) by arguing that many Yiddish words will survive by being incorporated into English (such as "nosh," "bagel," and "yenta."). This, I told her, does not a living language make. "So," she said, "it'll be a dead classical language, like Greek and Latin[!]."

The Fifth Dilemma:
How Do I Wish to Be Appreciated?

Given that my interest in the Women's Life Paths Studies and my interest in teaching at a historically Black college come from my own background, it is almost predetermined that some professional encounters will touch me very personally. Mostly, the work gives me joy and deep satisfaction. Sometimes, the work makes me feel awkward.

I find myself caught in a similar bind in both the Howard University and the New Zealand portions of the Women's Life Paths Studies. If I had not initiated the research it would not have been done. Everyone I work with in both places thinks it is useful work. Yet my role is seen by some people in both places as anomalous, and perhaps somewhat resented. I am sometimes given clues that my White/American identity is experienced by Black/New Zealand colleagues as a reminder of "imperialist" research.

In this role, I carry both too much and too little weight. I feel that I carry too much weight because the prototype questionnaire appeared to some colleagues as more fixed than I intended it to be. Although elaborate steps were taken to adapt it to the different research populations, it may be that more changes, additions, or deletions should have been made that were not. I also feel that I carry too little weight because the issue of preserving comparability across subject populations is one that I carried more than anyone else.

All of these issues can be seen as purely methodological, but they also af-fect the interpersonal dynamics of collaboration. Although I was aware, on and off, of this dilemma as we worked, I did not realize the full impact until my colleagues in New Zealand and at Howard University wrote their own versions of our process. These accounts made me feel like more of an out-sider than I had thought I was.

The same uncomfortable feeling of being misunderstood visits me some-times in my work at Howard. Back in the 1970s I wrote a paper for a Southeastern Psychological Association panel on multiple group member-ship that addressed the question of why Black women were less involved in the women's movement than White women. Although I know I am not the source of the ideas, I hear echoes of the ideas in that paper in some of what Black women are writing today. Yet I know that what some students hear when I talk about racism and sexism are colored by my own whiteness. Sometimes it means they cannot "hear" what I say, and sometimes it means that what they "hear" is different from what I mean.

Interethnic contacts, especially on work teams studying ethnicity, can prove disturbing in a number of ways. Old ideas are jostled, and deeply held, usually unarticulated, preconceptions surface. And personal feelings can be hurt.

Perhaps the visible dangers of interethnic collaborations are one reason why they are not more common in academia. It is with the hope that my own narrative may prove helpful to those who study ethnicity, whether or not they work in teams of mixed ethnicity, that I have revealed so much of my thoughts and feelings. I also expect these to change over time, with more experience.

Ultimately, there is nothing unique about my own constellation of being female; Jewish; upwardly mobile from a working-class background; first generation born in this country; and of a cohort shaped by the exodus from Europe, the Holocaust, leftist politics, and feminism. But the constellation does help explain my predilection for working on social justice issues, for working in ways and places that take me across boundaries and into anomalous situations. Perhaps anomalies are the stuff of learning.

References

Anzaldua, G. (1987). *Borderlands/La Frontera. The new Mestiza*. San Francisco, CA: Aunt Lute Books.

Chernin, K. (1983). *In my mother's house*. New York, NY: Ticknor and Fields.

Gurin, G. (1971, August). *A study of students in a multiversity*. Final report (Office of Education Contract No. OE-6-10-034). University of Michigan.

Hodari, A. (1994, August). Black women's affective reactions to racism and sexism. Paper presented at the American Psychological Association meeting, Los Angeles, CA.

Hull, G., Bell-Scott, P., and Smith, B. (1982). *All the women are White, all the Blacks are men, but some of us are brave: Black women's studies*. Old Westbury, NY: Feminist Press.

Marks, J. (1995). *Human biodiversity: Genes, race, and history*. Hawthorne, NY: Aldine de Gruyter.

Molnar, S. (1991). *Human variation: Races, types, and ethnic groups*. Englewood Cliffs, NJ: Prentice-Hall.

Playwrite. (1994, January 30). *Washington Post* (p. A20).

Pringle, J., Park, J., and Tangri, S. S. (in preparation). *The New Zealand women's life paths study* (working title).

Starhawk. (1993). *The fifth sacred thing*. New York, NY: Bantam Books.

Tangri, S. S. (1993). Remarks given at Chaim Schwartz's 90th birthday celebration. Los Angeles, CA.

Thomas, V. G., Tangri, S. S., and Mednick, M. T. (1992, August). Theoretical and methodological considerations in studying the lives of African American women. In D. Schuster, *Women's lives through time*. Symposium conducted at the meeting of the American Psychological Association, Washington, DC.

9

The Moral Self, Values, and Circles of Belonging

Mary M. Brabeck

For the most of us, if we do not talk of ourselves, or at any rate of the individual circles of which we are the centers, we can talk of nothing.
—Anthony Trollope, Framley Parsonage, *chapter 10*

I have been thinking recently about the image of circles as a metaphor for self and how that self relates to one's community, ethnic, gender, or cultural group. I have also been thinking about my work in Guatemala and how I, as a White middle-class American woman, have held ethnocentric assumptions about the self that have been close to what Trollope described. The Guatemalans with whom I have worked, and especially the Maya, have given me a vantage point to critique those assumptions. Thinking about different conceptions of the moral self, I have come to ponder variations in the social construction of personhood as more or less communal and relational.

I take it as axiomatic that people differ in the degree to which they are relational. Some people are highly relational: They construct the self as embedded in and indistinguishable from social relations. Relational people may be more or less affiliative. That is, they may seek the company of others often or seldom. But whether or not they are affiliative, relational people would view the circles of Anthony Trollope as nonsensical, because for them, center and periphery are one in the same. When someone is relational, the self does not exist apart from relationships. Furthermore, for relational people, moral issues arise when relationships are threatened. Moral philosophers (e.g., Noddings, 1984) and psychologists (e.g., Gilligan, 1982) argue that relational people are more likely to invoke the ethic of care to resolve moral issues (e.g., my care of self versus the need to care for you). In contrast, for the more individualistic person, whether high or low on the need for affiliation, the self is thought to be separate and separable from other, and the separate circumscribed moral self is described as principled, objective, rational, and universal. For these individuals, moral questions arise when there are conflicting claims to individual rights. Moral philosophers (e.g., Rawls, 1971) and psychologists (e.g., Kohlberg, 1969) have argued that the universal principle of justice is invoked to resolve such moral conflicts (e.g., my right to privacy versus your right to know).

The recognition that certain people are more relational than others leads to the question of whether certain categories of people are more relational than other categories of people. Is, for example, one gender more relational than the other? Or are some national or ethnic groups more relational than other national or ethnic groups?

In the first section of this chapter I look at how some feminists (Chodorow, 1978; Gilligan, 1982), especially Carol Gilligan, believe that women are more relational than men. These theorists claim that because of their greater concern with relationships, women are guided in their moral judgments by the ethic of care; men are guided by the principle of justice. They argue that differences in moral orientation (care ethic versus justice ethic) reflect differences in one's self (relational self versus individualistic self). However, the evidence, as I note, does not support their claim to gender differences in moral orientation.

After dismissing the idea of gender difference in moral self and moral orientation, I turn to recent psychological theories that have challenged the ethnocentric views of self as individualistic and autonomous and posited "Difference theories" of self and moral values attributable to different national groups. I then describe my own research with Guatemalan youths who are primarily Maya. The young men with whom I have worked, I argue, have a concept of moral self that, contrary to Gilligan's predictions about males, is more communal and relational than that of American youth. I present in some detail the evidence that led me to that conclusion. Finally, I confront the haunting question of the potential danger of error in my own work with Guatemalan youth. My inquiry into the validity of Gilligan's views of differences between women and men was motivated by a concern that such a dichotomy is harmful to women. In the last section of this chapter, I ask if my portrait of the Guatemalan Maya youth might also be detrimental, even if well intended. I reflect on how my role as outsider led me to a confrontation of the limits of my own circle of bounded assumptions.

"Difference" Feminism: The Historical View

In the nineteenth century, beliefs about different male and female selves and accompanying differences in moral orientations served as the basis for assigning males and females to separate spheres (Benderly, 1987). According to separate-spheres arguments, the public domain of work, achievement, and self-assertion, built on a notion of self as independent and autonomous, was deemed the male sphere, and the private domain of home, care, harmony, and relationships was deemed the female sphere. The theory of separate spheres was supported by the view of (White) women as "good mothers," known as the "Cult of True Womanhood" (Benderly, 1987; Scott, 1988). Women were defined as fit by nature for the separate sphere of home. There she was to be "tender, loving, pure, and inspiring in her home . . . to raise the moral tone of every household, to refine every man . . . to mitigate the harshness and cruelty and vulgarity of life everywhere" (an antisuffragist, 1908, quoted in Marshall, 1984, p. 570). "Good mothers" were to be a corrective to society (which was masculine) (Benderly, 1987; Scott, 1988), but they were to do so from the separate sphere of the home. Psychological (e.g., Sigmund Freud) and sociological (e.g., Talcott Parsons) theories, which asserted that there were essential and fundamental differences between males and females, bolstered the assignment of men and women to these different spheres.

The consequences of women being defined in this way have been described by a number of writers. For example, women's special traits have been used to deny them education (Deem, 1980) and to justify poor pay. Supposed gender differences have "explained" job segregation (Kahn and Yoder, 1989) and, more recently, accounted for the "mommy track" (Schwartz, 1989).

To reduce the likelihood that claims of difference could be used against women, feminist researchers (e.g., Hyde and Linn, 1986; Maccoby and Jacklin, 1974) have attempted to show that gender differences in personality and abilities are small, if they exist at all, and that they are attributable to differences in socialization and amenable to change. During the 1970s, the feminist goal of achieving political, economic, and educational equality was supported by refutations of essential gender differences and the burgeoning androgyny literature. Androgyny theorists (e.g., Heilbrun, 1985) claimed that society could get rid of the "macho–sex kitten dichotomy, the inevitable quarterback-cheerleader assignment of life's roles" (Heilbrun, 1985, p. 256) by doing away with separate gender roles completely and adopting the concept of androgyny. Buttressed by reports that the spheres of men and women were largely overlapping, that is, there were few clear differences in male and female traits (e.g., Maccoby and Jacklin, 1974), androgyny theorists suggested that women and men could be equally assertive, competitive, analytic, dominant, ambitious, and aggressive.

The corrective contained its own problems. By the end of the 1970s, feminist writers (Morawski, 1985) pointed out that androgyny theories maintained an androcentric view of the superior qualities of males by suggesting that these qualities could, and should be, adopted by women. Feminists questioned the validity of these "masculine" models, which failed to affirm the value of the feminine virtues. They argued that it is no advance for women to rush to be born again in the masculine norm, when that norm is fundamentally flawed (Miller, 1976; Morawski, 1985). They pointed to the inadequacy of the masculine, competitive, aggressive, autonomous model and sought a new norm that celebrated the alternative, feminine virtues (Ruddick, 1985).

In the postandrogyny period, the work of Carol Gilligan (1982) gained special prominence. Gilligan claims that the experiences of inequality and subordination, which circumscribe the lives of women, also give rise to a moral self grounded in human connections and characterized by concerns with relationship (Gilligan and Wiggins, 1988). Emphasizing the differences between men and women and boys and girls, Gilligan and her intellectual predecessors (Chodorow, 1978; Miller, 1976) and contemporaries (Noddings, 1984) celebrate that which they see as the essential "feminine" self and the feminine values associated with what they characterize as "the feminine voice." The "feminine voice," claims Gilligan, "emerges with great clarity, defining the self and proclaiming its worth on the basis of the ability to care for and protect others" (Gilligan, 1982, p. 79). This different moral voice develops because women "define their identity through relationships of intimacy and care" (Gilligan, 1982, p. 164.) In contrast, Gilligan argues, the masculine voice is concerned with abstract rules of justice. The male "I" is defined in separation (1982, p. 161). Gilligan writes, "Instead of attachment, individual achievement rivals the male imagination and great ideas or distinctive activity defines the standard of self-assessment and success" (1982, p. 163).

Gilligan's proposal that girls and women are relational resonates with national preconceptions about gender differences. American middle-class girls and women are expected to be more nurturing, more empathic, and more altruistic than boys and men (Shigetomi, Harmann, and Gelfand, 1981); furthermore, girls and women expect this of themselves (Eisenberg, Fabes, and Shea, 1989; Miller, 1976). Girls and women are more frequently sought for emotional support from both males and females and have a reputation among teachers, peers, and parents for being more helpful and empathic even though it is not clear that they are in fact so. Moreover, males expect females to make moral decisions from a more emotional perspective, while seeing male morality as based on law and order reasoning (Brabeck, 1989).

Evidence for Gender Differences in Moral Self

Do preconceptions about U.S. gender differences and Gilligan's conceptualizations accord with systematic evidence? It seems not. As I (Brabeck, 1983) and others (Greeno and Maccoby, 1986) have observed, Gilligan's characterizations are not substantiated by the data she collected and presented in her popular book *In a Different Voice*. Moreover, other researchers (Jadeck, Hyde, Moore, and Keller, 1995; Thoma, 1986; Walker, 1984, 1989; Walker, deVries, and Trevethan, 1987) have not been able to detect, even after much effort, systematic differences in how males and females reason about interpersonal or moral dilemmas. In studies using the Kohlbergian moral reasoning interview, males and females at equal age and educational levels have been shown to be equally able to resolve moral dilemmas by appealing to justice principles (Bebeau and Brabeck, 1987; Walker, 1984, 1989). Similar results have been obtained with the Defining Issues Test (DIT), the most frequently used objective test of comprehension of and preference for moral issues (Thoma, 1986). Failure to find reliable gender differences in the empirical literature on principled justice reasoning cannot be attributed to insensitive measures. The same measures that show gender similarities reveal differences resulting, for example, from education. Longitudinal work (Colby, Kohlberg, Gibbs, and Lieberman, 1983) has shown that women at the same educational level are as likely as men to advance in the sequential order of development predicted from Kohlberg's theory. Indeed, in cross-sectional studies, education is 250 times more powerful in predicting moral judgment level than gender (Thoma, 1986). The evidence for the claim that males, compared with females, are more principled in their reasoning, more concerned with conflicting rights, and more capable of justice reasoning can be summed up succinctly: The evidence does not support the assertion.

However, Gilligan makes a second assertion. She claims that women and girls are more relational and thus more likely to invoke a care ethic than men and boys. Gilligan's work to describe the ethic of care has made a contribution to moral development theory: It has drawn attention to beneficence as well as justice criteria for moral perspectives. However, the evidence to support or refute her assertion that the ethic of care characterizes female morality is problematic. In part, this is because there are so many different ways that care, as a psychological construct, is measured (Brabeck, 1989). Furthermore, in much of Gilligan's writing only girls' voices are presented and gender differences cannot be tested. Given these shortcomings, the available literature (e.g., Jadeck, Hyde, Moore, and Keller, 1995; Walker, deVries, and Trevethan, 1987) suggests that the majority of people, both males and females, can and do use both care and justice orientations. Some studies (Jadeck et al., 1995; Walker, deVries, and Trevethan, 1987) refute Gilligan's claims that girls and women are focused on care and concern for relationships. Other studies, especially those conducted by Gilligan and her colleagues (e.g., Gilligan and Attanucci, 1988) report that females tend to focus on the care orientation and males on the justice orientation, particularly in self-identified moral dilemmas. It appears that the topic of concern (e.g., an issue about a friendship, care for child), and not the gender of the person, is associated with care reasoning (Walker, deVries, and Trevethan, 1987). Thus, regardless of one's gender, if one is discussing a moral dilemma involving interpersonal dilemmas, one invokes an ethic of care. If the dilemma involves conflicting rights, one invokes justice reasoning. This has led me (Brabeck and Weisgerber, 1988; Bebeau and Brabeck, 1987) to argue that girls are socialized to attend more to interpersonal issues than males. Thus it is not moral orientation, moral reasoning, or moral self that differentiates men and women, but socialization to attend to some aspects of situations as more salient.

In sum, it is undoubtedly true that some people are more relational than others. But to the extent that we are interested in empirical data rather than provocative metaphors (Crawford and Gentry, 1989), we must refuse to go along with the gender-difference feminists. It seems to me that the enormous popularity of Carol Gilligan's work comes in part from its resonance with persistent, albeit subtle, sexism, reminiscent of the "good mother" theories of the past (Crosby, 1991, makes a similar point). The celebration of what we have historically associated with women but devalued is affirming to women and accounts in part for the positive response her theory has received among women. However, I want to suggest here that the relational focus that Gilligan describes as "feminine" and the view of self her theory reflects resonate with us because they address our discomfort with our contemporary cultural ethos, at least as it is experienced by White middle-class liberal America (Bellah, Madsen, Sullivan, Swidler, and Tipton, 1985).

The Ethic of Care
Situated in the Contemporary U.S. Context

The popularity of Gilligan's ideas (Hurd and Brabeck, in press) may be connected with a recent and growing sense of unease with the American ideal of individualism and separation. As Jean Bethke Elshtain (1986) suggests, ecofeminism and other forms of the difference feminisms illuminate "the possibility that liberal principles alone cannot sustain liberal democracy; that, in fact, our way of life ongoingly depends and has depended upon the survival of ties of community and obligation unacknowledged, even suspect, within the dominant ideology" (p. 58).

Feminists are not alone in noting the limits of American individualism. The influential book *Habits of the Heart* (Bellah et al., 1985) sounded the alarm that our stated concerns with individual right and liberties may be in the service of more selfish aims than we have cared to admit. U.S. citizens are increasingly expressing a longing for a sense of community, the need to join with others, to see one's self as part of a larger whole. This longing is joined by an equally strong impulse toward isolation and individualization. These tensions are detectable in the recent U.S. debates on affirmative action and on national health care. In these debates we see the clash of concerns for the common good, based on our recognition of our connections to others, and an equally strong stance that is self-protective and based on individual self-interest.

We are a society hungering for kindness and relationships and we are a community facing extraordinary needs for care: care for children, the homeless, the growing numbers of elderly, the victims of AIDS. We are also a society that has been reluctant to pay for this caregiving or to give up any individual rights to serve the common good. It is disturbing to think that there are those who will attribute to women's caring, relational self the answer to these tensions. However, the data require us to acknowledge that the typical American female is not less principled or less rational in her moral reasoning than her male counterpart. Her moral self is not characterized by a care orientation to a greater degree than the typical American male. To me this is good news because it spreads the responsibility of caring for others, and the responsibility to work toward social justice and equal rights, equally among men and women. Furthermore, it focuses attention on both care *and* justice aspects of the complex societal problems that confront us in the United States.

Cultural Differences:
Another Historical Perspective

Reflections on and critiques of our contemporary cultural ethos are also found in discussions about the nature of the person that are occurring within the field of psychology (Lykes, 1985; Sampson, 1977, 1985). In 1977, Edward Sampson argued that the American notion of the individualistic, self-contained person is stifling our ability to solve pressing social problems. More recently he boldly asserted: "Quite simply, understanding the individual qua individual is no longer relevant to understanding human life" (Sampson, 1989, p. 916).

Sampson (1988) described two conceptions of self. The first, which he labels "ensembled individualism," is characteristic of premodern understandings of self and develops out of societies with strong communal ties. Ensembled individualism is defined by fluid self-other boundaries, a sense of control that includes but goes beyond the individual, and a conception of other persons as included within one's notion of self. A second self is called "self-contained individualism." It is characterized by firm self-other boundaries, a sense of personal control, and a conception of self that excludes other people. Similar ideas were articulated by Wheeler, Reis, and Bond (1989), who distinguished between notions of self that they called "collectivism" on the one hand and "individualism" on the other. Similar distinctions have been drawn by Lykes (1985) in her study of "social individuality" and "autonomous individualism"; by Triandis (1989) in his discussion of public, private, and collective selves; and by Shweder (1991; Shweder and Bourne, 1984) in his analysis of "sociocentric" selves versus "egocentric" selves. Gilligan's work raised the possibility of a different moral self. Cross-cultural researchers suggest that the self is better described as collective or communal rather than individualistic. It is not clear how Gilligan's relational self is similar or different from a communal self. However, both challenge the notion of universality of an individualistic, autonomous self.

Psychologists have attempted to trace the origins and the developments of different views of self. Sampson (1989) placed the beginnings of our contemporary self-contained individualism in the fifteenth century, although "individualism" is a nineteenth-century word. Prior to that time, said Sampson, persons were understood as intrinsically and unalterably embedded in culture, and meanings of self, relationships, and values were derived within this context. Over the past three centuries, we have shifted from a notion of persons as molded within the particular experience of their culture to a notion of individuals who possess, as MacIntyre (1988) described it, "their identity and their essential human capacities apart from and prior to their membership in any particular social and political order" (p. 210). As individuals became detached from their communities, more affluent and mobile (Triandis, 1989), they were free to establish their own identities and rendered communities as derivative of the individual. In modern times community has come to be defined by the needs and the desires of the individual; the person is not created through his or her attachments within the community. Thus, the individual came to be seen, as Trollope described, as "individual circles of which we are the center."

Lykes (1989) located the origin of autonomous and social individualism in one's social reality, which includes conditions of power or powerlessness. Lykes's (1985, 1989) analysis of conceptions of self among "pink-collar" workers and Guatemalan women living in exile in Mexico demonstrates the critical roles that power status and material conditions exert over one's sense of self as social and individual. Luttrell's (1989) analysis of U.S. working-class Black and White "women's ways of knowing" also reveals distinctions in sense of self and ways of making meaning that are affected by ethnicity and class as well as by gender. In a similar vein, Toinette Eugene (1989) described how material reality (one's economic, social, and power status and one's cultural history) affects one's sense of self and gives rise to womanist ethic of liberational care found among Black women. Further equating ethic of care with powerlessness, Puka (1989) related Gilligan's ethic to women's subordinate positions and described care as a defensive response to sexism (Puka, 1989). These researchers view status, not gender, as the basis for development of moral self and associated ethical perspectives.

Cross-cultural theorists and researchers have, like Gilligan, associated different values with these different conceptions of self (Schwartz and Bilsky, 1990). For example, Triandis (1989) associated a collective self with the values of conservatism, hierarchy, harmony, and cooperation. In contrast, he claimed, individualistic selves are associated with autonomy, mastery, equality, and competition. Schwartz and Bilsky (1990) identified the interests that values serve (individual versus collective), the goal type (terminal versus instrumental), and goal motivation, which, they argued, distinguish different cultures or different sociohistorical contexts.

Values and Moral Self Among Guatemala Maya Youth

The idea that moral self and values are related to the sociohistorical context within which a person lives is supported also in my research (Brabeck, 1993). My own work has focused on values and conceptions of self. The particular question that guided my work when I began it was: What values are associated with psychological resiliency? My examination of the values of Guatemalan youth is guided by Ignacio Martín-Baró's (1988) concern about the effects of unjust systems on the development of the values of youth. This work addresses the question, What values help sustain and support individuals who have experienced the terrors of disappearances, extrajudicial deaths, massacres of loved ones, and the daily fear that any of these horrors may occur? I began with a question about values and psychological resilience, but a different question developed in the course of my work, which I will address at the end of this chapter. That is, what does stepping into the circle of another culture reveal about our Western notions of self?

Over the course of four years, I worked intermittently (usually one month at a time, although one stay was for four months) teaching English in a school for boys in Guatemala. This religiously affiliated school, run by North American priests, enrolled young men who were economically deprived and primarily Maya. These young men were between the ages of thirteen and twenty-one. Although the school was equivalent to a U.S. high school, the age range was large because the ongoing civil war, poverty, and lack of educational resources had disrupted schooling for many of these young men.

State-Sponsored Violence in Guatemala

It is estimated that between 1980 and 1984, the time referred to as "the violence," between 50,000 and 100,000 Guatemalans were victims of extrajudicial killings, reducing the population to 8 million people. Many of these persons were "disappeared"—forcibly taken from their homes, tortured, murdered, and left on the public highway to terrorize others into submission. In a country the size of Ohio, over 400 rural villages have been destroyed, and over 1 million people have been displaced and forced to leave their homes and villages (Lykes, 1989). Approximately 100,000 children have lost one or both parents. The vast majority of deaths and disappearances have been visited on the indigenous Maya, who make up approximately 60 percent of the population of Guatemala. Although the Maya are numerically a majority, their health, education, social, and economic statuses mark them as a subordinate group. Eighty-three percent (N = 34) of the students I interviewed are Maya. Seventeen percent (N = 7) were Ladino. Most fathers of these students work as campesinos (63 percent) on their own small farms, called milpas, or on fincas, which are larger farms, where the minimum wage is currently (during this election year) 10 quetzales (a little over $1.00 a day). The majority (76 percent) of the boys' mothers maintained traditional roles as homemakers, although many worked in the fincas during times of economic necessity. Families in this study were, with difficulty, supporting the education of the boys, or at least one boy, but many noted that their family could not afford to send girls to school.

The students responded to the question, "Have you ever been present in a violent situation?" The forty-one students had all been exposed, directly or indirectly, to the violence in Guatemala. Many relatives of these forty-one boys had been disappeared and/or murdered: 4 fathers, 5 aunts and uncles, 2 brothers, 1 godfather, 1 brother-in-law, and 5 cousins. Three boys had witnessed massacres; 4 spoke of open conflict in their town between guerrillas and the army; 8 noted the mutilated and/or dead bodies they had seen. Seventeen boys in this study mentioned that they knew individuals or had family members who were widows and orphans. Two boys had witnessed separate murders that resulted from fights between drunken friends; 3 described the fights between parents and physical abuse that occur when their fathers drink too much.

Every one of the forty-one students whom I interviewed had heard stories of torture and disappearances, some through the newspapers, many through talk with relatives and friends. One student described a friend who was in the military and had told him of the massacres and murders that the friend had witnessed. Ignacio Martín Baró (1988) has made the important point that state-sponsored violence affects all members within the state, regardless of whether they are direct victims of violence. However, many students had rarely talked about their own experiences of violence. At the close of the interview, after the tape recorder was shut off, I answered questions about the study. Seven students volunteered that this was the first time that they had talked about their experiences of and feelings about violence. Elizabeth Lira, a Chilean psychologist who works with survivors of torture, has suggested that talking about the violence, telling one's story, is an important aspect of the therapeutic process. Silencing, which is imposed from within because of fear of reprisals or from others because they do not know the importance of encouraging such communication—or because they, too, are afraid to talk about it—revictimizes the person because it does not allow reality testing.

Empirical Examination of Values and Moral Self

Even though I took pains to translate and back-translate the measure, and to use an interview developed with Guatemalan children and youth in mind (Becker, Morales, and Aguilar, 1994), the difficulty of finding culturally appropriate measures cannot be overemphasized. Therefore, my method was to use multiple measures (interviews, drawings, open-ended questions, and objective instruments). In a sense, I tried to take many "pictures" of the students and to look for patterns and themes.

One of the measures I used in my study is the Kinetic Family Drawing, which consists of instructions to "Draw everyone in your family, including yourself, doing something." It is followed by a series of questions. One of the questions in which I was most interested was, "What are the desires, hopes of your family?" Initially I began by asking the students, as per directions, to point to each member of the family and describe the individual's hopes and desires. The Maya students, whose ancient and contemporary culture emphasizes community and connection among all living creatures (Burgos-Debray, 1983), pointed obediently to each person and repeated exactly the same hopes and desires of each person in the family. For example, one of the boys (I will call him Diego) pointed to the picture of his father and said, "He wants me to get a good education and help the family, and he wants us to be happy." He pointed to his brother and said, "He wants me to get a good education and help the family, and he wants us to be happy." And so it went with each member of the family. Diego was defining the collective desires of his family and attributing them to each individual. This happened so often that without making a conscious decision, I changed the question and asked, "What are the hopes and desires of all the people in your (i.e., collective) family?"

As I listened to the interviews, I realized how my interviewing had been affected by the students' connected understanding of the individual members of the family. These intelligent, socially adept, autonomously active students revealed a connection to their families in which their hopes and desires were not merely similar but were the same. These students reflected the African adage that Sandra Crump, a colleague at Boston College, recently described for me: "We are, therefore, I am." This is a reversal of our Western philosophy that community arises out of and in order to meet the needs of individuals. For the Maya boys in Guatemala, self arises from and has meaning within the community. This is similar to Lykes's notion of "social individuality," Sampson's notion of "ensembled individualism," and Sweder's "sociocentric" or "collective" self.

The following year I further examined my emerging belief that the interviews revealed a collective sense of self. One hundred five students (84 percent Maya and 16 percent Ladinos[1]) completed Harter's "Social Support Scale for Children" and the "Adolescent Self-Perception Profile" along with two values inventories and an open-ended question about goals and qualities of a good person. These instruments were translated and back-translated by a team that consisted of both native Spanish speakers and native English speakers. Harter's (1988) self-perception profile consists of subscales (scholastic competence, romantic appeal, conduct and morality, close friendship), factors related to self-worth, and a global self-worth scale. The overall mean global self-worth among the Guatemalan boys was high (M = 3.154, SD = .59) and compares favorably with global self-worth scores from U.S. samples of boys in parochial school who range from 2.91 to 3.43 (Harter, 1988). There were no significant differences among the Maya and Ladino groups of students in global self-worth.

Self-esteem was associated with social supports. A 2 (high global self-worth [divided at the mean] by 2 (Maya versus Ladino) ANOVA showed that students with high global self-worth perceived significantly greater support from their parents ($p < .001$) and from their teachers ($p < .004$), though there was no effect for perceived support from friends or classmates, no main effect for ethnic group, and no interactions. Examination of the sources of self-worth (the Harter subscales) indicated that boys with high self-worth perceived themselves as more physically attractive, more moral, and were more likely to have a close intimate friendship.

The possibility that one's evaluation of self as a moral agent may be derived from one's social interactions was investigated further. Perceptions of moral worth were positively correlated with perceived parental support ($p < .0006$), support from classmates ($p < .008$), support from friends ($p < .008$), social acceptance ($p < .0006$), and close friendships ($p < .001$). These correlations suggest that supportive social relationships and a trusting environment in which to discuss personal beliefs, feelings, and experiences, even those that result from political action, may affect one's sense of self as a moral agent. These correlations also suggest that for these Guatemalan youth, one's sense of self as a moral agent may be derived from social interactions.

We examined these observations further through analysis of an open-ended question, "What characteristics or ways of being do you consider positive in a person?" This question was first used by Ignacio Dobles Oropeza (1988, 1989), a Costa Rican psychologist who investigated the values associated with a positive sense of self among Latin American youth. To examine values and a sense of self in two cultures, the responses of Guatemalan students were compared with a sample of North Americans in a suburban school (junior and senior high school) that is predominantly White and middle class. In this sample, 106 were male and 99 were female students; they were between the ages of 15 and 17. These students are part of a longitudinal study examining the development of self and attachments during the adolescent years (Kenny, Moilanen, Lomax, and Brabeck, 1993; Brabeck, Kenny, Stryker, Tollefson, and Stern-Strom, 1994). To analyze the open-ended responses, we developed a strategy for conducting a content analysis.[2] Each of the Spanish responses were translated into English and two teams of raters, three in each group, read all the responses and identified key concepts. From these group efforts, we developed a list of key concepts. Then raters individually rated each response by identifying the concepts expressed in each complete thought.

In each team of three raters there was at least one native Spanish-speaking person who read the original responses of the Guatemalan youth in Spanish. There was at least one native English speaker for the U.S. sample in each team so that all teams had at least one person who was a native speaker of the language in which responses were originally written. However, it must be noted that although the Guatemalan youth wrote in Spanish, the majority of these students are Maya and for them Spanish is a second language. Their first language is a Maya dialect, such as Mam, Kaqchikel, or Kiché.

The importance of moral self and the centrality of social relations in self-definition was evident in both U.S. and Guatemalan samples from Dobles Oropeza's open-ended question, "What characteristics or ways of conducting yourself do you consider to be positive in a person?" The list of ideal characteristics indicates that both the Guatemalan and U.S. samples viewed behavioral conduct/morality characteristics as of central importance to the students (Guatemalan sample: 83 percent of characteristics, 484 citations; U.S. sample: 70 percent of characteristics, 135 citations). Each also rated social acceptance characteristics as important (Guatemalan sample: 9 percent of characteristics, 54 citations; U.S. sample: 8 percent of characteristics, 14 citations).

Yet further examination of the responses reveals some striking dissimilarities in the content of their responses. Although both samples repeatedly mention moral behavior and social acceptance as important, the Guatemalan students mention these characteristics in relation to helping others and bettering the community, whereas the U.S. students' responses reflect more individualistic concerns. For example, under the category of "equal," a typical Guatemalan student's response is "to pay attention to any person, don't discriminate if they are rich or poor, indigenous or Ladinos." Here the focus is on the other person. In contrast, a U.S. student's response, coded under the same category of "equal," is "it is important to let everyone *express their own opinion*." Here the focus is on the individual self.

The category of "respect" also illustrates a difference between the focus of the two groups. One Guatemalan student states that "it is necessary and our duty that each one be respectful to those who are older . . . respect parents in any work they send us to do." In contrast, a U.S. student mentions respect in the context of "people should be respectful, but they shouldn't be wimps. You have to *stand up for what you believe in*."

Under the category of "morals" a Guatemalan student responds with "it is important to give the best of yourself to others, to have good morals," whereas a typical U.S. response in that category is "do unto other as you'd have done to you." There is a subtle difference in emphasis: The Guatemalan response focuses on what one gives to *others;* the U.S. response takes the experience of the *individual self* and draws a rule from that individual focus (as you'd have done to you).

One final example: A comparison of descriptions coded as "happy" provides more evidence of these content differences. One U.S. student mentions the characteristic of "happy" as "being happy with yourself." In contrast, a Guatemalan student mentions the same characteristic as "to help any person that needs us, without asking for something in exchange because if we have something that is good that we can help others, well that's good, *we will always feel happy helping others*."

The Guatemalan students framed their ideal personal characteristics as those that help others and that actualize the larger collective goal of developing Guatemala. In contrast, the U.S. students' responses reflect a more individualized sense of self and an understanding of others in relation to that self. Examining the qualitative content of these responses adds additional support to the claim that the U.S. students' values reflect an individualized sense of moral self whereas the Guatemalan students' values reflect a sense of moral self that is communal and connected to others. Consistent with previous research from other cultures (Triandis, 1989), our examination of the sense of moral self found among these Mayan youth raises questions about the universality of our psychological models of an individualistic, separate self. Again the Guatemalan youth were demonstrating Lykes's

(1985) notion of "social individuality" and Sampson's (1988) notion of "ensembled individualism." Clearly, the portrait of Guatemalan youth that I am painting here is one that emphasizes their strengths. This strength may be tied to their connection to others and a view of self as a moral agent responsible for the well-being of others. It must be acknowledged that this work is descriptive of a selective group. Their values and sense of self may be attributable to the religious education that they are receiving; alternatively, these values may be attributable to their socialization within a culture that emphasizes the well-being of the group over that of the individual. Yet examination from outside the circle of Guatemalan community of the sense of self found among these Mayan youth raises questions about the universality of our psychological models that posit an individualistic, separate self as the end point of development.

Reflections

My work has positioned me inside the circle of feminist psychology. From this perspective, I have examined the work of Carol Gilligan and found the essentialist claims she makes about women's psychology restrictive, empirically unsupported, and politically dangerous. Her theory, in emphasizing what differentiates men and women, creates a circle around women that confines and limits possibilities by emphasizing similarity and minimizing diversity. Hare-Mustin and Marecek (1990) would perhaps label my perspective "beta bias," for in attempting to enlarge the diversity within the circle of women's psychology, I de-emphasize differences dichotomizing men and women. I have suggested here that Gilligan's assertions that the feminine self is more relational, more connected to others, and more caring may be dangerous. Gilligan's view, which ignores differences among women, and similarities between men and women, leaves open the possibility that we can assign the pressing needs for care and relationships to the "separate sphere" of women. With Unger (1990) and others, I believe that the circle that circumscribes the group "women" is organic and expandable because it is socially constructed by class, gender, sexuality, and history. With Lorde (1984) and others I believe that identities are not single and determined but multiple and changing.

My work inside Gilligan's theory led me to ask, Who has the power to define whom (McCarthy and Crichlow, 1993, p. xvi)? And who benefits from the definitions? My work outside the circle in Guatemala raises a similar set of questions. I have come to believe that speaking for others (for women, for Maya youth) inevitably is to negate through an act of otherizing. Gilligan tried to revalue women by celebrating ways in which they are different from men. Her attempt failed. It failed in part because it has not been empirically upheld. Furthermore, it failed because whatever "woman" is, or however she is defined, she will be devalued in a patriarchal society where the standard and the privilege will be those that are accorded to men. The same may be inevitable in cross-cultural comparisons, such as my work comparing Maya and U.S. youth. Not being part of a culture may blind me to the impact of my observations, which are from a standpoint of a dominant position as White, middle-class, and North American.

As Triandis (1989) noted, all humans are ethnocentric. We assume that our culture is the standard and we compare all cultures against our own. This is particularly dangerous when dominant cultures (by virtue of economic condition and size of army) attempt to define less-dominant societies. Patriarchy has resulted in men labeling women from their standpoint (and out of their needs). This can limit women's options and shape their conceptions of self. So it is, too, with ethnocentric researchers from dominant cultures.

Dualistic categorizations of self as offered by cross-cultural researchers and difference feminists are insufficient because they fail to capture the instability of power status (Brabeck and Brown, in press), the multiplicity of selves (Hsu, 1985), and the changes that occur within shifting contexts. Like the process of gendering, culture is multiply determined, and therefore essentialist claims are doomed to fail. McCarthy and Crichlow (1993) wrote,

> The challenge before us is to move beyond tendencies to treat race as a stable, measurable deposit or category. Racial difference is to be understood as a subject position that can only be defined in what Homi Bhabha calls "performative terms"—that is, in terms of the effects of political struggles over social and economic exploitation, political disenfranchisement, and cultural and ideological repression. (p. xxi)

As with gender, emphasizing group homogeneity over the diversity among members of a group has dangers.

What then, is the White researcher to do? The task, I believe, must be changed. The position of outsider to the circle of culture can create the condition of being "the other," and this has potential to be a source of insight. My work in Guatemala led me to challenge some of my basic assumptions about the centrality of the autonomous self and to see, with Geertz (1993), the "oddity" of our celebration of individualism. Looking at my psychological theories from this perspective made me more self-critical and clarified my distinct and particular standpoint. This de-centering of my experience by becoming the "other" revealed previously hidden assumptions and the limits of my own thinking. It expanded the circle of my understanding to include acknowledging what I cannot know, to understanding the limitations of my own ethnocentrism.

In the extraordinary biography of Nobel peace prize winner Rigoberta Menchú (Burgos-Debray, 1983), Rigoberta tells the story of her family during "the violence." Her book is about Guatemala during the time period that I asked the young men in my study to describe to me. From the birth ceremonies of the Quiché to the horrific details of the torture and murder of her family members, Rigoberta tells her story. The first words of the book make it clear that this honesty is not to honor an individual journey but to tell the story of a people:

> My name is Roberta Menchú. I am twenty-three years old. This is my testimony. I didn't learn it from a book and I didn't learn it alone. I'd like to stress that it's not only my life, it's also the testimony of my people. . . . The important thing is that what has happened to me has happened to many other people too: My story is the story of all poor Guatemalans. My personal experience is the reality of a whole people. (p. 1)

To give testimony on behalf of her people, Rigoberta tells in painful detail the story of her family during the time of the violence. She breaks the silence of a repressive system and reveals the institutional lies of the powerful military that ran the government. Rigoberta tells her story out of respect for those who disappeared, were tortured, and died in the horrors of that time. And yet, after revealing her most intimate throughts, experiences, and pain, she writes in the last line of her biography, "I'm still keeping secret what I think no-one should know. Not even anthropologists or intellectuals, no matter how many books they have, can find out all our secrets" (Burgos-Debray, 1983, p. 247). Rigoberta's words remind us that after all has been told, the secret of culture remains with those within the circle of that lived, and living, reality.

In a sense I have been trying to break out of the circle that defines "women" as a group, to expand our understanding of that group by calling attention to within-group differences. My standpoint, multiply affected by many economic, political, sexual, and educational contexts, is one among many. Through my work in Guatemala I have come to recognize that the position of outsider can illuminate what is problematic about the familiar. Working in the unfamiliar can make one aware of what is not noticed until it is missing or differently arranged, as with the fish who is unaware of water until removed from it (Rogoff and Morelli, 1989). My Guatemala work, from the vantage point of my critique of Gilligan's theory, has led me to reflect on my own ethnocentrism. I wonder if the circles I have drawn of U.S. and Guatemalan youth have missed the secrets, the variation, and the infinite diversity that explodes the perimeters of circles.

Notes

1. "Ladino" is a term used in Guatemala to refer to individuals who are mixed race, Spanish and Maya, or who have abandoned their Maya culture and adopted Western customs. Communal values are associated with Maya to a greater degree than with Ladinos.

2. Rater agreement was high (.87 across ratings). Discrepancies among ratings were resolved through discussion and each idea was coded. Next all responses were separated out by key constructs and a sort was then performed to list all response codes under each category together. Finally, the responses of Guatemalans and North Americans were separated for comparison.

References

Bebeau, M., and Brabeck, M. (1987). Integrating care and justice issues in professional moral education: A gender perspective. *Journal of Moral Education*, 16, 189–203.

Becker, D., Morales, G., and Aguilar, A. I. (1994). *Trauma psicosocial y adolescentes latinoamericanos: Formas de acción grupal.* ILA: Instituto Latinoamericano de salud mental y deréches humanos, Santiago, Chile.

Bellah, R., Madsen, R., Sullivan, W. M., Swidler, A., and Tipton, S. (1985). *Habits of the Heart.* New York, NY: Harper and Row.

Benderly, B. L. (1987). *The myth of two minds.* New York, NY: Doubleday.

Brabeck, M. (1983). Moral judgment: Theory and research on differences between males and females. *Developmental Review, 23,* 274–291.

Brabeck, M.(1993). Models of self among young men in the Guatemalan Highlands. In G. M. Avalrado and A. S. Gonzalez (Eds.), *Challenges of cultural and racial diversity to counseling* (pp. 12–19). Washington, DC: American Association for Counseling and Development.

Brabeck, M. (Ed.), (1989). *Who cares? Theory, research and educational implications of the ethic of care.* New York, NY: Praeger Publishers.

Brabeck, M., and Brown, L. (in press). Feminist theory of feminist practice. In N. Johnson and J. Worell (Eds.), *Feminist visions: New directions for education and practice.* Washington, DC: American Psychological Association Press.

Brabeck, M., Kenny, M., Stryker, S., Tollefson. T., and Stern-Strom, M. (1994). Human rights education through the "Facing History and Ourselves" Program. *Journal of Moral Education, 23,* 333–347.

Brabeck, M., and Weisgerber, K. (1988). Responses to the Challenger tragedy: Subtle and significant gender differences. *Sex Roles, 19* (9/10), 639–650.

Burgos-Debray, E. (Ed.), (1983). *I, Rigoberta Menchú: An Indian woman in Guatemala.* London, England: Verso.

Chodorow, N. (1978). *The reproduction of mothering: Psychoanalysis and the sociology of gender.* Berkeley, CA: University of California Press.

Colby, A., Kohlberg, L., Gibbs, J., and Lieberman, M. (1983). A longitudinal study of moral judgment. *Monographs of the Society for Research in Child Development, 48* (1–2, Serial No. 200).

Crawford, M., and M. Gentry (Eds.) (1989). *Gender and thought: Psychological perspectives.* New York, NY: Springer-Verlag.

Crosby, F. J. (1991). *Juggling: The unexpected advantages of balancing career and home for women and their families.* New York, NY: Free Press.

Deem, R. (Ed.) (1980). *Schooling for women's work.* London, England: Routledge and Kegan Paul.

Dobles Oropeza, I. (1988). Psicología social desde centroámerica: Retos y perspectivas. *Revista Costarricense de Psicología, 8–9,* 71–76.

Dobles Oropeza, I. (1989). *Orientaciones axiologicas en estudiantes de secudaria de San Jose, Costa Rica.* Unpublished paper.

Eisenberg, N., Fabes, R., and Shea, C. (1989). Gender differences in empathy and prosocial moral reasoning: Empirical investigations. In M. Brabeck (Ed.), *Who cares? Theory, research and educational implications of the ethic of care* (pp. 127–143). New York, NY: Praeger.

Elshtain, J. B. (1986). *Meditations on modern political thought: Masculine/feminine themes from Luther to Arendt.* New York, NY: Praeger.

Eugene, T. (1989). Sometimes I feel like a motherless child: The call and response for a liberational ethic of care by Black feminists. In M. Brabeck (Ed.), *Who cares? Theory research and educational implications of the ethic of care* (pp. 45–62). New York, NY: Praeger.

Geertz, C. (1993). *Local knowledge: Further essays in interpretive anthropology.* New York, NY: Basic Books.

Gilligan, C. (1982). *In a different voice.* Cambridge, MA: Harvard University Press.

Gilligan, C., and Attanucci, J. (1988). Two moral orientations: Gender differences and similarities. *Merrill-Palmer Quarterly, 34,* 223–237.

Gilligan, C., and Wiggins, G. (1988). The origins of morality in early childhood relationships. In C. Gilligan, J. V. Ward, and J. M. Taylor, *Mapping the moral domain* (pp. 111–138). Cambridge, MA: Harvard University Press.

Greeno, C. G., and Maccoby, E. E. (1986). How different is the "different voice"? *Signs: Journal of Women in Culture and Society, 11,* 310–316.

Hare-Mustin, R. T., and Marecek, J. (1990). Gender and meaning of difference. In R. Hare-Mustin and J. Marecek, *Making a difference* (pp. 22–64). New Haven, CT: Yale University Press.

Harter, S. (1988). *Manual for the self-perception profile for adolescents.* Denver, CO: University of Denver.

Heilbrun, C. (1985). Androgyny and the psychology of sex differences. In H. Eisenstein and A. Jardine (Eds.), *The future of difference* (pp. 258–286). New Brunswick, NJ: Rutgers University Press.

Hsu, F.L.K. (1985). The self in cross-cultural perspective. In A. J. Marsella, G. De Vos, and F.L.K. Hsu (Eds.), *Culture and self* (pp. 24–55). London, England: Havistock.

Hurd, T. L., and Brabeck, M. M. (in press). The presentation of women and Gilligan's ethic of care in college textbooks, 1970–1990. *Teaching of Psychology.*

Hyde, J. S., and Linn, M. C. (Eds.) (1986). *The Psychology of gender: Advances through meta-analysis.* Baltimore, MD: Johns Hopkins University Press.

Jadeck, R. A., Hyde, J. S., Moore, C. F., and Keller, M. L. (1995). Moral reasoning about sexually transmitted diseases. *Child Development, 66,* 167–177.

Kahn, A. S., and Yoder, J. D. (1989). The psychology of women and conservatism. *Psychology of Women Quarterly, 13,* 417–432.

Kenny, M., Moilanen, D., Lomax, R., and Brabeck, M. (1993). Contributions of parental attachments to view of self and depressive symptoms among early adolescents. *Journal of Early Adolescence, 13*, 408–430.

Kohlberg, L. (1969). Stage and sequence: A cognitive developmental approach to socialization. In D. E. Goslin (Ed.), *Handbook of socialization theory and research* (pp. 347–480). Chicago, IL: Rand McNally.

Lorde, A. (1984). *Sister outsider.* Trumansberg, NY: Crossing Press.

Luttrell, W. (1989). Working-class women's ways of knowing: Effects of gender, race and class. *Sociology of Education, 62*, 33–46.

Lykes, M. B. (1985). Gender and individualistic vs. collectivist bases for notions about the self. *Journal of Personality, 53*, 356–383.

Lykes, M. B. (1989). The caring self: Social experiences of power and powerlessness. In M. Brabeck (Ed.), *Who cares? Theory research and educational implications of the ethic of care* (pp. 164–180). New York, NY: Praeger.

Maccoby, E., and Jacklin, N. (1974). *The psychology of sex differences.* Stanford, CA: Stanford University Press.

MacIntyre, A. (1988). *Whose justice? Which rationality?* Notre Dame, IN: University of Notre Dame Press.

Marshall, S. E. (1984). Keep us on the pedestal: Women against feminism in twentieth century America. In J. Freedman (Ed.), *Women: A feminist perspective* (pp. 567–580). Mountain View, CA: Mayfield Publishing Company.

Martín-Baró, I. (1988). La violencia política y la guerra como causas del trauma psicosocial en El Salvador. *Revista de Psicologiá de El Salvador, 7,* 123–270.

McCarthy, C., and Crichlow, W. (Eds.) (1993). *Race, identity and representation in education.* New York, NY: Routledge.

Miller, J. B. (1976). *Toward a new psychology of women.* Boston, MA: Beacon Press.

Morawski, J. G. (1985). The measurement of masculinity and femininity: Engendering categorical realities. *Journal of Personality, 53*, 196–223.

Noddings, N. (1984). *Caring: A feminine approach to ethics and moral education.* Berkeley, CA: University of California Press.

Puka, B. (1989). The liberation of caring: A different voice for Gilligan's "different voice." In M. Brabeck (Ed.), *Who cares? Theory research and educational implications of the ethic of care* (pp. 19–44). New York, NY: Praeger.

Rawls, J. (1971). *Toward a theory of justice.* Cambridge, MA: Harvard Univerisity Press.

Rogoff, B., and Morelli, G. (1989). Perspectives on children's development from cultural psychology. *American Psychologist, 44*, 343–348.

Ruddick, S. (1985). Maternal thinking and the practice of peace. *Journal of Education, 167*, 97–111.

Sampson, E. E. (1977). Psychology and the American ideal. *Journal of Personality and Social Psychology, 35*, 767–782.

Sampson, E. E. (1985). The decentralization of identity: Toward a revised concept of personal and social order. *American Psychologist, 38*, 279–298.

Sampson, E. E. (1988). The debate on individualism: Indigenous psychologies of the individual and their role in personal and societal functioning. *American Psychologist, 43,* 15–22.

Sampson, E. E. (1989). The challenge of social change for psychology: Globalization and psychology's theory of the person. *American Psychologist, 44,* 914–921.

Schwartz, F. N. (1989). Management women and the new facts of life. *Harvard Business Review, 89,* 65–76.

Schwartz, S. H., and Bilsky, W. (1990). Toward a theory of the universal content and structure of values: Extensions and cross-cultural replicators. *Journal of Personality and Social Psychology, 58,* 878–891.

Scott, J. W. (1988). *Gender and the politics of history.* New York, NY: Columbia University Press.

Shigetomi, C. D., Harmann, D. P., and Gelfand, D. M. (1981). Sex differences in children's altruistic behavior and reputations for helpfulness. *Developmental Psychology, 17,* 434–437.

Shweder, R. A. (1991). *Thinking through cultures: Expeditions in cultural psychology.* Cambridge, MA: Harvard Univeristy Press.

Shweder, R. A., and Bourne, E. J. (1984). Does the concept of the person vary cross-culturally? In R. A. Levine and R. A. Schweder (Eds.), *Culture theory: Essays on mind, self, and emotion.* Cambridge, England: Cambridge University Press.

Thoma, S. (1986). Estimating gender differences in the comprehension and preference of moral issues. *Developmental Review, 6,* 165–180.

Triandis, H. C. (1989). The self and social behavior in differing cultural contexts. *Psychological Review, 96*(3), 506–520.

Unger, R. (1990). Imperfect reflections of reality: Psychology constructs gender. In R. T. Hare-Mustin and J. Marecek, (Eds.), *Making a difference: Psychology and the construction of gender* (pp. 102–149). New Haven, CT: Yale University Press.

Walker, L. J. (1984). Sex differences in the development of moral reasoning: A critical review. *Child Development, 55,* 677–691.

Walker, L. J. (1989). A longitudinal study of moral reasoning. *Child Development, 60,* 157–166.

Walker, L. J., deVries, B., and Trevethan, S. D. (1987). Moral stages and moral orientations in real life and hypothetical dilemmas. *Child Development, 58,* 842–858.

Wheeler, L., Reis, H. T., and Bond, M. H. (1989). Collectivism-individualism in everyday social life: The middle kingdom and the melting pot. *Journal of Personality and Social Psychology, 57,* 79–86.

10

Intraethnic and Interethnic Diversity: Researching the Japanese American and Mexican American Communities

Guadalupe Gutierrez and Donna K. Nagata

What people believe and value influences how they behave, and cultures exert a strong influence on what it is that people believe and value (Kluckhohn, 1962; Triandis, 1972). The very definitions of "normal" and "abnormal" behavior depend on cultural context (Marsella, 1979). Each culture perceives certain patterns of behavior as acceptable or laudable, and not all patterns of behavior are equally valued in all cultures.

Researchers have become increasingly aware of the need to understand the role of ethnicity and culture in psychological experience (McGovern, Furumoto, Halpern, Kimble, and McKeachie, 1991). As the United States acknowledges how multicultural it is, the effort to document mental health statistics among ethnic minorities gains the endorsement of such arms of the establishment as the American Psychological Association and the American Psychological Society.

Although making progress, psychologists still have a way to go. Most of the empirical work involves comparisons between ethnic-minority groups and non-Hispanic Whites. Such ethnic-minority–White comparisons are limited in two ways. First, they often presume that there is little or no variation within the ethnic group, an assumption that is not warranted

167

(Betancourt and Lopez, 1993). Second, they imply—more or less subtly—that ethnic-minority groups are interesting mostly as a foil to White America (see Allen, this volume).

We take a rather unconventional route in addressing these problems. We address questions of ethnic identity, worldview, and acculturation among minority individuals by presenting portions of two specific research studies conducted independently by the first author (GG) and by the second author (DN). Nagata's research explores the cross-generational impact of the Japanese American internment of World War II upon the adult offspring of former internees. For the purposes of this chapter, we look at some of the factors that may be linked to differences in acculturation among third-generation Japanese Americans. Gutierrez's project explores the worldviews of college-aged Mexican Americans in the Midwest. Whereas Nagata's project treats acculturation primarily as a dependent variable, Gutierrez's frames it as an independent variable.

The chapter begins by describing the two projects, one after the other. We summarize the rationale, methodologies, and results from Nagata's Japanese American project and from Gutierrez's Mexican American project. Although there are many differences between these groups and their experiences in the United States, both represent bicultural populations that must negotiate between their ethnic heritage and the dominant majority society. In the second, shorter, part of the chapter, we discuss briefly how the results and issues raised by each of the separate studies inform our understanding of the other, especially concerning the issues of acculturation, identity, and behavior variations. Because neither Mexican Americans nor Japanese Americans are part of the numerically dominant cultural group in the United States, the comparisons across the two investigations can be mutually enriching in a nonhierarchical way. Finally, we share our thoughts on our roles as researchers, looking through the lens of gender and ethnicity. We both identify with the communities we study and we bring this perspective to the work.

A Tale of Two Research Projects

Studying the Japanese American Internment

The incarceration of more than 110,000 Japanese Americans in desolate internment camps during World War II represents the single most dramatic historical event in that group's history. Shortly after Japan bombed Pearl Harbor, over 90 percent of those Japanese Americans living on the U.S. mainland were abruptly interned, forced to leave businesses, homes, and friends. The government claimed that all persons of Japanese American ancestry along the West Coast presented a threat to national security. Internment was portrayed as a military necessity and, as a result, Japanese Americans spent an average of two to four years imprisoned behind barbed wire.

Over two-thirds of the interned were U.S. citizens born in this country. Yet citizenship offered no protection against internment. No charges were made; nor did Japanese Americans have the right to a trial. Forty years later, the Commission on Wartime Relocation and Internment of Civilians (CWRIC) investigated the circumstances surrounding the internment. Upon reviewing hundreds of documents and hearing the testimonies of former internees, the commission concluded that the evidence did not support a military need to intern. Rather, "race prejudice, hysteria, and a failure of political leadership" (Commission on Wartime Relocation and Internment of Civilians [CWRIC], 1983, p. 18) shaped the internment, and "a grave injustice was done to American citizens and resident aliens of Japanese ancestry" (CWRIC, 1983, p. 18).

"Before camp" and "after camp" are phrases that continue to punctuate time, particularly for many first-generation (Issei) and second-generation (Nisei) members in the Japanese American community (CWRIC, 1983). Given the magnitude of the internment, it seemed likely that its effects would extend into the lives of the third generation (Sansei) born after the war. It also seemed likely that the internment experience might have had a range of differing effects. Nagata's Sansei Research Project examined these possibilities by investigating the cross-generational impact of the internment upon the Sansei generation.

The Sansei Research Project included data from over 500 survey participants and over 40 interviewees from across the U.S. mainland and Hawaii. Participants were recruited primarily with the assistance of the Japanese American Citizens League (JACL), a national organization with chapters across the country, the Young Buddhists Association, and through the JACL newspaper. The return rate for the survey was close to 60 percent, with an approximately equal representation of women and men. The average respondent age was thirty-two years. Participants fell into one of three main groups: (1) those who had both parents interned during the war (the Two-Parent group), (2) those who had only one parent interned (the One-Parent group), and (3) those who had neither parent interned (the No-Camp group). Although over 90 percent of mainland Japanese Americans were interned, a small percentage escaped internment because they lived in areas outside the government's exclusion areas. These included, for example, persons living in the Midwest or East Coast at that time. In addition, since fewer than 1 percent of Hawaiian Japanese were interned (Ogawa and Fox,

1986), Sansei in the No-Camp group included individuals whose parents were in Hawaii during the war. Comparisons between the three different groups of Sansei assessed the degree to which extensiveness of direct family experience with the internment may have influenced subsequent perceptions and behaviors.

Survey questions explored a range of internment-related issues. Detailed information about the project, its methodology, and the full range of results is available in book form (Nagata, 1993). However, two primary areas of relevance to the present chapter were the intergenerational impact of the internment on family communication and its impact on Sansei ethnic identity and acculturation. Family communication had already been identified in literature on the children of Holocaust survivors as an important issue to explore in the intergenerational transmission of trauma (e.g., Danieli, 1988; Lichtman, 1984; Robinson and Winnik, 1981) and seemed equally important in studying the effects of the Japanese American internment. In addition, descriptive writings by Miyoshi (1980) highlighted the need to explore the communications about camp, particularly between Nisei parents and their Sansei children. Ethnic identity and acculturation represented equally important and logical areas to investigate since the internment and its aftermath directly challenged the ethnic identity of Japanese Americans. Japanese ancestry alone dictated imprisonment, whereas citizenship, demonstrated loyalty, and level of acculturation were disregarded. "Japaneseness" became identified with the enemy and potential disloyalty for the Nisei. Such pressures might well have filtered down to affect the identity of the Sansei after the war.

Within the context of the Sansei Research Project, several questions emerged in trying to explore the intragroup diversity of internment effects. In what ways did the internment affect family communication, ethnic identity, and acculturation? Would Two-Parent Sansei experience the most severe consequences from their parents' combined internment legacy when compared to the One-Parent or No-Camp Sansei? Did the gender of the interned parent make a difference within the One-Parent group, and did Sansei males and females report different impacts?

Several findings from the larger Sansei Project (Nagata, 1993) are noteworthy here. Family communication did, indeed, represent one major area of impact. Communication about the internment was more frequent and longer in the families of Two-Parent and One-Parent Sansei when compared to the No-Camp group. Yet what appeared even more significant was that even for these individuals, conversations were relatively rare (approximately ten conversations in their lifetime) and brief (about fifteen minutes in duration) with their parents. Interviewees confirmed that a shroud of secrecy or silence seemed to surround the topic of internment in their families. As one woman described it, "It's like a secret or maybe more like a skeleton in the closet—like a relative in the family who's retarded or alcoholic" (Nagata, 1993, p. vii). Gender analyses suggested that Sansei males reported having shorter internment conversations within their families than did Sansei females. In addition, the vast majority of Sansei, regardless of camp group, perceived their mothers as talking more about the camps than fathers.

One might conclude that the relative absence of direct communication about the internment spared the Sansei from the effects of that event. However, this was not the case. In fact, the *absence* of discussion signaled the presence of a trauma too difficult to share. Many Sansei perceived an unstated sense of shame, hesitancy, sadness, and discomfort in their parents' perceptions, which then affected the Sansei's own sense of ethnic identity and acculturation process. Interviewees reported that they believed the internment experience led their parents to minimize Japanese culture and language in raising the Sansei. Others felt that the effects went beyond the loss of language and customs and extended to an "inherited" sense of inferiority or a need to prove oneself as 200 percent American within the White-majority society. The internment served as a reminder, noted one individual, that she can never really assimilate in this country.

In addition, survey results showed that Sansei who had a parent interned (Two- and One-Parent respondents) expressed a significantly greater ethnic preference for associating with other Japanese Americans over Caucasian Americans and had less confidence in their rights than the No-Camp Sansei. Two-Parent Sansei were also more likely to see a future Japanese American internment as possible than One-Parent and No-Camp Sansei. Other potential indices of acculturation, however, did not reveal differences between those whose parents were interned and those whose parents were not. Rates of outmarriage, level of ability to understand the Japanese language, and current involvement in Japanese American community groups did not differ significantly between the groups.

Sansei gender differences were largely nonsignificant on acculturation variables. Although ethnic preference data showed that Sansei males had a stronger preference for interacting with other Japanese Americans over Caucasian Americans, no gender differences were found for sense of confidence in one's rights or for outmarriage rates.

Gender effects were also examined according to the gender of the interned parent. These analyses divided the One-Parent group into those who had a father interned and those who had a mother interned. Results suggested that those Sansei who had only a father in camp may have experienced particularly strong effects. This group had the highest outmarriage rate, the lowest degree of confidence in their rights, and were least likely to report positive impacts from their parent's internment. Additional data suggested that having a father in camp might have had particularly severe consequences: Twice as many fathers who were interned (across the Two-

Parent and One-Parent groups) died before the age of sixty years than did fathers in the No-Camp group.

Finally, intragroup differences were also evaluated according to the geographic residence of the Sansei participants by dividing the sample into four groups: California, East Coast, Midwest, and Northwest. Several interesting regional differences emerged (although caution should be used in generalizing from these results since the sample sizes for the non-California groups were significantly smaller than the California sample). For example, although Sansei in the study expressed generally high agreement that they would actively resist a future internment, the East Coast Sansei reported the highest resistance ratings and the lowest level of confidence in their rights. By contrast, California Sansei were, relative to the other geographic groups, the least likely to resist future internment and reported the highest ethnic preference for Japanese Americans, highest degree of socializing with other Japanese Americans, and lowest outmarriage rate. Having contact with a larger Japanese American community did not, it seems, necessarily engender a greater likelihood to resist another internment.

Nagata's work broadens our perspectives on Japanese Americans by documenting the ways in which the past internment continues to shape the present-day views and experience of the Sansei generation. By examining a variety of intragroup variables (e.g., internment status, acculturation and ethnic identity, gender of the respondent and the interned parent, and geographic residence), we can generate a rich picture of the diversity within the Japanese American community. The Sansei Project shows us the importance of current perceptions that are linked to an ethnic group's past. Yet, as we shall see in the next study, everyday perceptions about life more generally are also significant in cultural experience.

Exploring the Worldviews of Mexican Americans

Gutierrez's research also sought to expand our understanding of the intraethnic diversity within ethnic-minority group experiences but did so by focusing upon the broader current worldviews of Mexican Americans rather than the psychological sequelae to a specific historical event. The term "worldview" refers to a group or individual's approach to life as dictated by the cultural norms, values, and beliefs (Ibrahim and Kahn, 1987). Mexican Americans, however, are a culturally and psychologically distinct population, not simply half Mexican and half North American. They are bicultural, bilingual, and bicognitive, which indicates not only a unique merging of cultural norms and language but also a unique mode of thought and perception that is distinct (Bernal and Knight, 1995; Ramirez, 1983).

To explore the worldviews of Mexican Americans, Gutierrez interviewed 113 English-proficient Mexican Americans from Chicago and Detroit. Participants included approximately equal numbers of females and males.

The mean age of the respondents was twenty-four years, and the majority came from working-class or lower-middle-class backgrounds. The average number of years residing in the United States was 20.57 years, and the majority of the sample were second generation, born of immigrant parents. The participants were recruited from community service agencies in Chicago and from a Latino youth center in Detroit.

Participants completed Hofstede's (1980) measure of worldviews. Hofstede's measure was selected because it had already been administered to large samples in forty countries, including the United States and Mexico. This provided comparative data for the Mexican Americans surveyed in Gutierrez's study. Furthermore, Hofstede's measure produced four specific factors, called cultural dimensions, that existed to varying degrees in all the nations/societies sampled previously. These four dimensions were Power Distance, Individualism, Masculinity-Femininity, and Uncertainty Avoidance. Power Distance referred to superior-subordinate relations. For this dimension, respondents were asked to rate the type of approach they prefer in an authority figure, as exemplified in the following item: "I prefer an authority figure to tell people what to do when making decisions." Items were presented in two forms. Some items on this scale assessed respondents' preferred Power Distance, whereas others assessed their actual experience of Power Distance. The current scale provided both perceived and actual Power Distance scores. The Individualism dimension addresses the relationship between the individual and the collective. It indicates the position of respondents on a continuum from concern only for self to primary concern for the collective, one's community. The basic psychological issue is definition of the self as "I" or as "we." A sample item from this dimension reads "It is important for me to have freedom to do what I want." The scale labeled Masculinity-Femininity is really a misnomer. It actually inquires about respondents' preference for competitive materialism versus cooperative emotional security. A typical item reads: "I think wealth and power are a good thing." The scale's label indicates what was originally designated to evaluate sex-role orientation per traditional Western norms. Finally, the fourth cultural dimension, Uncertainty Avoidance, refers to the tolerance of ambiguity. A sample item from this scale is "I am able to tolerate (put up with) not knowing exactly what is going to happen in the future or in daily situations."

What influences variations among Mexican Americans in their feelings about power, their individualism, their competitive materialism, and their desire to avoid uncertainty? Given the dynamic influences of biculturalism, two particular factors that seem especially likely to produce variations along the cultural dimensions are acculturation (Kaplan and Marks, 1990) and gender (Amaro and Russo, 1987).

Previous psychological research on Mexican Americans has looked primarily at the cognitive style, self-esteem, and effects of SES and acculturative stress on mental health (Rogler, Malgady, Costantino, and Blementhal, 1987). As a Chicana born in the United States of Mexican immigrant parents, Gutierrez also noted acculturation differences between women and men. In the process of immigration and acculturation, sex-role norms are upset and enter a stage of transition. The increased employability of women and the loss of status and authority of males, particularly the paternal figures, can create conflicts around issues of gender roles and obligations (Espin, 1987). This observation, along with a survey of the literature indicating that little attention had been paid to Mexican American women's experiences of biculturalism, led to a focus on how gender and acculturation might interact on the cultural dimensions to be assessed. In addition to the worldview scales, then, respondents also completed an acculturation scale. Items within this scale assessed the level of behavioral acculturation (e.g., level of English spoken, preference of Anglo versus Mexican media, socialization with Anglos versus Mexicans) (Cuellar, Harris, and Jasso, 1980).

Gutierrez hypothesized that gender and acculturation would significantly influence the Mexican American value orientations she was studying. Because Mexican American women are exposed to shifting norms, it was expected that gender would most significantly affect scores on the Individualism and Power Distance scales. In particular, women would express more individualism and a stronger preference for less Power Distance as compared to the men in the sample. Furthermore, it was predicted that acculturation level would most significantly affect scores on the Uncertainty Avoidance and Masculinity-Femininity scales. According to Hofstede's original study, U.S. Anglo subjects were more tolerant of unspecified or vague situations (high Uncertainty Avoidance) than were Mexicans. Therefore, Gutierrez predicted that the greater the reported Anglo behaviors (indicating increased acculturation), the greater the expected level of Uncertainty Avoidance and the greater the expected tendency toward a Masculine value orientation of competitive materialism.

Two of the four hypotheses were supported by the data. Gender showed a significant effect on the Individualism index. Women in the sample indicated a greater orientation toward autonomy than did men. Acculturation also had a significant effect on this scale. Participants who reported more Anglo behaviors were more likely to value individualism over collectivism. No differences were found in how men and women evaluated the actual Power Distance they experienced. The sample, as a whole, tended to perceive that there were marked power differentials. Regardless of acculturation level or gender, they felt there were clear lines drawn between themselves and persons in power. However, when asked about their preferred Power Distance (what they felt it should be), the women indicated a significantly stronger preference for democratic and egalitarian power structures than the men.

Originally it was hypothesized that acculturation level would have an effect on the Masculinity-Femininity index. In fact, neither acculturation level nor gender showed a significant effect for this scale. The women and men both wanted worlds in which they would be equally valued. They wanted material goods and interpersonal security. Uncertainty Avoidance was predicted by gender but not by acculturation. Women wished for certainty more than men did, but acculturated Mexican Americans did not desire certainty more than others.

The patterns of results of Gutierrez's study show a complex interplay of acculturation and gender in the worldviews of the Mexican Americans in her sample, suggesting the need for further research on these intragroup variables. They also support the theoretical premise that Mexican Americans as a population are qualitatively different from Mexican or U.S. Anglo populations. For some dimensions of the worldviews measure, Mexican Americans in Gutierrez's study tended to answer in the middle ranges, between the Mexican and U.S. Anglo scores. For example, Hofstede's (1980) original research found that Mexicans tended to perceive high Power Distance in their lives whereas U.S. Anglos perceived low Power Distance. The Uncertainty Avoidance dimension showed a similar pattern. Mexicans rated high in Uncertainty Avoidance, U.S. Anglos rated low, and Mexican Americans' scores fell in between the two other groups. Other dimensions suggested that Mexican Americans' worldviews are closer to those of U.S. Anglos. For example, U.S. Anglos scored the highest of all countries on the Individualism scale, whereas the Mexican sample scored at the lower end and favored a collectivist worldview. In this case, Mexican Americans' ratings revealed a trend toward individualism rather than collectivism and tended to be closer to the U.S. Anglo perspective. Gutierrez concluded that overall, Mexican Americans were not entirely Mexican or Anglo, nor were they consistently placed between these two groups. Rather, Mexican Americans demonstrated their own combination of attributes that require closer examination. In addition, the fact that gender differences occurred among Mexican Americans in their worldviews suggests that researchers should avoid conceptualizing the acculturation process as homogeneous.

Learning from Each Other

The studies described here differ in the ethnic groups they assessed, the generations studied within those groups, and the context of their focus (historical reference versus present-day worldviews). At the same time, these differences are embedded within the framework of important similarities: Both look at intragroup phenomena related to acculturation and gender within ethnic-minority populations. The simultaneous disparity and similarity of the studies provides a special opportunity for us to inform each other about the varying perspectives through which data can be viewed and how we might expand future research efforts.

Although Nagata's research appears most directly anchored in a historical perspective, in actuality both studies are affected by historical past. For example, Sansei in Nagata's study reported an inherited sense of shame and loss of culture and language stemming from the internment. Although the Mexican American population does not share a single traumatic historical event like the internment, the loss of culture and language, experiences of shame, inferiority, and identity diffusion are familiar given their experiences with mainstream America. Dramatic events that significantly affect identity and acculturation can occur at both the group level (internment) and at the individual level (crossing the border). Sociopolitical past, then, is present in the worldviews of Mexican Americans even if we do not explicitly study it.

At the same time, recognizing that worldviews and historical context are intertwined, Gutierrez's study suggests that it may be fruitful to tap the more general worldviews of Japanese Americans, more particularly in relation to Nagata's work, the Sansei generation. This would allow for a more complete assessment of Sansei perceptions, not just those related to ethnic identity, family communication, and acculturation.

Regional differences, as suggested by Nagata's work, can provide an important level of intragroup variation. Mexican Americans in the Southwest, having a larger community and closer contact to the home country, may well provide different worldviews from those of the Midwestern community tapped by Gutierrez's work. Hence, replication of her research in other areas of the country would be especially useful.

The measurement of acculturation itself also varies between the two studies. Gutierrez employed a scale that directly assessed behavioral indices of acculturation, whereas Nagata relied on both behavioral indices and less direct "psychological" indices, such as the Sansei participants' degree of confidence in their country and stated likelihood to resist a future internment. The inclusion of such psychological indices may also be useful in future evaluations of the degree to which Mexican Americans feel secure or vulnerable about their status in the United States.

It is also interesting to compare the level of focus for each of the investigations. Gutierrez examined the value orientations within a single generation, whereas Nagata took a broader view of intergenerational dynamics. Hence, although Gutierrez's data lay an important foundation for understanding the worldviews of second-generation Mexican Americans, it does not tell us how those worldviews were transmitted from previous generations. Nagata's research also shows us that sometimes silence is a form of communication that can shape subsequent ethnic identity and acculturation processes. Similarly, it would be interesting to learn more from the Mexican American respondents about the dynamics that underlie their worldviews.

How, for example, do second-generation Mexican Americans learn about their parents' immigration experiences, and what lessons, cautions, or guidance are communicated verbally or nonverbally about identity, acculturation, and gender roles? The inclusion of in-depth interviews could greatly enhance our understanding in this area.

Through the Lens of Ethnicity and Gender

Both of us are female members of the ethnic groups we studied, and both included gender analyses in our research. We felt it would be instructive to "step back" and look at our respective research experiences through the lens of ethnicity and gender since both issues are an integral part of the studies presented. Several key questions guided our thoughts. To what extent is gender secondary to our main goals and theory as researchers? How was gender assessed within our projects and what other contextualizing variables enhance our understanding of intragroup diversity? What were the "gender dynamics" in conducting research within our respective communities as women?

Is Gender Secondary?

Both authors began their research with the primary goal of describing the perceptions of members from specific ethnic groups, noting the need for research psychologists to expand their knowledge base of historically underrepresented groups. In this sense, the lens of ethnicity was most prominent in the rationale of the studies presented. Nagata, for example, was interested in documenting the intergenerational internment effects for Japanese Americans more generally. Her experience as a Sansei whose parents were interned suggested that there was much to learn about the camps' long-term impacts. The degree to which gender influenced such effects was a logical but secondary question to pursue. Earlier writings discuss the ways in which the internment affected first-generation (Issei) Japanese American women differently from the Issei men (e.g., Matsumoto, 1984) and the experiences of Nisei women within the camps (Nakano, 1990). However, in the absence of formal studies investigating the long-range effects of the internment and the interaction between gender and these effects, Nagata focused first upon uncovering data at a more general level.

Gutierrez also had a broader goal of describing the worldviews of Mexican Americans, but in contrast to Nagata, she identified gender as a key variable in her initial hypotheses. Gender was not an overriding concern at the initial stages of her research. However, as she explored her premises for doing the research and her own experiences as a Mexican American, she became more focused on potential gender differences as a significant psychosocial factor. A review of literature suggested that the role of gender in the bicultural Mexican American experience was just beginning to emerge. Her study seemed a perfect opportunity to explore her own curiosity and to help fill the gap in the literature of women's experience of biculturalism.

Although one might say that gender was secondary to ethnicity in the initial conceptualizations of the studies, gender was an important variable in both projects and, along with other variables, helped to contextualize the construct of ethnicity. Gutierrez's study directly assessed gender differences among her respondents with respect to the four cultural dimensions included in her survey. By evaluating acculturation effects as well, she was able to determine the relative contributions of gender and acculturation to her results, although she recognizes that SES, age, educational background, and generational status interact with gender and acculturation and that it would be useful to look comparatively at gender within these additional variables. Her results portray gender and acculturation level as two dimensions of a multidimensional phenomenon. Similarly, Nagata (1993) explored age, SES, and educational background differences within her sample, although those results are not presented here.

The importance of these multiple contextualizing variables clearly affects the degree to which we can generalize from our results. Gutierrez, for example, found that Mexican American women in her sample were significantly higher than their male counterparts on the Individualism scale. However, her respondents included young, U.S.-born, English-proficient, and college-bound women. Different results might occur with a non–English proficient and non–college bound group of women who hold similar generational status.

Nagata assessed potential gender effects not only by looking at gender differences among Sansei respondents but also by evaluating the potential gender differences created by having a father versus a mother interned. Her research adds another variable to consider in refining our understanding of ethnic communities, that of tracking the impact of gender differences in the cross-generational transmission of values, experiences, and attitudes.

Gender Dynamics of Research Within the Authors' Ethnic Communities

Both Gutierrez and Nagata conducted research within their respective ethnic communities, and it appeared that being a member of the community to be studied played an important role in gaining access to the populations of interest. Because Nagata's survey was sent and returned by mail, she did not come into direct contact with her respondents. However, her in-depth interviews did require face-to-face and telephone contact, and in these cases gender was apparent. It is interesting to note that although survey data indicated that Sansei males had shorter conversations with their parents about camp, Nagata did not detect differences in male and female interview lengths or in an overall ability to identify the impacts of a parent's internment. What appeared to be most critical in Sansei's willingess to participate in both portions of the study was the awareness that Nagata herself was a Sansei interested in Sansei perceptions of the internment.

Gutierrez directly approached community respondents for her study. As such, her interpersonal relations with participants were integral to her data collection. Gutierrez acknowledged that as a researcher it was not her place to challenge the existent ways of conduct in the Mexican American community. Rather, she saw her role as working within those ways and studying the people who practiced them. On the front line of data collection, she made several interesting observations. First, her participants were apprehensive and aloof until she identified herself as a Latina and spoke her name with the appropriate Spanish pronunciation. Once respondents heard that she spoke Spanish, they were more willing to assist by completing the survey. Gutierrez also observed that the women respondents were more open to participation than the men. Men participated in the study but took longer to convince. She hypothesized that this may be because of traditional expectations of compliance in the women as well as because of a sense of helping out a "sister," a bond between Latina women. Gutierrez also noted that her personal knowledge as a Mexican American helped to maximize her survey response. Knowing the importance of patriarchal lines, she used gestures and language that simultaneously presented her professional status but maintained a respect toward the men approached in the community.

Summary and Conclusions

Comparing the research experiences of Nagata and Gutierrez, we see the rich data that can emerge when we study intraethnic diversity. Gender differences, acculturative influences, and intergenerational dynamics all contribute to the study of ethnic communities. How one goes about studying these issues can vary considerably, as is evident in the two studies presented in this chapter. Ultimately, however, the more we expand our research efforts and learn from each other's efforts, the more we will learn how to document and appreciate the complexity of the communities we study.

References

Amaro, H., and Russo, N. F. (1987). Hispanic women and mental health. *Psychology of Women Quarterly, 11,* 393–407.

Bernal, M. E., and Knight, G. P. (Eds.) (1995). *Ethnic identity: Formation and transmission among Hispanics and other minorities.* New York, NY: SUNY Press

Betancourt, H., and Lopez, S. R. (1993). The study of culture, ethnicity, and race in American psychology. *American Psychologist, 48,* 629–637.

Commission on Wartime Relocation and Internment of Civilians (CWRIC) (1983). *Personal justice denied.* Washington, DC: U.S. Government Printing Office.

Cuellar, I., Harris, L. C., and Jasso, R. (1980). An acculturation scale for Mexican American normal and clinical populations. *Hispanic Journal of Behavioral Sciences, 2*(3), 199–217.

Danieli, Y. (1988). Treating survivors and children of survivors of the Nazi Holocaust. In F. M. Ochberg (Ed.), *Post-traumatic therapy and victims of violence* (pp. 278–294). New York, NY: Brunner/Mazel.

Espin, O. M. (1987). Psychological impact of migration on Latinas. *Psychology of Women Quarterly, 11,* 489–503.

Hofstede, G. (1980). *Culture's consequences: International differences in work related values.* Beverly Hills, CA: Sage Publications.

Ibrahim, F. A., and Kahn, H. (1987). Assessment of worldviews. *Psychological Reports, 60,* 163–176.

Kaplan, M. S., and Marks, G. (1990). Adverse effects of acculturation: Psychological distress among Mexican-American young adults. *Social Science Medicine, 31*(12), 1313–1319.

Kluckhohn, C. (1962). *Culture and behavior.* New York, NY: Free Press.

Lichtman, H. (1984). Parental communication of Holocaust experiences and personality characteristics among second-generation survivors. *Journal of Clinical Psychology, 40,* 914–924.

Marsella, A. J. (1979). Cross-cultural studies of mental disorders. In A. J. Marsella, R. G. Tharp, and T. J. Cibrowski (Eds.), *Perspectives in cross-cultural psychology.* New York, NY: Academic Press.

Matsumoto, V. (1984). Japanese American women during World War II. *Frontiers, 8,* 6–14.

McGovern, T. V., Furumoto, L., Halpern, D. F., Kimble, G. A., and McKeachie, W. J. (1991). Liberal education, study in depth, and the arts and science majors: Psychology. *American Psychologist, 46,* 598–605.

Miyoshi, N. (1980, December 19–26). Identity crisis of the Sansei and the American concentration camps. *Pacific Citizen,* pp. 9, 41, 42, 50, 55.

Nagata, D. K. (1993). *Legacy of injustice: Exploring the cross-generational impact of the Japanese American internment.* New York, NY: Plenum.

Nakano, M. (1990). *Japanese American women: Three generations, 1890–1990.* Berkeley, CA: Mina Press.

Ogawa, D. M., and Fox, E. C., Jr. (1986). Japanese internment and relocation: The Hawaii experience. In R. Daniels, S. C. Taylor, and H.H.L. Kitano (Eds.), *Japanese Americans: From relocation to redress* (pp. 135–138). Salt Lake City, UT: University of Utah Press.

Ramirez, M. (1983). *Psychology of the Americas: Mestizo perspectives on personality and mental health.* New York, NY: Pergamon Press.

Robinson, S., and Winnik, H. Z. (1981). Second generation of the Holocaust: Holocaust survivors' communication of experience to their children, and its effects. *Israeli Journal of Psychiatry and Related Sciences, 18,* 99–107.

Rogler, L. H., Malgady, R. G., Costantino, G., and Blementhal, R. (1987). What do culturally sensitive mental health services mean? The case of Hispanics. *American Psychologist, 42*(6), 565–570.

Triandis, H. C. (1972). *The analysis of subjective culture.* New York, NY: John Wiley and Sons.

11

Rethinking Psychological Theory to Encompass Issues of Gender and Ethnicity: Focus on Achievement

Amy J. Dabul and Nancy Felipe Russo

What accounts for differences in achievement among people? Why do some people persist in their efforts to achieve despite great odds, whereas others retreat at the sign of difficulty? Why does a person persevere in some situations but not in others? Questions such as these have long intrigued psychologists. But for decades, researchers predominately defined and examined achievement issues in terms of men and boys (e.g., McClelland, 1961). Fortunately, the second wave of the women's movement in the 1970s proved to be an important catalyst for the development of new scholarship on women's careers and achievement (Betz, 1993; Nieva and Gutek, 1981; Green and Russo, 1993; Mednick and Thomas, 1993).

Also during this period, researchers with an interest in achievement theory began to explore attributional processes in earnest. Causal attributions are the explanations that people give for the causes of behavior—behavior of others and of themselves—in order to make sense out of their worlds. Attributions have been found to influence everyday decisionmaking, with far-reaching consequences for success, well-being, and life satisfaction in a variety of personal, educational, and professional domains (Forgas, Bower, and Moylan, 1990; Fry and Ghosh, 1980; Weiner, 1985). Thus, attribution theory has potential for helping us understand how the meanings that we give to our behaviors can affect the strength of our motivation for and satisfaction with our achievements.

However, we contend that attribution theory has not realized its potential for illuminating why some, but not all, people are motivated to persist in the face of obstacles. The reason for this failure is that attribution theory, like most research on achievement motivation, does not sufficiently incorporate the role of context and culture in its analyses. Yet the same behavior might have different meanings in different contexts and for people of different cultures. Specifically, we believe that attribution theory, like most American psychology, has viewed the world through a lens of individualism.

This chapter falls into four parts. We first selectively review earlier research on achievement attributions. Next, we turn to cross-cultural issues, identifying work on cultural constructions of the self that raises questions for attribution theory and research. We then elaborate a new model of achievement and specifically of achievement attributions. Our model, based on the first author's (AJD's) conceptualizations developed under the guidance of the second author (NFR), moves away from individualistic assumptions and reflects a multilevel approach to the issue of achievement. We conclude by reflecting on how our own experiences and backgrounds enter into our understandings of achievement and of achievement accounts among individuals of diverse cultural identities and in varying contexts.

Attribution and Achievement

Traditional attribution research has suggested that achievement attributions are related to affect as well as performance. That is, attributions to internal causes (ability and effort) are considered to increase feelings of pride in success, whereas attributions to external causes are not (McFarland and Ross, 1982; Weiner, Russell, and Lerman, 1978). In essence, the assumption has been that particular attributions will lead to particular affective evaluations, with some attribution patterns considered more "adaptive" than others (the most adaptive patterns being those most often used by individualistic males). Thus, attributing internal causes to success and external causes to failure (called a self-serving bias) is considered to produce the most ego-enhancing and favorable affective and performance outcomes. The reverse pattern, attributing external causes to success and internal causes to failure (called the self-derogating bias), is considered to lead to unfavorable affect and future performance.

One problem with the traditional approach is that it does not produce consistent results for women and men and across cultures. For more than a decade, scholars have noted inconsistent relationships between achievement attributions and behavior across gender (e.g., Frieze, Whitley, Hanusa, and McHugh, 1982; Mednick and Thomas, 1993; Travis, Phillippi, and Henley, 1991). For example, women often demonstrate self-derogating attributions while still maintaining levels of objective achievement comparable to that of men (Erkut, 1983; Gitelson, Petersen, and Tobin-Richards, 1982). Originally, explanations of gender inconsistencies focused on factors related to research designs and settings. Deaux's early work is typical in this regard. For example, Deaux and Emswiller (1974) hypothesized that observers would attribute the success of a target who completed a gender-consistent task to skill, but the success of a target who completed an opposite-gender task to luck. However, they found that regardless of whether the task was masculine or feminine, in general, successful men were more likely to be perceived as skillful, and successful women were more likely to be perceived as lucky.

Recent examinations of gender, attributions, and achievements have focused less on methodological artifacts and more on "real-world" contextual factors. Consider a study conducted by Russo, Kelly, and Deacon (1991) of 200 males and 42 females in senior positions in public administration. Contrary to simplistic conventional wisdom, these researchers did not find that men made internal and stable attributions for their successes while women assigned their successes to good luck or hard work. Rather, Russo et al. found that both women and men in the sample generally explained their achievements in terms of a combination of hard work and ability—a combination the researchers labeled the Alger factor after Horatio Alger. Both women and men, furthermore, attributed some of the successes of their colleagues to the Alger factor. But they also clearly perceived the importance of professional contacts. In fact, the women believed that professional contacts explained more about the variations in success of their male colleagues than did ability and hard work. Acknowledging the issue of context brings us to a fascinating and disturbing observation. Achievement attributions have typically been studied in situations where individuals compete against each other. Perhaps without intending it, and certainly without identifying it as such, researchers have tended to reproduce in their laboratories the individualism that is so much a part of the larger society.

What happens if one adopts a more complex, multilevel perspective, one that incorporates an interpersonal lens in the analysis? When intergroup contexts have been studied, group-related attributions become critical in explaining individual performance. For example, Chambers and Abrami (1991) reported that team outcomes in a cooperative learning setting influenced subsequent individual achievement. Group attributions were as important to future success as attributions to individual behavior. Similarly, Croxton and Klonsky (1982) found that team attributions were used just as often to explain individual success as were self-attributions. These findings suggest that expanding the definition of achievement settings beyond the traditional individualistic competitive model may provide greater understanding of the achievement attribution process.

Research has also shown that the highly individualistic and often competitive values traditionally endorsed in U.S. culture do not necessarily lead to the most favorable achievement outcomes. Indeed, as Spence (1985) has noted, the extreme individualism of the West may ultimately prove destructive at both local and global levels. Viewing the self as totally distinct from others is neither universal nor universally considered good.

Looking Across Cultures

Although there may be many aspects of the self that differ across individuals and cultures, a value orientation that reflects the level of collectivism or individualism present in a culture has particular implications for understanding achievement. Whether a culture operates with collectivistic or individualistic values has to do with the degree to which the self is viewed as connected with others or as disengaged from others. This value orientation is thought to be important at both the group level (comparing cultures with one another) as well as at the individual level (comparing individuals within cultures with one another). At the group level, this distinction is referred to as individualism-collectivism (Hofstede, 1980; Triandis et al., 1986, 1988), although the cultural labels of cooperation-competition (Mead, 1934, 1967) and collaterality-individualism (Kluckhohn and Strodtbeck, 1961) have also been used. At the individual level, the terms independent and interdependent are often used (Markus and Kitayama, 1991). Allocentrism-idiocentrism, individual-relational, and personal-collective are other labels that have also been used to refer to similar psychological constructs at the individual level. Here we will refer to individualism-collectivism when referring to the group or cultural level and independent-interdependent when referring to the individual level.

The distribution of cultures into collectivistic and individualistic categories has to do with the emergence of certain themes that occur consistently within a culture. These themes have been studied and measured by a variety of researchers (Hofstede, 1980; Hui and Triandis, 1986; Triandis, Leung, Villareal, and Clack, 1985). A few of the important distinctions are the way behavior is regulated within a culture, the level of connectedness between individuals, the way that individuals are taught to perceive and define themselves, and the goals or tasks that individuals in that culture are expected to reach. In individualistic cultures, the individual tends to be the unit of analysis. In other words, behavior is regulated primarily by the individual, and personal goals take precedence and are largely unrelated to group goals. The major task in individualistic cultures is to reinforce internal attributes of the self (Markus and Kitayama, 1991; Kitayama, Markus, and Kurokawa, 1994). Individuals strive toward independence and uniqueness, seeing themselves as separate entities from the group (Dumont, 1965; Lukes, 1973). Western cultures, primarily North American and European cultures, are usually considered to be individualistic (Singelis, 1994; Triandis, 1983; Triandis et al., 1988).

Alternatively, in collectivistic cultures, the group is the primary unit of analysis. The individual is guided by group goals and cooperation is the desired pattern of social behavior. Fitting in with the group and preserving group harmony while downplaying internal attributes is the primary cultural task. Individuals perceive themselves as appendages of the in-group and changes to the self are thought to occur primarily through interpersonal relationships. Collectivistic tendencies have been found in Asian (Bond, 1988; Kondo, 1990; Lebra, 1993; Triandis, 1983), Hispanic (Marin and Triandis, 1985; Triandis, 1983), and African (Boski, 1983) cultures. It is important to note that individualism and collectivism have been represented as a continuum, such that some cultures can be identified as highly individualistic or collectivistic and others can be identified as falling somewhere in between. For example, Boski (1983) examined three different tribal divisions in Ethiopia and found that these groups varied greatly in levels of collectivism and individualism even though they were relatively close in geographic proximity.

Diversity is found within as well as across cultural groups. An independent construal of the self is characterized by an emphasis on personal freedom, expression, and independence (Johnson, 1985; Miller, 1988; Markus and Kitayama, 1991). The individual defines himself or herself as separate from the social context and works to reaffirm internal attributes. In contrast, those with a more interdependent view of the self emphasize the importance of social relationships and the maintenance of interdependence and group harmony (DeVos, 1985; Miller, 1988). A summary of the key differences between these construals of the self at the individual level, as characterized by Markus and Kitayama (1991), is presented in Table 11.1.

Attaining success, in the sense of achieving the primary tasks emphasized in a culture, is different in different cultures. By definition, in individualistic cultures, being unique and standing out is important for positive cultural evaluation (unless you are female, where a norm of modesty may prevail). In collectivistic cultures, maintaining group harmony and fitting in are viewed as the primary cultural tasks that lead to favorable evaluations of the self. Given these differences, value orientations at both the individual and cultural levels would be expected to affect definitions of achievement, attributions for achievement, and affective responses to attributions.

TABLE 11.1   Summary of Key Differences Between an Independent and an Interdependent Construal of Self

Feature Compared	Independent	Interdependent
Definition	Separate from social context	Connected with social context
Structure	Bounded, unitary, stable	Flexible, variable
Important features	Internal, private (abilities, thoughts, feelings)	External, public (statuses, roles, relationships)
Tasks	Be unique Express self Realize internal attributes Promote own goals Be direct: "Say what's on your mind"	Belong, fit in Occupy one's proper place Engage in appropriate action Promote other's goals Be indirect: "Read other's mind"
Role of others	Self-evaluation: others important for social comparison, reflected appraisal	Self-definition: relationships with others in specific contexts define the self
Basis of self-esteem[a]	Ability to express self, validate internal attributes	Ability to adjust, restrain self, maintain harmony with social context

[a]Esteeming the self may be primarily a Western phenomenon, and the concept of self-esteem should perhaps be replaced by self-satisfaction or a term that reflects the realization that one is fulfilling the culturally mandated task.
SOURCE: Markus and Kitayama (1991), p. 30. Used by permission.

Cross-Cultural Studies of Attributions and Achievements

For more than two decades, researchers have reported linkages between interpersonal factors and achievement that differ across ethnic groups. For example, Hawaiians (Gallimore, 1974; Gallimore, Weiss, and Finney, 1974) and Japanese (DeVos, 1985) have been found to associate achievement more with affiliation than competitive, individualistic goals. Mexican Americans and African Americans score higher on needs for family achievement and lower on needs for academic achievement than do their Anglo counterparts (Ramirez and Price-Williams, 1976). We know from early research that individuals from collectivistic cultures are more likely to use context-bound or relational attributions than individuals from individualistic cultures (Miller, 1984; Schweder and Bourne, 1982). But do self-derogating attributions undermine achievement of individuals in collectivistic cultures? We suggest not. For example, following success, Japanese individuals show an attributional pattern opposite to the traditional individualistic prediction but have no decrement in achievement motivation and behavior (Kashima and Triandis, 1986). In another study, Black individuals who demonstrated a more "self-defeating" attributional pattern than White individuals actually expected to perform better in the future, showing greater persistence and expectations for future success (Whitehead and

Smith, 1990). Clearly, models that consider the interaction between the internal self-structure and aspects of the external social structure are needed if understanding of the attribution process across gender, ethnicity, and culture is to be obtained.

Developing a New Model

Researchers have also expressed concern with the failure of psychological theories to recognize the individual as existing within a network of social groups (e.g., Miller and Prentice, 1994; Sherif, 1979; Spence, 1985; Zaccaro, Peterson, and Walker, 1987). The level of analysis in achievement contexts may be an important factor for several reasons. First, achievement goals and motivations may differ from context to context. For example, an athlete who competes in an individual sport, such as golf, where performance outcomes are independent of others, may adopt different motivational, attributional, and affective strategies than an athlete who is a member of a basketball team and whose performance outcome is dependent on the performance of others. Second, because of the differential role of the group in collectivistic and individualistic cultures, this factor may interact with the value orientation of the self discussed previously. Taken in combination, these two factors highlight the importance of the role of both the individual as well as the social context in the explanation of social behavior.

Work on achievement attribution has direct, practical application. Findings in the attributional literature have been used to develop interventions designed to train individuals to discard maladaptive causal perceptions and adopt self-enhancing attribution patterns. "Reattribution" training programs have involved token reinforcement or self-instructional cognitive interventions (e.g., Henker, Whalen, and Hinshaw, 1980; Renshaw, 1990). These programs rest on the assumption that modesty interferes with the motivation to succeed. However, for individuals who hold interdependent self-construals, the values associated with modesty may be the values that provide the motivation for future performance. Training individuals from collectivistic cultures to engage in self-enhancing attributions may undermine their achievement by disengaging achievement values from those associated with social support. In addition, reattribution training programs may unintentionally contribute to value conflicts in interdependent individuals who must struggle between a construal of the self that promotes self-effacement and the imposed self-enhancing attributional style. This discomfort may also lead to decrements in motivation. The development of different attribution training programs for independent and interdependent individuals may be a way of validating both attribution patterns, by retaining the values that may lead to future persistence and task performance.

In AJD's comprehensive examination, chaired by NFR, she set about to develop a model that would indeed include both individualistic and interpersonal dimensions of achievement (Dabul, 1994). She developed an alternative, multilevel framework for understanding achievement attribution behavior that recognizes roles for the self and the social context in the attribution process (see Table 11.2). The extent to which an individual has an independent or interdependent self-construal is crossed with three levels of analysis—personal, interpersonal, and intergroup—creating a theoretical matrix. Within each cell of the matrix, a variety of predictions may be made regarding motivational, attributional, and affective components. For example, an independent individual in an intergroup context may show a tendency to be motivated by the desire for personal enhancement, may make group-serving attributions, and may experience self-focused emotional responses. These predictions are specific to this cell in the matrix. Using her model, she can make affective, cognitive, and attributional predictions across cells that can be empirically tested. Areas of attribution research that have received heavier attention as well as those areas that remain underdeveloped both theoretically and empirically become illuminated when viewed through the lens of this framework. We have developed several research projects, including AJD's dissertation, to explore how aspects of her model might help us to understand both self- and social attributions. We believe that the ways that we understand and interpret the causes of (i.e., give meaning to) our behavior and that of others is a primary guiding element in how we construct and interact with our culture. In addition to work examining the self-attributions of individuals across gender and ethnicity, we are also interested in looking at how individuals who may not fit the individualistic cultural mold are perceived by our larger society. We emphasize the importance of recognizing that our gender and ethnicity serve as stimulus variables, and perceptions by others can ultimately determine our achievement opportunities and experiences through complex avenues.

One of our current projects that seeks to explore those avenues focuses on the costs and benefits associated with holding collectivistic values in the workplace. Are individuals who are perceived as having collectivistic values at a disadvantage? If so, how is that disadvantage manifested?

For our study we created a series of vignettes describing a company employee who had been identified as the most productive employee during a three-month period. Background information for the employee varied. In some cases, the employee was described as having independent values (e.g., stressing the importance of individual goals, workplace competition, and self-promotion); in some cases the employee was described as having interdependent values (e.g., stressing the importance of group goals, cooperation, and modest responses to achievement). In addition, sometimes the em-

TABLE 11.2 A Dimensional Framework of Achievement Attributions Based on the Social Context and Personal Value Orientation

	Level of Analysis		
	Personal	Interpersonal	Intergroup
Independent/individualistic value structure			
Motivation/goal structure	Accuracy/improvement Mastery Personal enhancement	Self-enhancement Superiority over others Success versus failure Strongest motivational context for independent individuals	Competition between groups Success versus failure Self-enhancement via group membership
Attributions	Self-serving attributional bias	Self-serving attributional bias	Group-serving attributional bias
Affective responses			
Success	Pride-competence	Pride, competence	Pride, competence
Failure	Frustration, anger	Frustration, anger	Frustration, anger
Interdependent collectivistic value structures			
Motivation/goal structure	Social obligations of duty	Group goals become individual goals Maintenance of social relationships	Acceptance versus rejection Cooperation, group harmony Strongest motivational context for interdependent individuals
Attributions	Self-effacing attributional bias	Self-effacing attributional bias	Group-effacing attributional bias
Affective Responses			
Success	Gratitude, thankfulness	Gratitude, thankfulness	Gratitude, thankfulness
Failure	Shame/guilt-related constructs	Shame/guilt-related constructs	Shame/guilt-related constructs

ployee was described as male, sometimes female, and sometimes the gender was not specified. We then asked 160 male and 160 female Anglo college-student participants to place themselves in the role of a company executive and assess the likelihood of assigning various workplace tasks and rewards to the successful employee. These tasks and rewards ranged from increasing social contacts with the employee to recommending the employee for advancement opportunities.

We found that the type of activities and rewards assigned were influenced by the perceived value orientation of the target employee. The good news was that independent and interdependent individuals were equally likely to be assigned workplace rewards leading to individual job advancement (e.g., they received support for a promotion, were given increased work responsibilities). The bad news was that interdependent employees were also significantly more likely to be assigned socioemotional leadership tasks for the group that do not lead toward job advancement (e.g., organizing the company picnic, mediating disputes between other employees). This interaction is presented in Figure 11.1.

We suspect that the differential assignment of socioemotional tasks to employees perceived as having collectivistic values is a contributor to the

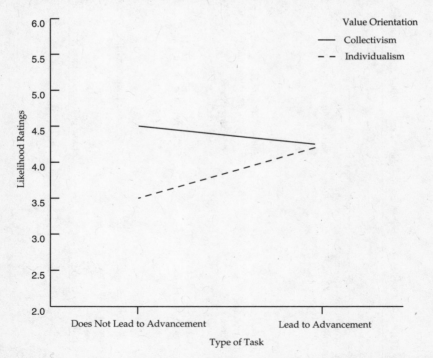

FIGURE 11.1   Ratings of Tasks and Rewards by Perceived Value Orientation of Target Employees

"glass ceiling effect," given the individualistic norms of the typical workplace. In other words, if collectivistic individuals become engaged in time-consuming interpersonal tasks that are not important in the workplace, they have less time to spend on the tasks that are necessary for upward advancement in that context. Although this data set has not been fully analyzed and our ultimate aim is to obtain data from actual managers, this one finding provides a compelling demonstration of the complexity of the path between the perceptions of others and one's path to success in traditional contexts. These data suggest that although it may appear that even if both people with independent and interdependent values are equally valued as people and similarly rewarded for their workplace performances, the additional tasks that interdependent individuals—whether they be men or women—may be expected to perform in the workplace could undermine their chances for job advancement.

We selected this specific finding to give a concrete example of what is coming out of our broader perspective because it demonstrates the interrelationship between our intellectual work and our daily experience. We are high achievers who hold collectivistic values. As such, we are more sensitive to the fact that women are asked to do time-consuming socioemotional tasks that are not "counted" in the academic context and then they are "punished" for not publishing enough. For example, we have seen several instances of young assistant professors (women and minorities) being asked to be on committees or to become involved in university activities who were then negatively evaluated for not publishing as much as those who focused on developing their personal research programs. We marvel at the attribution that such individuals "can't get it together to do research" so they focus on service. We believe that such events occur in diverse circumstances and for diverse individuals who hold interdependent values that have diverse origins, including gender and ethnicity. We are interested in exploring the exquisite double bind for individuals with interdependent values who are asked to do socioemotional tasks that take away time from "real work" of publishing and who will be punished no matter how they respond. At the personal level, we believe that the knowledge that we gain from our work will ultimately make us better teachers and mentors (in the service of our interdependent values). At the political level, we believe that knowledge about the interpersonal dimensions of achievement will enable us to redesign educational and occupational settings to enable individuals of diverse value orientations and skills to achieve success.

Making Research Part of Our Lives

The opportunities for scholarship and advocacy around women's achievement created by the second wave of the women's movement in 1970 laid the groundwork for the development of interests that have led to our collaboration. Nancy Felipe Russo (NFR) "grew up" professionally during that period, devoting a substantial portion of her career to conducting research and developing action programs to understand issues related to women, achievement, and work and to promote women's advancement (Russo, 1994, and Russo and Cassidy, 1983, present information about some of these activities). These experiences led her to have an intense interest in the relationship of gender and ethnicity to achievement and how the meanings of our achievement-related experiences may differ depending on other gender- and ethnic-related values that we may hold (Russo, Kelly, and Deacon, 1991). The work reported in this chapter reflects the convergence of those interests with those of Amy Dabul around ethnic identity, gender, and achievement.

Amy J. Dabul (AJD) attributes her interest in studying the psychology of ethnicity and gender to her childhood experiences as a biracial female. The feelings of marginality and exclusion associated with simultaneous membership in multiple social categories has led to an ongoing interest in understanding the links between gender and ethnicity and the ways in which dual minority status may influence achievement. Much of her earlier graduate work focused on the perceptions of ethnic individuals with multiple social identities (Saenz and Dabul, 1994; Saenz, Dabul, and Nassar, 1995). More recently, however, her work has evolved to reflect a growing interest in the creation of psychological models that consider both gender-related and cultural aspects of achievement. As she prepares to leave graduate school and begin her academic career, she feels fortunate to be "growing up" professionally during a time in which the importance of this kind of work is beginning to be recognized and supported.

We believe that our gender and ethnicity have affected the research topics that interest us, the questions we ask, and the way that we test those questions in multiple and complex ways. The knowledge that we seek reflects our scientific, social, and personal agendas and is intended to serve multiple purposes. In the interest of contributing to science, this research enables us to think more complexly about gender and ethnicity in achievement domains. It does more than fill a gap in the existing literature on how meanings of achievement behavior are influenced by gender and ethnicity: It charts a course for future research needed to attain a multilevel understanding of the relationship of achievement attributions that encompasses diverse cultural values and contexts. In keeping with our social agenda, this research seeks to promote the achievement of women and ethnic minorities by increasing understanding of the links between achievement attribution patterns and achievement behavior in diverse ethnic groups. We believe that current attribution training programs may hinder the achievement progress of women and ethnic minorities and undermine their own purpose by contributing to inequities in achievement outcomes. Thus, promoting understanding of achievement attributions in such populations may be critical for reducing biases in intervention programs. Finally, at a personal level, we hope that learning about how diverse populations respond in achievement settings will increase our effectiveness as mentors and teachers. We recognize that we play an active role in constructing the social context in our classrooms and in our individual relationships with students, and we have made a personal commitment to promote an atmosphere that is conducive to success for all students.

This work is not without its costs, however. Because much of our work is driven by the questions we believe are most important to address with respect to the real-world experience of women and ethnic minorities, these are not always the questions that are the quickest and easiest to study. Obtaining research participants with diverse backgrounds is often difficult. For example, even when academic achievement is the type of achievement of interest and student attributions are relevant, it may be difficult to recruit sufficient numbers of ethnic research participants. Further, when studying achievement behavior, college samples are not likely to produce a sufficient range of differing achievement levels and attributional styles. For example, ethnic minorities attending college are likely to have cultivated achievement strategies that are necessary for success in individualistic academic contexts and may not be similar to their noncollege cohorts. When access to real-world samples is obtained, as in the Russo, Kelly, and Deacon (1991) study, the use of randomized experimental designs may not be feasible without destroying the phenomenon that one is studying. This can make publication of results in traditional journals—the ones needed for tenure—more difficult.

Despite the difficulties associated with this research, the knowledge that we hope to gain and put to practical use far outweighs the potential costs, and it is one of the reasons that our working relationship has been and continues to be productive. We both share a desire to promote the study of the psychology of women and ethnic populations by understanding the way in which the social context shapes our experience. By our engaging in this research, the underlying message is that the psychological experiences of individuals that stem from their experience as a social being and member of multiple, crosscutting groups are important, valuable, and central to psychological theory.

These values have become part of the mentoring process, contributing to AJD's experience of graduate training as both validating and empowering. The incorporation of interdependent values, and a movement away from traditional mentoring styles that emphasize inequitable power structures, have not only led to an interpersonally enjoyable relationship for us but have contributed to our high level of productivity as a research team. Our experiences provide a living example of how interdependent values may contribute to the overall effectiveness and productivity of workplace activities.

At the same time that we recognize and value the interdependence that we see as a basic human need found in all people, we do not aim to homogenize the members of all social groups. We also recognize and value the fact that each person is an individual, with a unique perspective. As psychologists, we see our task as constructing new models that will help us understand the ways that multiple factors interact and result in both commonality and diversity in perspectives across time, place, and person. This too is reflected in our working relationship. Although we value our collaboration, we also value diversity of perspective and independence of thought—which makes for stimulating discussions and two-way learning. Arizona State University is fortunate in having some of the top people in their fields, and AJD has been encouraged to work with a variety of faculty members and to learn all the skills needed to conduct an independent research program. This independence, in turn, has enhanced the productivity of our collaboration. For example, her learning about multivariate analyses and new methods of multiple regression that were developed after NFR left graduate school has been particularly helpful and has enabled NFR to acquire knowledge of new statistical techniques rapidly and painlessly.

By the time you read this, our official adviser-student relationship will have ended, but our ability to learn from each other and continue to collaborate will not. We plan to continue research—individually and collectively— aimed at extending attribution theory and research to include the interpersonal side of achievement. More important, we hope to generate knowledge that can be used to construct contexts at school, at work, and in the community that support achievement of individuals in all their diversity.

References

Betz, N. (1993). Women's career development. In F. L. Denmark and M. A. Paludi (Eds.), *Psychology of women: A handbook of issues and theories* (pp. 627–684). Westport, CT: Greenwood Press.

Bond, M. H. (1988). Finding universal dimensions of individual variation in multicultural studies of values: The Rokeach and Chinese value surveys. *Journal of Personality and Social Psychology, 55,* 1009–1015.

Boski, P. (1983). A study of person perception in Nigeria: Ethnicity and self versus other attributions for achievement-related outcomes. *Journal of Cross-Cultural Psychology, 14,* 85–108.

Chambers, B., and Abrami, P. C. (1991). The relationship between student team learning outcomes and achievement, causal attributions, and affect. *Journal of Educational Psychology, 83,* 140–146.

Croxton, J. S., and Klonsky, B. G. (1982). Sex differences in causal attributions for success and failure in real and hypothetical sport settings. *Sex Roles, 8,* 399–409.

Dabul, A. J. (1994). The influence of independent and interdependent self-orienta-tions on achievement attribution: A framework for understanding attribution processes across gender and cultural lines. Unpublished manuscript.

Deaux, K., and Emswiller, T. (1974). Explanations of successful performance on sex-linked tasks: What is skill for the male is luck for the female. *Journal of Personality and Social Psychology, 29,* 80–85.

DeVos, G. A. (1985). Dimensions of the self in Japanese culture. In A. Marsella, G. DeVos, and F.L.K. Hsu (Eds.), *Culture and self* (pp. 149–184). London, England: Tavistock.

Dumont, L. (1965). The modern conception of the individual: Notes on its genesis. *Contributions to Indian Sociology, 8,* 13–61.

Erkut, S. (1983). Exploring sex differences in expectancy, attribution, and academic achievement. *Sex Roles, 9,* 217–231.

Forgas, J. P., Bower, C. H., and Moylan, S. J. (1990). Praise or blame? Affective in-fluences on attributions for achievement. *Journal of Personality and Social Psychology, 59,* 809–819.

Frieze, I. H., Whitley, B. E., Jr., Hanusa, B. H., and McHugh, M. (1982). Assessing the theoretical models for sex differences in causal attributions for success and failure. *Sex Roles, 8*(4), 333–343.

Fry, P. S., and Ghosh, R. (1980). Attributions of success and failure: Comparison of cultural differences between Asian and Caucasian children. *Journal of Cross-Cultural Psychology, 11,* 343–363.

Gallimore, R. (1974). Affiliation motivation and Hawaiian-American achievement. *Journal of Cross-Cultural Psychology, 5,* 481–491.

Gallimore, R., Weiss, L. B., and Finney, R. (1974). Cultural differences in delay of gratification: A problem of behavioral classification. *Journal of Personality and Social Psychology, 30,* 72–80.

Gitelson, I. B., Petersen, A. C., and Tobin-Richards, M. H. (1982). Adolescents' ex-pectancies of success, self-evaluations, and attributions about performance on spatial and verbal tasks. *Sex Roles, 8,* 411–419.

Green, B. L., and Russo, N. F. (1993). Work and family roles: Selected issues. In F. L. Denmark and M. A. Paludi (Eds.), *Psychology of women: A handbook of is-sues and theories* (pp. 685–720). Westport, CT: Greenwood Press.

Henker, B., Whalen, C. K., and Hinshaw, S. P. (1980). The attributional contexts of cognitive intervention strategies. *Exceptional Educational Quarterly, 1,* 177–193.

Hofstede, G. (1980). *Cultures' consequences: International differences in work-re-lated values.* Beverly Hills, CA: Sage.

Hui, C. H., and Triandis, H. C. (1986). Individualism-collectivism: A study of cross-cultural researchers. *Journal of Cross-Cultural Psychology, 17,* 225–248.

Johnson, F. (1985). The western concept of self. In A. Marsella, G. DeVos, and F.L.K. Hsu (Eds.), *Culture and Self.* London, England: Tavistock.

Kashima, Y., and Triandis, H. C. (1986). The self-serving bias in attributions as a coping strategy: A cross-cultural study. *Journal of Cross-Cultural Psychology, 17,* 83–97.

Kitayama, S., Markus, H. R., and Kurokawa, M. (1994). Cultural views of self and emotional experience: Does the nature of good feelings depend on culture? Unpublished manuscript.

Kluckhohn, F. S., and Strodtbeck, F. L. (1961). *Variations in value orientations.* Evanston, IL: Row, Peterson.

Kondo, T. (1990). Some notes on rational behavior, normative behavior, moral behavior, and cooperation. *Journal of Conflict Resolution, 34,* 495–530.

Lebra, T. S. (1993). *Above the clouds: Status culture of the modern Japanese nobility.* Berkeley, CA: University of California Press.

Lukes, S. (1973). *Individualism.* Oxford, England: Basil Blackwell.

Marin, G., and Triandis, H. C. (1985). Allocentrism as an important characteristic of the behavior of Latin Americans and Hispanics. In R. Diaz-Guerrero (Ed.), *Cross-cultural and national studies in social psychology* (pp. 85–104). Amsterdam, Netherlands: North-Holland.

Markus, H. R., and Kitayama, S. (1991). Culture and the self: Implications for cognition, emotion and motivation. *Psychological Review, 98,* 224–253.

McClelland, D. C. (1961). *The achieving society.* New York, NY: Free Press.

McFarland, C., and Ross, M. (1982). Impact of causal attributions on affective reactions to success and failure. *Journal of Personality and Social Psychology, 43,* 937–946.

Mead, G. H. (1934). *Mind, self, and society.* Chicago, IL: University of Chicago Press.

Mead, M. (1967). *Cooperation and competition among primitive people.* Boston, MA: Beacon.

Mednick, M. T., and Thomas, V. G. (1993). Women and the psychology of achievement: A view from the eighties. In F. L. Denmark and M. A. Paludi (Eds.), *Psychology of women: A handbook of issues and theories* (pp. 585–626). Westport, CT: Greenwood Press.

Miller, D. T., and Prentice, D. A. (1994). The self and the collective. *Personality and Social Psychology Bulletin, 20,* 451–453.

Miller, J. (1984). Culture and the development of everyday social explanation. *Journal of Personality and Social Psychology, 46,* 961–978.

Miller, J. (1988). Bridging the content-structure dichotomy: Culture and the self. In M. Bond (Ed.), *The cross-cultural challenge to social psychology.* Newbury Park, CA: Sage Publications.

Nieva, V., and Gutek, B. (1981). *Women and work: A psychological perspective.* New York, NY: Praeger.

Ramirez, M., and Price-Williams, D. R. (1976). Achievement motivation in children of three ethnic groups in the United States. *Journal of Cross-Cultural Psychology, 7,* 49–60.

Renshaw, P. (1990). Self-esteem research and equity programs for girls: A reassessment. In J. Kenway and S. Willis (Eds.), *Hearts and minds: Self-esteem and the schooling of girls.* London, England: Falmer Press.

Russo, N. F. (1994). The evaluation of a feminist psychologist, advocate, and scholar. In P. Kellar (Ed.), *Academic careers: Career decisions and experiences of psychologists* (pp. 105–119). New York, NY: Lawrence Erlbaum.

Russo, N. F., and Cassidy, M. (1983). Women in science and technology. In I. Tinker (Ed.), *Women in Washington: Advocates for public policy.* Sage Yearbooks in Women's Policy Studies, 7, 250–262.

Russo, N. F., Kelly, R. M., and Deacon, M. (1991). Gender and success-related attributions: Beyond individualistic conceptions of achievement. *Sex Roles, 25,* 331–350.

Saenz, D. S., and Dabul, A. J. (1994). The effects of physical attractiveness on attribution and social categoricalization: Across-race comparison. Manuscript submitted for publication.

Saenz, D. S., Dabul, A. J., and Nassar, R. (1995). Perceptions of biracial targets as a function of their self-labels: Similarity can be costly. Manuscript submitted for publication.

Schweder, R. A., and Bourne, E. J. (1982). Does the concept of person vary cross-culturally? In A. J. Marsella and G. M. White (Eds.), *Cultural conceptions of mental health and therapy* (pp. 257–291). Dordrech, Holland: D. Riedel.

Sherif, C. W. (1979). Bias in psychology. In J. A. Sherman and E. T. Beck (Eds.), *The prism of sex: Essays in the sociology of knowledge.* Madison, WI: University of Wisconsin Press.

Singelis, T. M. (1994). The measurement of independent and interdependent self-construals. *Personality and Social Psychology Bulletin, 20,* 580–591.

Spence, J. (1985). Achievement American style. *American Psychologist, 12,* 1285–1295.

Travis, C., Phillippi, R. H., and Henley, T. B. (1991). Gender and causal attributions for mastery, personal, and interpersonal events. *Psychology of Women Quarterly, 15,* 233–249.

Triandis, H. C. (1983). *Allocentric vs. idiocentric social behavior: A major cultural difference between Hispanic and Mainstream* (Tech. rep. No. ONR-16). Champaign, IL: University of Illinois, Department of Psychology.

Triandis, H. C., Bontempo, R., Betancourt, H., Bond, M., Leung, K., Brenes, A., Georgas, J., Hui, C. H., Marin, G., Setiadi, B., Sinha, J.B.P., Verma, J., Spangenberg, J., Touzard, H., and de Montmollin, G. (1986). The measurement of etic aspects of individualism and collectivism across cultures. *Australian Journal of Psychology, 38,* 257–267.

Triandis, H. C., Bontempo, R., Villareal, M. J., Asai, M., and Lucca, N. (1988). Individualism and collectivism: Cross-cultural perspectives on self-ingroup relationships. *Journal of Personality and Social Psychology, 54,* 323–338.

Triandis, H. C., Leung, K., Villareal, M. J., and Clack, F. L. (1985). Allocentric versus idiocentric tendencies: Convergent and discriminant validation. *Journal of Research in Personality, 19,* 395–415.

Weiner, B. (1985). An attributional theory of achievement motivation and emotion. *Psychological Review, 92,* 548–573.

Weiner, B., Russell, D., and Lerman, D. (1978). Affective consequences of causal ascriptions. In J. H. Harvey, W. J. Ickes, and R. F. Kidd (Eds.), *New directions in attribution research, Vol. 2.* Hillsdale, NJ: Erlbaum.

Whitehead, G. I., and Smith, S. H. (1990). Causal attributions of blacks and whites. *Journal of Social Psychology, 130,* 401–402.

Zaccaro, S. J., Peterson, C., and Walker, S. (1987). Self-serving attributions for individual and group performance. *Social Psychology Quarterly, 50,* 257–263.

About the Book

Having agreed that gender constitutes a fundamental category of analysis, feminists are now paying attention to variations among women. This book is part of that effort. In this volume, seventeen women psychologists address issues of diversity while exploring the effects of essentialism—the presumed sameness of all women. By exposing the ways in which their own work incorporates their gender and ethnicities, the contributors invite us on a journey of awareness, a journey built on communication and collaboration.

This accessible, lively book explores dilemmas of gender and ethnicity facing psychologists. It looks at various ethnic communities, including African Americans, Japanese Americans, and Mexican Americans, within settings involving issues of parenting, education, and personal and professional achievement. It should appeal to those exploring the role of women, especially ethnic-minority women, from feminist as well as cultural perspectives.

Index